# SHARKS IN THE DESERT

# SHARKS IN THE DESERT

## The Founding Fathers and Current Kings of Las Vegas

# JOHN L. SMITH

BARRICADE
BOOKS

Fort Lee, New Jersey

Published by Barricade Books Inc.
185 Bridge Plaza North
Suite 308-A
Fort Lee, NJ 07024

www.barricadebooks.com

Library of Congress Cataloging-in-Publication Data

Smith, John L., 1960-
    Sharks in the desert : the founding fathers and current kings of Las Vegas / John L. Smith.
        p. cm.
    Includes bibliographical references and index.
    ISBN 1-56980-274-2 (hardcover)
        1. Gambling--Nevada--Las Vegas. 2. Casinos--Nevada--Las Vegas. 3. Organized
    crime--Nevada--Las Vegas. 4. Businessmen--Nevada--Las Vegas. 5. Central business
    disricts--Nevada--Las Vegas. 6. City planning--Nevada--Las Vegas. I. Title.

HV6721.L3S55 2005
979.3'135--dc22

Third Printing
Manufactured in the United States of America

# DEDICATION:

*To Amelia, my Little Miss Marker.*

*To Tricia, my best friend.*

# Contents

# Contents

# Publisher's Preface

T he book you are about to read is replete with stories of men and women who made fortunes in the casino business. By comparison, their fortunes dwarf those of the Carnegies, Vanderbilts, and Rockefellers of the last two centuries.

*Sharks in the Desert* presents the complete grand drama of Las Vegas. It depicts the people and the intrigues that go beyond anything William Shakespeare might have conceived even on his most-imaginative day.

From the made men to the corporate tough guys—they're all here. Things only appear to have changed. The corporate hard-asses have the same goal as the mobsters who preceded them: to make as much money as possible without regard to who gets destroyed in the process.

In this introduction, I'll explain how so many men got so rich in what author John L. Smith calls "the casino racket." No other industry has created as many billionaires as the casino business. And they got rich by taking your money.

Always keep in mind that casino games were not designed

to favor the player. Those people on the other side of the tables didn't build their billion-dollar palaces as gifts for the welfare of mankind. Casino games were carefully designed for no other purpose than to separate you from your cash.

During the past decade, a dramatic change has taken place. When it became apparent that some visitors would partake of the cheap rooms, food, and shows, but wouldn't gamble, someone got a novel idea. "Let's not depend only on casino revenue, let's actually make a profit on the services we provide!"

It was a revolutionary concept. And it reshaped the way things work now. There are still bargains to be found, but generally, prices have skyrocketed. It's not unusual for rooms to costs several hundred dollars a night, shows to charge $100 a seat, and the bill for a gourmet meal for two to reach $300. Today more than half the profits on that bottom line come from room, food, and beverage sales.

If casino owners could slip into your bedroom at home and empty your pockets, checking accounts, and piggy bank, do you believe they'd be heartbroken because now you could no longer afford to come to Las Vegas to let them entertain you?

The approach is more delicate today, but some years ago the man who was running Binion's Horseshoe on Fremont Street told me candidly, "We're not doing our job until the customer's last check bounces for lack of funds."

The egocentric Bob Stupak, whom you'll read about in these pages, said it as well as anybody: "I target everybody. I'm in the business of taking their money. It makes no difference to me if it's a Social Security check, a welfare check, or a stock-dividend check. It's our duty to extract as much money from the customers as we can and send them home with smiles on their faces."

If you understand this, you'll understand why so many billionaires have been made in one desert town.

Let me be specific.

You hand me a dollar, and I give you ninety-eight cents change. And each time you hand me a dollar, you get back ninety-eight cents. You'd be pretty crazy or dumber than dumb to keep handing me dollars, wouldn't you?

Yet that's exactly what happens in every casino. Each time you bet a dollar, the casino keeps a percentage of it. Except that they do it as painlessly as possible by providing you with an atmosphere of bright lights, soothing music, free alcohol, and pretty ladies who don't overdress.

◆  ◆  ◆

I should point out that I'm not some social critic or antigambling fanatic. On the contrary, I've been a heavy gambler myself with Las Vegas credit lines exceeding $1 million. I've been gambling (gaming is a euphemism to disguise the harsh reality) since the 1950s when Las Vegas had a population of less than 25,000. There were no traffic lights on Las Vegas Boulevard, little McCarran Airport's entrance was just off the Strip, and one had to climb steps on the field to get into or out of a plane.

I was a "whale" then. Each time I flew New York to Las Vegas, I was given two first-class round-trip airline tickets. My food, room, and beverage were provided for me without charge. Limousines transported me to and from the airport. My clout was so strong that I once took twenty-four members of my book-publishing staff to Vegas, put them up at four hotels, and wasn't asked to pay a penny for anything.

On the other hand, I've bet as much as $40,000 on a hand at blackjack. Nor were my wagers of $20,000 a hand at baccarat unusual.

Being a savvy gambler, I very often went home a winner. Which brings me to a subject over which I used to argue with Victor Lownes.

◆  ◆  ◆

Let me tell you about Victor. He was the #1 man in Hugh Hefner's Playboy empire. He ran the Playboy Club in London when that casino was the most profitable in the world. The *Guinness Book of Records* listed him as the highest-paid executive in England. (Victor is an American.)

Victor insisted that no one can beat a casino. In rebuttal, I cited my own winning forays. Victor would smile and say, "We love people like you. When you go home with some of our money, we know you're only making a high-interest loan because you'll return with what you've won and more."

There is a casino owner's philosophy that says profits come from winners rather than from losers. Sounds paradoxical? Let me explain. Two people each wager $100 at the dice table. One wins, and one loses. But the winner, who should be getting $100 actually is paid $95. Got it?

Here's how it works: At the craps table, you bet $100 on a 4 or a 10. Your number is thrown, and you are paid $180. You are paid 9 to 5. The true odds are 2 to 1. So if the casino was an even playing field, you would have been paid $200. The casino kept $20 on your winning wager. That's how they pay for those impressive chandeliers.

The casino profits that way on every game.

In casinos today, two-thirds of the gambling income is gathered from slot machines. These function this way: A random-numbers enumerator spins hundreds of combinations per second. The fact is that you can hit a jackpot twice in a row. The odds are millions to one against that happening, but it could happen, because every spin is independent. No matter. Over a period of time, the machine will keep the percentage at which it was set. Given enough time, it will swallow all your money.

Victor Lownes insists that casino gambling is expensive entertainment. Nothing more, nothing less.

That little "per" (percentage) that the casino earns on every wager you make is what has garnered the millions and the billions.

Casino owners argue about many things, but they'll all agree on this truism: The way to make money in a casino is to own it.

Short of that, you don't have a chance. You're a sardine in shark-filled waters. Turn these pages, and you'll understand why.

—Lyle Stuart
May 2005

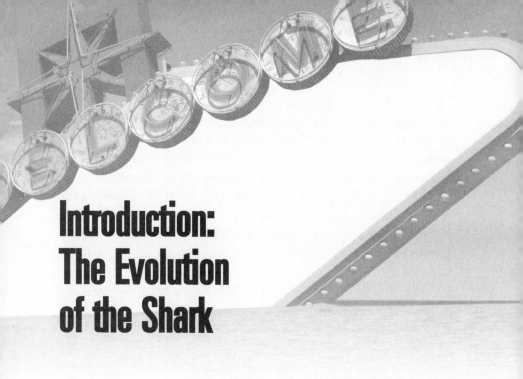

# Introduction:
# The Evolution
# of the Shark

E ach morning at the Mandalay Bay Casino and Resort on the Las Vegas Strip, throngs of gawking tourists line up to tour "Shark Reef," a handsome aquatic attraction featuring crocodiles, piranha, and other species of the ocean's most dangerous predators. Legions of visitors stand impressed and safe from behind the glass walls of the enormous aquarium.

Consider that tank a million-gallon metaphor for the unseen waters of Las Vegas and the green-felt sharks that swim there in an atmosphere as treacherous as any existing in the deep blue sea. When it comes to the business of feeding, great whites and hammerheads have nothing on the sharks of Las Vegas.

Whereas the oceangoing sharks didn't much evolve over many millennia, the toothy-grinned predators of American gaming have mastered the art of rapid adaptation, transmuting from street-smart sharpies to Ivy League MBAs and from

1

Damon Runyon's *Guys and Dolls* characters to Dun and Bradstreet silk suits in a single generation.

By the year 2000, flamboyant casino prince Steve Wynn would have his Mirage Resorts swallowed whole by Kirk Kerkorian's MGM Grand. Kerkorian, the ultimate shark, would go feeding again less than four years later by gobbling up the sparkling Mandalay Resort Group. And Harrah's Entertainment, whose namesake William Harrah had created the first authentic publicly traded gaming stock, would make a successful takeover offer for the gigantic Caesars Entertainment. The Securities and Exchange Commission office was riddled with consternation, but the higher gods of Wall Street smiled on the action.

Not long after gambling was legalized in Nevada in 1931, racket bosses and bootleggers flocked into the state seeking refuge from the law. They faced a problem. During Prohibition, dividing liquor territory was done the old-fashioned way: with Tommy guns and grenades. But if the racket boys were to survive as tailored and manicured gambling aficionados in their desert sanctuary, they had to get along. Bloodshed was the surest way to crap out everyone and brand Las Vegas as nothing more than a hustler's paradise and a killing field.

A decision was made early on by the Syndicate bosses. With infinite wisdom, they mandated that contract murders were to take place outside of Nevada so as to avoid law-enforcement heat. While this rule was not always followed, it was a simple rule for a simpler time. Thus, when the decision was made to eliminate Bugsy Siegel in June 1947 and Gus Greenbaum in December 1958, the rituals were performed elsewhere.

Volatile men weren't accustomed to reasoning together, but former Cleveland bootlegger Moe Dalitz understood the need for a united front. Like his friend and fellow Las Vegas investor Meyer Lansky, Dalitz knew that the best method to ensure a level of collegiality was to blend. And so, close partnerships were created when Mafia made men married off their sons and daughters into rival clans in the cause of self-preservation.

Dalitz understood the importance of the rule of law—even if that law was unwritten and unknown to straight society. For years, Dalitz was the chief arbiter for the men who owned Las Vegas.

"Differences were ironed out peaceably in those early days," a Dalitz associate recalled. "For instance, when they were building the Stardust Hotel, which was the largest one then, Dalitz complained that it would give too much competition to his Desert Inn. The man behind the Stardust was an old bootlegging colleague, Antonio Stralla, or as we knew him, Tony Cornero.

"An old-fashioned war threatened to break out until Meyer [Lansky] called a meeting. We all flew in for it. Dalitz, and his right-hand man, Morris Kleinman were there, as was Longy Zwillman and other biggies. We worked out a deal that gave each group an interlocking interest in each other's hotels. Our lawyers set it up so that nobody could really tell who owned what."

Dalitz's rule of comportment became obsolete when the Chicago Outfit reasserted its authoritarian rule of the street rackets during the bloody era of Anthony "Tony the Ant" Spilotro—played so famously by Joe Pesci in the film, *Casino*. The action was shortsighted, for just as the founding fathers had feared, the high-profile violence led to the fall from grace of the traditional mob in casino front offices.

"It should have been so sweet," hoodlum Frank Cullotta told *Casino* author Nicholas Pileggi with sadness in his voice. "Everything was in place. We were given paradise on earth, and we fucked it up."

But Cullotta was a blue-collar criminal with a gutter's-eye view of the inner workings of the gambling industry. By the time his pal Spilotro was murdered in 1986, the template of the postmob Las Vegas had been set for several years. Hands-on hoodlums had always been problematic for a pariah racket that hungered for respectability on the national stage. After Spilotro, the tough guys became certified dinosaurs.

Using the mob's downfall as the ultimate point of demarcation in Las Vegas history missed the city's greater—if less easily quantified—influence on American life. It was something Sally Denton and Roger Morris noted in their book, *The Money and the Power: The Making of Las Vegas and Its Hold on America, 1947-2000.*

"Whatever the hoary compromises of the Washington regime, the face of the Syndicate was changing in the eighties as so much else in the country," they wrote. "By the natural attrition of aging feudal barons, by the periodic prosecutions of crime lords in New York and elsewhere, the previously recognizable mob was fading.

"A new, educated, more refined, carefully groomed, and legalized postmodern Syndicate was already emerging. Financed and purchased by the political economy created by the Reagan revolution, Las Vegas was no longer to be its outpost colony or clearinghouse, but its sparkling capital. And alongside, out of the ethos and easy money of the decade, came a new brand of capitalists and capitalism, intent, like the Strip, only on making money, no longer constrained like their Wall Street or corporate predecessors of the decades before to disguise or conceal the obscenity of their investments or their profits.

"When these postmodern speculators and predators met the postmodern Syndicate, it would be the most spectacular Las Vegas wedding of all."

The Denton and Morris book made for compelling reading, but in the new century, Las Vegas was far more likely to be the subject of a cheesecake-adorned Travel Channel segment, the latest action from the "Binion's World Series of Poker" tournament on ESPN, or a gushing feature story in *Time* magazine, than it was to be lambasted as an island of sin and post-Syndicate shenanigans. Its dark heart hadn't changed, but its facelift projected around the world had done a 180-degree image switch in less than a decade.

4

This was due, in no small part, to America's changed perception of Las Vegas. While the city continued to attract critics, it had largely shaken its stigma because forty-seven other states now offered some form of legalized gambling, and even the raciest Strip floor shows were tamer than the sex movies offered on late-night cable channels.

Las Vegas was no longer the outlaw city. It had become a community that prospered because it remained intriguing and was able to constantly reinvent itself.

The traditional mob element faded from Las Vegas just as it had in society generally. In part, this was due to attrition and prosecution, and in part to the growth of the corporate animal in Nevada. The old-school gambling muscle men vanished, replaced in the corporate casino hierarchy by former FBI men and federal prosecutors. These often were the very people who had teamed up to tackle and destroy the mob.

"Today in Las Vegas," Pileggi concludes, "the men in fedoras who built the city are gone. The gamblers with no last names and suitcases filled with cash are reluctant to show up in the new Las Vegas, for fear of being turned in to the IRS by a 25-year-old hotel school graduate working casino credit on weekends."

Although longtime Las Vegas visitors often complain about the rigid structure of today's corporate culture, the Strip is not without its characters. None are more intriguing than Steve Wynn and Sheldon Adelson. Wynn is credited with ushering in the new Las Vegas with the opening of the Mirage and its man-made volcano and upscale atmosphere.

Wynn built Mirage Resorts into the most dynamic casinos in town, but in March 2000, his personal excesses and tumbling stock price made him vulnerable to a surprise and unwelcome $6.7-billion buyout by Kirk Kerkorian's MGM Grand. Wynn received a huge amount of cash, but lost his power base. Time passed. Wynn recovered and boasted that he would again change the Las Vegas skyline.

5

Sheldon Adelson understood that heaps of money could be drained from conventions. His annual COMDEX trade show ranked among the world's largest conventions, and its huge profits gave him the cash that allowed him to create the Venetian. This became an enormous success and totally confounded the skeptics on Wall Street and Las Vegas Boulevard.

With gambling a legal and accepted part of life by a majority of Americans, understanding the gambler's role in society offers an insight into society itself. To get there, we need to understand the men who founded Las Vegas, nursed its explosive growth, and, in the name of corporate expansion, exported the dark magic of gaming to city after city and onto Indian reservations.

The new Las Vegas is paved with the dust of imploded icons such as the Dunes, Sands, and Hacienda. These were replaced by the Bellagio, Venetian, and Mandalay Bay. Even Bugsy Siegel's Flamingo has vanished. Today all that remains of the house Benny built is a plaque in a commemorative rose garden. Yet, like Coleridge's "Ancient Mariner," some of the first-generation casinos such as the Riviera, Frontier, and Tropicana have survived. To understand today's sharks, it's instructive to know the survivors' stories as well.

Meyer Lansky biographer Robert Lacey portrayed the first-generation operators as a hoodlum element of men whose time had come and gone. These men were destined to be replaced by even more aggressive sharks. This happened as gaming evolved from mobbed-up vice to all-American entertainment. "It was like the legal state lotteries which proliferated in the 1970s and 1980s, instantly dwarfing the numbers games they mimicked," he wrote. "The corporate inheritors of Las Vegas proved that the legitimate world can run a racket better than any crook."

The legitimate guys and crooked guys had so much in common that it was difficult even for experienced observers to tell them apart. That similarity, and the stigma it generated, kept publicly traded gaming companies from being taken seriously by Wall Street.

The Public Gaming Research Institute concluded in 1980, "Casino gaming expansion to other states was stalled for almost three decades because of the public and political perceptions of the problems associated with controlling it, and with the history in Nevada of criminal influences in the industry."

Moral and ethical standards changed so rapidly that by 1994, *Time* magazine pronounced Las Vegas "the All-American City."

Which, David Johnston observed in his book, *Temples of Chance*, said as much about America as it did about the gambling subculture.

"The issue," Johnston wrote in 1992, "is how to deal with this third wave of gambling fever. Gambling will always be with us, legal or not. To make wagering among friends a crime is to create vice. But to make the noblest expression of our civility, the democratic state, a partner in wagering is to encourage pathologies to enrich the state's coffers, a Faustian bargain.

"Bad as the mob is, having Corporate America dominate the casino business is worse. The mob was limited to Nevada, and its own incompetence at managing a business as complex as casinos limited its profits. Most of those murdered were themselves mobsters or their associates. Many people who now play on credit at corporate-owned casinos would never have signed a marker in the days when the mob dispatched enforcers to collect them.

"Corporate America has access to skilled managers and it can employ the same marketing clout that sells dandruff shampoo, to push casinos and create an appearance of respectability. But licensing an enterprise does not change its nature."

◆ ◆ ◆

Las Vegas has experienced dramatic changes since Benny Siegel's time. Today's operators are licensed by state authorities and are far more likely to have an ex-sheriff or former FBI special agent on their payrolls than some knuckle-dragging ne'er-do-well. And yet, the heart of the business—and the personality it takes to successfully run that business—hasn't changed. In Las Vegas, what passed for collegiality in Moe Dalitz's day has gone the way of the penny slots and the $2 steak. Egotistical corporate titans are driven by the promise of profits and no longer feel compelled to hang together with their casino industry counterparts.

The result has been a feeding frenzy of multibillion-dollar takeovers and unprecedented competition as Las Vegas celebrated its centennial in May 2005. The sharks of old Las Vegas wouldn't recognize the new place, but they have plenty in common with the corporate bosses who run things today. The truth is that the corporate era would make the days of Meyer and Moe appear tame by comparison.

# Benny's Dream
# (Part One)

*"I got it. I got it. It came to me like a vision. Like a religious epiphany. ...
I am talking about the single biggest idea I ever had ... What do people
fantasize about? Sex, romance, money, adventure. I'm building a monument to all of it. ... I've found the answer to the dreams of America ... I'm
talking about a hotel. I'm talking about a place where gambling is allowed,
where everything is allowed. The whole territory is wide open. I'm talking
about a palace, an oasis, a city. I'm talking about Las Vegas, Nevada!"*

—Ben Siegel, as portrayed by
Warren Beatty in the movie *Bugsy*

**B**enjamin Siegel would have gone bug-eyed over the title of
the movie based on his bloody life, but he surely would have
been pleased at being portrayed on film by a handsome
leading man and elated to know he'd finally made the grade on
the big screen in Hollywood.

Given the Siegel legend, it's easier to believe that he created
Las Vegas than the other way around. It's almost believable that
this eccentric hired killer drove out into the Mojave Desert like
some Moses with a rap sheet and had a vision of an emerald oasis
rising from the sage and sand. Yes, that must be it: Siegel designed
and built the fabulous Flamingo in the desert just off U.S.
Highway 91. And, just like that, Las Vegas went from a tumble-
weed-strewn whistle stop to a neon-lighted gambling Mecca.

9

The problem is that the Hollywood version was inaccurate. It was based on decades of romantic, but revisionist press hype. Las Vegas was incorporated in 1905. Casino gambling was legalized in 1931. Siegel didn't have a substantial finger in anything in Las Vegas until 1941. The Flamingo was a dismal flop when it opened in December 1946—years after the successful premieres of the Old West-themed El Rancho Vegas, the Hotel Last Frontier, and a string of sawdust joints in downtown's Glitter Gulch.

But let's not let facts get in the way of the fable. The Siegel legend became a beacon that drew the press and public. Casino bosses were reluctant to correct it. In Las Vegas, the only thing that really matters is the number of dollars that fall to the bottom line.

So let's overlook that before taking on the Nevada project, the only thing Siegel ever built was his reputation as a vicious killer. Forget, too, that Trocadero nightclub creator and *Hollywood Reporter* newspaper founder Billy Wilkerson had already poured the foundation for his fabulous carpet joint in the desert. When Wilkerson's own gambling problems thoroughly drained his bankroll, he needed the kind of cash transfusion that only Murder Incorporated could provide in the days when banks declined to finance the casino industry. Thus Wilkerson's foundation became the foundation for the Flamingo.

Before Valley Bank expedited Teamsters Pension Fund loans, and before Michael Milken created high-risk, high-yield junk-bond financing, and before Wall Street jumped into the gaming game, there were only the Syndicate boys with their suitcases full of illicit cash. But forget all that.

In the beginning, there is the legend of Benjamin Siegel.

Siegel was born on February 28, 1906, in Brooklyn. In his childhood, he befriended a boy named Meyer Suchowljansky, who shortened his last name to Lansky. Siegel and Lansky formed the "Bug and Meyer" mob as little more than teenagers and assembled a group of contract killers.

What made Murder Inc. unique was that it killed for a fee,

and there was never any connection between the killer and his victim. It took a decade before Murder Inc. became a household name in America and police understood what they'd been facing in unsolved killings.

Murder Inc. was a force based primarily in New York and Philadelphia. It was feared everywhere else. In short order, its rulers, Lansky and Siegel, were respected figures among the Syndicate's governing body. Being Jewish, both men were associates of, but never could be members of the Sicilian Mafia.

Lansky was satisfied to let others do the heavy work on the street and take the risks involved. As reckless as he was handsome, Siegel couldn't keep his hands out of the bloody activity associated with bootlegging, prostitution, political corruption, extortion, and drug running.

Meyer was rat-faced and introverted, but Ben had movie-star good looks and an appetite for the ladies. At a time when Hollywood was glorifying the sneering gangster image in its first talkies, Siegel fit the image as if he'd been typecast. He dressed in the finest clothes and hung his hat at the Waldorf-Astoria in the 1930s, setting a trend that saw half the upper echelon of New York's mob families keep an apartment at that ritzy high-rise.

He also drew attention to himself. While Lansky was obsessive about keeping a low profile, Siegel made for splashy headlines with his violent temper and champagne lifestyle.

In part to avoid the heat in New York City and in part to organize the rackets on the West Coast, Siegel was sent to California in 1937. His assignment was to sell the mob's lucrative racing wire service to bookmakers. It took no time to intimidate the bookies, and they all knew they had to subscribe to his race wire service or spend weeks in hospital beds with broken arms and legs. Subscriptions poured in.

In a short time, Siegel became bored with the mundane rackets even as he fell in love with Hollywood. No stranger to his mirror, he was a sucker for a new suit of clothes, and soon he had a string of willing starlets on call.

He spent time with tough-guy movie star George Raft. Raft was the street kid who turned the sneer and snappy patter he'd learned on the streets of Brooklyn into a substantial fortune and international fame. Raft was also the man who taught a generation of mobsters and wannabes how to walk the walk, talk the talk, and dress in mob-style class.

Siegel was the fellow who taught Raft a thing or two about the way real hoodlums worked. They became close friends.

Given Siegel's sometimes irrational mental state, their relationship didn't stop him from nearly shooting Raft one day because the actor joked about Bugsy's thinning hair. As Raft later recalled, Siegel pulled a pistol and said, "I oughta blow your brains out, you son of a bitch." Raft calmed the sociopath by calling him "baby blue eyes."

"That 'baby blue eyes' line pleased him, and whenever I used it in critical situations, Benny would soften up," Raft said. "But after that, I never kidded him again about personal matters, For example, I never mentioned that I knew he was using face creams, eye shades, and other things in an attempt to keep his youthful look."

◆　◆　◆

Cleveland Syndicate insider Lou Rothkopf dispatched diminutive muscleman Mickey Cohen from Cleveland to Los Angeles to assist Siegel and guard his back. He was to be a fail-safe for the Syndicate's interests.

"I was getting a hundred dollars a week at first," Cohen recalled in his autobiography, *In My Own Words*, written with John Peer Nugent. "Whenever they called on me for a piece of work, I always got a little extra. Sometimes I pulled heists out in Los Angeles for Benny Siegel, not for the money so much as to put certain persons in line. Sometimes I also had to break a head.

"They wanted somebody like me to be with Benny. The Cleveland people were strong with me. When Benny got knocked off, they were stronger with me than ever.

"When I was told to come out here and that Benny was out

**12**

here, I actually wasn't told that I was fully under Benny's arm," Cohen said. "I figured I'd come out here and do whatever piece of work I wanted to do on my own. But my understanding was that I would be with Benny if it was necessary—if he had to call upon me or vice versa. I understood that Benny was sent out here by the outfit. But from what I understand, he came here to put this part of the country—Vegas and Nevada and all those places—in line with the organization's way of doing things back East."

Cohen was as much feared as his boss. Las Vegas credit jeweler Mickey Leffert was a Beverly Hills jeweler who early on migrated to Las Vegas and opened Clover Jewelers on downtown's Fremont Street. He was the third credit jeweler in a town with a population of no more than 20,000. Today Las Vegas has hundreds of jewelry stores.

Leffert told of the time he bought a small nightclub in Los Angeles "mostly for the girls." He recalled: "I was having fun with it when one day Cohen walked into my office unannounced. I knew who he was immediately.

"'I'm taking over,' he told me. 'Take your shit and get out of here in an hour.'"

Leffert, a onetime heavyweight boxer, was tall and powerfully built. Cohen was a shrimp. But his reputation preceded him. Leffert quietly "took his shit" and left the place.

Cohen was the new club owner, and no money had changed hands.

Cohen was a very active fellow. After a stickup of a group of gamblers and lesser wise guys, one of whom, Dago Louie Piscopo, had substantial connections, Cohen was summoned to a meeting with Siegel in which he experienced Bugsy's diplomatic side.

"Lookit, do me a favor," Siegel said. "Ya made a good score. Jolly good for you. But I want you to kick back Dago Louie's stickpin. It was his family heirloom; it's a thing that the guy can't replace. You're gonna get nothing for it anyway. If ya want something for it, of course I'll ante up."

Cohen was only too happy to comply and their friendship

13

was strengthened. Cohen was becoming fiercely loyal to Siegel.

With Cohen as his messenger boy, it took Siegel little time to shake up the rackets in laid-back Los Angeles, a city that had been run in slipshod fashion by a soft mob figure named Jack Dragna.

Cohen recalled, "[Dragna] wasn't able to put things together to the satisfaction of the Eastern people, or even keep things together for himself. He wasn't pulling the counties or the political picture together. There wasn't even an [illegal] casino operating in the whole territory. There was no combination; everyone was acting independently."

Siegel straightened out Dragna and the West Coast mob in a matter of days.

When World War II came, Siegel talked of putting a hit on Mussolini. It turned out to be only talk. He traveled often during a time when most Americans were conserving gasoline. He brought Moe Sedway west to further establish the Trans-America wire service on behalf of the Capone outfit. Sedway migrated to Nevada, which had legalized gambling since 1931, but because of its tiny population, had been overlooked by James Ragen's Continental Wire Service.

In Nevada, Siegel's scout found that not only was there intense interest in a reliable source of racing information—many of the licensed gambling hall operators were bookmakers—but it was a service that gave the boys entrée into the casinos themselves. In no time, Sedway managed to finagle a piece of the Golden Nugget, Fremont, and El Cortez for his bosses Siegel and Lansky.

By the time Benny Siegel took over the construction of Billy Wilkerson's foundering hotel and casino project, he already had interests in the town. Now he busied himself with rewriting his personal history. For that job, he hired a young lawyer and former Broadway ticket scalper named Hank Greenspun, who was publishing a slender magazine called *Las Vegas Life* and collecting advertising dollars from the casino operators.

Greenspun would later go on to become known as the firebrand publisher of the *Las Vegas Sun*. The *Sun* was started by the printers' union as competition for the *Review-Journal* when that conservative paper fought all attempts to unionize its staff. The *Sun* hemorrhaged money, and finally, in disgust, the union's president sold the paper lock, stock, and press to Greenspun for $1,000.

Greenspun sat at his desk for the first time and opened a drawer. He found a bankbook with a little more than $1,000 on deposit. This meant that he'd bought the newspaper for nothing.

When Greenspun died in 1989, he was one of the wealthiest men in Nevada. But in those days before he became a newspaper publisher, he wasn't too proud to shill for Benny.

"Youngish, baby blue-eyed Benjamin 'Ben' Siegel has spent a great deal of his 40 years running around the periphery of bigtime respectability," Greenspun wrote in his magazine. "The few encounters he has had with it were either head-on or passing through.

"It was obvious after a few years that you don't get in the blue book by making book, so Ben decided to go into the hotel business. The result of this Siegelian course of action is the Flamingo—the world's most lavish conception of hotel resort, casino, café and playground all rolled into one."

But even Greenspun's breathless prose couldn't change the fact that underneath those custom-tailored suits, Las Vegas's newest playboy and entrepreneur was a street hood with at least a dozen murders to his credit and a psychopathic streak that wouldn't quit.

Any perceived slight resulted in a smack on the face or a pistol butt to the skull. Tales of Siegel's violence and intimidation were commonplace in Las Vegas. One oft-repeated story concerned a tourist who failed to refer to the boss by his proper name and instead addressed him as "Bugsy."

Siegel beat the man bloody with his ever-present .38 revolver.

Siegel once made hotel publicist Abe Schiller crawl on his hands and knees around the pool after a perceived slight. Loose talk about Siegel's past cost casino man Sandy Adler a pistol-whipping. Anytime he was called "Bugsy," he went into a temper tantrum.

But tough guys don't last long in Las Vegas where making money transcends all else. Siegel couldn't beat and batter his way into a successful construction project. He had to use a different part of his brain.

Siegel was running a business—and the business suffered under his hand. That meant big problems for the man his admirers once described as "Benny who knocked out plenty."

Stories vary, and even the official confidential government reports aren't precise, but it was clear that Siegel's partners were displeased with the way their investment dollars were evaporating at the Flamingo.

Siegel had named the hotel for his girlfriend, Virginia Hill, who always dressed colorfully. Rumors persisted that she was on the payroll for big money for just being there.

The budget for building the Flamingo had been $1 million. Costs had swollen to nearly $6 million, and not a single roulette wheel was spinning, and not a pair of dice was being flung, and not a single card was being dealt anywhere on the premises.

Despite Siegel's ferocious reputation, the Flamingo suffered problems typical of other construction projects in the post World War II era. Materials were difficult to find, and those that were legally available came at inflated prices. Being resourceful, Siegel turned to the thriving postwar black market for building supplies and even raided Long Beach, California, shipyards for scrap metal to build his palace.

The palace, meanwhile, was riddled with architectural flaws, and Siegel's maniacal micromanagement didn't keep costs down. In many ways, the foundation and walls of the Flamingo reflected the paranoia of their major influence: They were made of concrete poured extra thick (so thick that years later when a wrecking crew came to knock them down, the crew was frustrated and had to bring in heavier equipment to do the job). Siegel was not just building a posh hotel casino at the edge of the

Mojave Desert; in his mind, he was creating a fortress to provide him with a safe haven from his mounting world of problems.

He never dreamed that subcontractors would be gutsy enough to drive materials in through the front gate, receive credit for their delivery, and then drive away with them out the back gate. They'd return the next day to sell him the same material a second time.

Siegel's paranoia manifested itself in his decision not to surround himself with savvy builders. There were men for hire who had shepherded dozens of big construction jobs and could spot the frauds and goldbricks. Siegel believed he could do it all himself.

He lacked knowledge of design and any real sense of the mounting price of his construction naiveté. For example, he insisted that every bathroom in the 147-room hotel have a separate sewer line. Plumbing cost: an additional $1 million. Nor did he understand basic architectural and structural concepts. Result: stairways leading nowhere (which were later declared purposeful designs by their cagey creator) and a beam in the boss's master suite that lowered part of the ceiling to five-feet-eight inches. Removing structural flaws alone added thousands of dollars to the costs.

As a result, Siegel's dream was awash in a sea of red ink. He traveled East on fund-raising tours of Chicago, New York, and Miami. His personal stake in the Flamingo shrank as his agitated partners began to wonder out loud what they'd gotten themselves into by trusting Meyer's best friend.

Builder Del Webb recalled, "He told me at lunch one day, while I was trying to collect money long overdue me, that he had personally murdered twelve men. He must have noticed my facial response because he laughed and reassured me by saying, 'You don't have to worry, Del. We only kill each other.'"

Siegel knew better than anyone that his future depended on the outcome of the project. In addition to the construction cost leakages, Siegel had to deal with his girlfriend, Virginia Hill.

Benny and Virginia were a match made in hell. Together, they were the picture of dysfunction with his violence and paranoia and her pill-popping histrionics. Benny envied his friend, Mickey Cohen, who managed to keep two beautiful women, stripper Candy Barr and actress Liz Renay, at small expense and with almost no trouble.

Cohen admired Siegel's wife, but he didn't care much for Hill, whom he recognized as a pure gold digger. He had watched her work tough guys like Joe Epstein, Joe Adonis, Siegel, and others, and had seen every man get hurt—some worse than others—by her conniving ways and wiles. He knew that she was a supremely Machiavellian operator who used sex to extract major money from major players.

Contrary to the way Hollywood portrayed her years later in the person of actress Annette Bening, the affection Hill showed for Siegel didn't equal her greatest love, which was money. Her lust for cash seemed unquenchable.

Five years after Siegel's death, a U.S. Senate committee chaired by Estes Kefauver asked Hill why she was such a favorite with Benny and the boys. She paused only a moment before replying under oath, "Senator, I'm the best goddamn cocksucker in the world."

♦  ♦  ♦

Occasionally, Siegel attempted to mingle with the locals. He bought ads in Greenspun's magazine where he was lauded for creating hundreds of construction jobs.

"We played gin rummy, and I won eight bucks," Las Vegas events coordinator Herb McDonald recalled. "I knew him as just another card player. When I saw him again at the El Rancho, he asked me when I was going to give him a chance to win some of his money back. I said, 'Any time you think you're good enough.'"

An El Rancho casino supervisor overheard McDonald's smart-aleck remark and quickly schooled him.

"Don't you know who that is?" the casino employee asked. "That's Bugsy Siegel, the president of Murder Incorporated."

McDonald's knees nearly buckled with fear.

# Benny's Dream
# (Part Two)

After millions of dollars in cost overruns, the Flamingo opened on December 26, 1946—one day after Christmas and historically among the slowest days of the year for Las Vegas casinos.

Not even Siegel could control the weather, and it was so stormy that several flights carrying movie stars from Los Angeles couldn't land. Worse yet, the casino lost money by the bucketful to lucky gamblers. Even the swinging sounds of Xavier Cugat's band and the comedy of Jimmy Durante couldn't save the evening. Opening night was a dark failure.

After that, Siegel discovered that Charlie "Lucky" Luciano, the boss of bosses, would no longer take his calls. Benny now had reason to worry.

With the Flamingo finally open, Siegel tried to give it a touch of class. Even the bellmen were required to wear tuxedos.

So when Siegel strolled through the pool area late at night and saw a man in black tie sleeping on a lounge, he exploded. After being badly battered, the frightened fellow was able to stammer that he wasn't a bellman, but rather a g-g-guest at the hotel.

Bugsy fidgeted while his pal Lansky and other underworld bosses discussed their belief that Siegel had skimmed hundreds of thousands of dollars of their investment from the Flamingo.

The bosses then held a meeting in Havana to discuss Siegel's future.

They concluded he didn't have one.

"He used to vacation in Los Angeles every two weeks," Don Garvin, the original engineer at the Flamingo, said. "He'd have me change the locks to the door of his suite almost every week. He and Virginia would sit in the hall while I worked. It became ridiculous. It got to where I would pretend to change it and hand him the same key."

But the "don't draw heat in Nevada" mob directive would have assured safety in Las Vegas for Siegel even if Garvin had removed the door from its hinges. By late spring 1947, casino profits (called the hold) at the Flamingo began to equal the gold-mine percentages generated at the El Rancho and Hotel Last Frontier. The casino's accounting problems seemed to be corrected, and things were looking up.

With the profit problem fixed, Siegel believed he was home free. He showed no shortage of confidence. After all, he surmised, now that the Flamingo was a success, he should be a hero in the eyes of his investors.

Mickey Cohen didn't agree. He knew that the eyes of certain investors hadn't liked what they saw. He knew that if they felt betrayed, they had small capacity for forgiveness. He said nothing and went along with Benny's bravado.

For all his violence and rough edges, Siegel wanted to gain entrée into legitimate society. He was not only enamored of the Hollywood celebrities and starlets, but also sought the approval of business owners, politicians, and judges—and not just for the purposes of influence and extortion. He once told Mickey

Cohen, "Don't you know you gotta do business with these coppers? Ya wanna be a goddamn gunman all your life?"

Chronicling accurate personal memories of Siegel was never a simple matter. Few who saw him regularly knew him well, and remembrances generally reinforce the image of Siegel as a short-fused maniac.

In his memoir, *With All My Might,* Erskine Caldwell, author of *Tobacco Road,* recalled a visit to the Flamingo shortly after it opened. He was both awed and repulsed by Siegel. "Bugsy appeared that night in the casino bar of the Flamingo, accompanied by two ever-ready, gray-suited bodyguards," Caldwell wrote. "He drew considerable attention. Later in the evening at a blackjack table, his presence did not have to be heralded. If Al Capone and Lucky Luciano, with some of their troops had walked into the Flamingo at that moment, they would have had to make a slam-bang entrance to attract as much attention as Bugsy did merely by quietly appearing with his ever-present, half-smoked cigar clutched between two fingers of his left hand.

"Bartenders, cocktail girls, busboys, porters, and even hard-drinking barstool customers recognized Bugsy either with lingering glances of awe or with unconcealed signs of apprehension," he recalled.

Caldwell had come to Las Vegas from his home in Arizona to relax, but instead witnessed local history being made.

"I was one of several players seated at a blackjack table when Bugsy decided to deal a few rounds of twenty-one for the house," Caldwell wrote. "He took charge of the game by silently dismissing the table dealer with a flip of his thumb. With a smile barely visible through the pale skin of his face, Bugsy deftly shuffled the cards several times with the ease of a magician demonstrating how the hand could be quicker than the eye. After each shuffle, the cards were cut and the first card to be turned face up each time was an ace. Some of the players applauded with polite smiles while others regarded him with tight-lipped suspicion.

"'Don't worry friends,' Bugsy said with reassuring glances

and smiling pleasantly for the first time. 'This is the Flamingo. What you saw can happen somewhere else in town, but never at the Flamingo. When you want an honest game, come to the Flamingo for it.'"

Caldwell played quietly and listened as a player asked the dealer if he was actually Ben Siegel. Another tourist interjected, "I've heard about you. And I've seen your picture in the papers, too. I know who you are. You're Bugsy Siegel—that's who! Calling yourself Ben something else won't fool me—Bugsy!"

Siegel snapped his fingers, and two bodyguards quickly ushered the tourist from the casino much against his futile protests.

"Nothing more was heard from him after, with feet dangling high above the floor, he was being hustled into the night," Caldwell wrote. "By then, Bugsy had gone back to the bar and had calmly relit his cigar. After calling for a drink, he blew a puff of smoke at a passing cocktail waitress."

In December 1946, FBI agents monitored major mob figures closely enough to notice them traveling to Miami, then on to Havana, where they gathered at the Hotel Nacional with Lucky Luciano. Those who assembled comprised an all-star team of Mafia men and associates. The roll call included Frank Costello, Vito Genovese, Joe Adonis, Willie Moretti, Albert Anastasia, Joe Profaci, Joe Bonanno, Tommy Lucchese, Joseph Magliocco, Tony Accardo, Charlie Fischetti, Carlos Marcello, Santo Trafficante, Moe Dalitz, and Meyer Lansky.

All those bosses, but no Ben Siegel. Not only had he insisted on running the Flamingo without interference, but he'd refused to close his Trans-America wire service after the murder of James Ragen made Moe Annenberg's Continental Wire Service "available."

It is also possible that the Syndicate bosses had more important items on their agenda: namely, the division of the drugs being smuggled from Europe into the United States.

News of the Havana mob gathering didn't convince FBI

Director J. Edgar Hoover of organized crime's existence. Hoover was no stranger to Costello or mob-run racetracks, where he was known to stiff bookies if his hunches failed him. However, he showed no interest in crossing swords with the Syndicate because, as rumor has it, they had photographs of him in women's clothing playing the role of "Mary" in a homosexual relationship.

While all this was happening, Siegel continued to travel to Beverly Hills to relax at Virginia Hill's North Linden Drive mansion. On the last night of his life, he had dinner at a new restaurant called Jack's with his friend, Syndicate conduit Al Smiley. He and Smiley returned to the North Linden Drive home with a copy of the morning newspaper.

Virginia was conveniently in Europe.

Bugsy didn't manage to turn to his favorite comic-strip page before shots rang out. Someone with a .30-caliber rifle had nailed Siegel from just outside the living-room window. A single bullet slammed into the back of his head and knocked out one of his baby blues, sending the eyeball across the room. Within seconds, Siegel was as dead as any man who'd ever crossed him.

The killing made national news headlines, and his name was burnished in Las Vegas history. Before his body was cold, and some say before word of his death had even reached Las Vegas, the boys installed a new management team at the Flamingo headed by former Phoenix-based bookmaker, Gus Greenbaum.

The Siegel murder was never solved, but wisecrackers said he died of natural causes. Although most theorize Siegel was undone by his partners, one view has Moe Dalitz getting the go-ahead to kill him because of the way he abused Virginia Hill. Still another theory, one endorsed by Smiley, had one of Virginia's brothers doing the shooting to avenge Siegel's rough treatment of his sister.

What emerged from Siegel's death was an immortal Las Vegas legend.

Benny Siegel didn't invent Las Vegas. He didn't even originate the idea for the Flamingo. But in death, he was credited with all of it. In reality, Lansky and several lesser-known racketeers, together with some plain old transplanted gamblers, played much greater roles than Siegel.

"If it was in my power to see Benny alive, he would live to be as old as Methuselah," Lansky told Israeli reporter Uri Dan in a rare interview.

Beyond bucking astronomical odds and going against his Hollywood typecast, the presence of an AARP card-carrying Bugsy Siegel would have taken much of the hype and mystery away from the fable of the creation of Las Vegas. The fact is, Siegel's ghost was good for business even if it was bad for the image of the gambling town that has never stopped swearing it isn't populated with characters who are "connected."

Benny Siegel wasn't the last tough guy associated with the city. But few of those who followed him fared much better.

# Greenbaum's Gamble and Marshall's Law

A fter the big bosses "retired" Benny Siegel, a job opening was created that the mob spent decades trying to fill: the duty of chief enforcer in an open city where associates of many crime families could operate in peace side by side.

Siegel's murder sent the announcement that the boys were not to be trifled with by one of their own. It was a lesson Siegel's affable replacement, Gus Greenbaum, learned the hard way.

Hours after Siegel's demise, Greenbaum drove the dirt road to Las Vegas from Phoenix, where he had been an intimate pal with future U.S. Senator Barry Goldwater and movie industry fixer-turned snitch Willie Bioff.

To say Las Vegas brought out the Caligula in Greenbaum is an understatement. In addition to being known as "the Mayor of Paradise," he developed a heavy drinking problem that he enhanced with pills and eventually heroin addiction. He took charge of the Flamingo and let it be known that he took orders from no one in legitimate authority.

At one point in the years that followed, and when he'd been replaced at the Flamingo and moved to the Riviera, Greenbaum made the decision to leave Las Vegas.

He flew to Phoenix and sent word that he would not take on the management of the Riviera, despite the mob's orders. Only then did he discover that departure wasn't an option for him.

His sister-in-law also lived in Phoenix. She was found smothered to death in her bed.

Once again came the order to return to the Riviera. By now he'd gotten the message. He packed his bags and returned.

Greenbaum's job was to front the Chicago mob's creation of the Riviera, which opened in March 1955. For all the world, he appeared to be a legitimate casino operator. Legitimacy, however, is a relative term in Las Vegas.

Willie Bioff's cooperation with a federal investigation of labor corruption in the movie business put several mobsters behind bars. These included John Rosselli and Paul De Lucia, also known as Paul "the Waiter" Ricca. Nevertheless, their many influential contacts resulted in their early release from their ten-year sentences.

When Bioff turned up at Greenbaum's side, Chicago Outfit boss Tony Accardo, who had his personal fortune invested in the Riviera, became understandably nervous. He knew that Rosselli and DeLucia were not men who took a double cross in stride. He ordered diminutive hit man Marshall "Johnny Marshall" Caifano to Las Vegas to warn Greenbaum against using bad judgment when choosing with whom to associate.

On November 4, 1955, in Phoenix, someone—possibly Caifano—personally delivered a message. Bioff turned the key to the ignition of his pickup truck and was blown to pieces.

Now it was Gus Greenbaum who was understandably nervous. He tried to cut a more conservative path, but the pressures inherent in pleasing his masters had driven him to drug addiction.

In December 1958, in his well-appointed home outside of Phoenix, the bodies of Gus Greenbaum and his wife, Bess, were found. If he was suspected of talking too much, it was a certainty he'd never talk again. His throat had been cut so severely that his head was nearly severed from his body. As a reward for her loyalty to her husband, Bess Greenbaum's throat was also cut.

At their joint funeral service, Gus was remembered as a good and humble man whose life had been full of charitable deeds. It was almost as if he hadn't been in the dice racket at all.

◆　◆　◆

First Siegel, then the Greenbaums. The men behind the men who ran Las Vegas knew how to make money, but obviously they were still working out the kinks of their retirement plans. The boys had no shortage of applicants interested in the unique challenge of casino operations in the era of Johnny Marshall.

Frankie Carbo was a suspect in Siegel's 1947 murder. Both he and Caifano had been in the Beverly Hills area that June night and had known Al Smiley, the man sitting next to Benny when he was killed. Caifano was also a go-to guy for Accardo, Ricca, and emerging boss Sam Giancana. And Caifano was fascinated with car bombs such as the one that killed Ricca-snitch Willie Bioff. For that matter, he was no stranger to up-close work with a knife and was capable of sending a message to anyone who spoke too much about Outfit business.

Caifano was the prime suspect in the 1943 torture and arson murder in Chicago of backroom casino moll Estelle Carey, with whom he had shared a bed. Carey's boyfriend was suspected of cooperating in a police investigation against the Outfit. She was burned in sensitive places with a cigarette lighter and then ice-picked to death.

It was clear to those who could read the signs that Marshall Caifano had become the chief predator in town and suffered no shortage of prey.

When boxing trainer Johnny Tocco moved to Las Vegas in the 1950s with the blessing of St. Louis mob chief John Vitale, he checked in with Caifano. Tocco, who was rumored to have been offered the chance to become a made member of La Cosa Nostra, described Marshall as one of the toughest characters he'd ever encountered.

"Serious as a heart attack," Tocco remarked. Those were strong words coming from an understated man who had worked the corners of the fight ring for many champions and was Sonny Liston's last trainer.

An attorney who often provided legal representation for the Outfit observed, "Of all the men I've met from that world, Marshall Caifano was the most frightening. He just sat there, said nothing, and you could feel the heat from him. He always seemed to be smoldering and ready to explode."

Benny Siegel was tough, but he neglected business. Gus Greenbaum thought being connected made him tough. But the man born Marchello Caifano in New York City in 1911 was a pure psychopath. At a touch over five-feet-five, the gray-eyed ex-boxer had a criminal record dating back to childhood and after moving to Chicago, grew up in Giancana's 42 Gang.

His penchant for violence marked him as a man on the rise in the Outfit, and in short order, Caifano was dispatched to collect debts large and small. He rarely disappointed his bosses. What's more, he enjoyed the work. That is, he had a sadistic side that was as effective as it was unnerving to those around him.

"Johnny Marshall" didn't operate his one-man chamber of horrors unnoticed. When he arrived in Las Vegas, he was given an option from cowboy Sheriff Ralph Lamb: "Keep a low profile, or get out of town." But like Siegel before him, Marshall was not only in love with the life of money, lust, and blood, he was also a vain fellow who, like Benny, hadn't killed all those people in order to keep the fact a secret.

He was eager to be known as the Outfit's main man in Las Vegas, a wise guy who had carte blanche at any place in town and, despite his diminutive frame, could make it with the most statuesque showgirls in Sin City. He did this loudly, intimidating dancers, dealers, and casino bosses with his razor-sharp glare and tough-guy patter.

"We were all terrorized by the guy," former Riviera publicist and organized-crime expert Ed Becker recalled. "If he walked into your hotel, you made sure he got whatever he wanted. You never approached him. He always looked at you like he was looking for a gun in your hand. He was such an evil son of a bitch that you didn't dare cross his line. His attitude was, 'I'm a mob guy. Don't fuck with me.'"

And few did.

But Las Vegas isn't an island unto itself. Until the Mafia conference at Apalachin, New York, in 1957, an embarrassed FBI Director J. Edgar Hoover had for many years ignored the presence of organized crime in American society. Now mob activity was being more closely scrutinized. And that meant mad dogs like Johnny Marshall threatened to expose Las Vegas as a casino town run by men who fronted for the hoodlum element.

Even in the 1950s, the casinos generated a large portion of the taxes that kept the lights on in Nevada. In those years, licensees were approved despite numerous minor gambling violations and even reputations for violence. They were catalogued by the Tax Commission. With a handful of exceptions, the only real scrutiny they received came from a satellite office of the FBI.

Visiting journalists grinned and wisecracked at the presence on the casino floor and in the front office of so many racket guys. They remembered them from back home, places like Covington, Steubenville, Cleveland, Boston, Providence, Miami, Chicago, and New York.

One of the notable exceptions to Nevada's laissez-faire oversight happened in 1957 when the Tax Commission suspended the license of the Thunderbird, which was manipulated behind the scenes by Jake and Meyer Lansky. In that case, U.S. District Judge Charles Merrill declared, "For gambling to take its place as a lawful enterprise in Nevada, it is not enough that this state has named it lawful. We have offered it the opportunity for lawful existence. The offer is a risky one, not only for people of this state, but for the entire nation."

After the Apalachin meeting and the grisly Greenbaum murders in 1958, there was an increase in federal law-enforcement interest in mob activity generally and especially in the high-profile action in Las Vegas. That focus, coupled with the endless threat of federal taxation on the pariah gambling fraternity, led to a countermeasure by Nevada politicians: the creation of a two-tiered system of casino regulation in the form of the Gaming Control Board and the Gaming Commission.

The board's function was investigative in nature. It collected data and weighed information, then made a recommendation to the commission, which had the final say. Although the members of the board and commission were appointed by the governor, and thus, were subject to a certain degree of willful blindness, the new regulatory structure had two positive effects on Nevada. It kept the Feds at arm's length, and for the first time since gambling was legalized in 1931 gave Nevada a modicum of credibility when it came to controlling its top industry.

The rise of the gaming regulatory apparatus led to the fall of Marshall Caifano in Las Vegas. Caifano had been arrested many times since 1929, but it was an administrative process that led to his inclusion as one of eleven original members of the Black Book of notorious people banned from setting foot in Nevada casinos that would lead to his exile. If he couldn't operate inside the casinos, he would have a very difficult time communicating with and intimidating the Outfit's people. Although Caifano fought the state in court, he lost, and a precedent was set.

Caifano had qualified for the List of Excluded Persons by reputation rather than any single act. In addition to the Estelle Carey mutilation, he was suspected in the 1950 murder of ex-Chicago police Lt. William Drury, the 1952 strangulation of hoodlum gambler Russian Louie Strauss, and the shotgun assassination of Chicago rackets insider Teddy Roe.

As a Riviera publicist, Ed Becker recalled seeing Caifano in Las Vegas casinos in the mid-1950s, just when the killer legally changed his name to "Johnny Marshall." A new surname, however, couldn't disguise his volatile nature or the real reason he was in Las Vegas. He wasn't there for the waters, but to shake down casino bosses like Benny Binion and Beldon Katleman on behalf of the boys in Chicago.

Even after his inclusion in the Black Book, Caifano couldn't resist the neon. By 1961, he'd popped onto the FBI's 10 Most Wanted List and decided to hide out at the Desert Inn where he had friends and allies. The staff apparently also contained at least one informant. After a few days of eating room-service cuisine, he was discovered and yanked from the premises.

Caifano's high profile meant increased media scrutiny, and that led to an accidental encounter with *Las Vegas Sun* photographer Frank Maggio. When Caifano was escorted from the Desert Inn, Maggio drew the assignment. Maggio approached Caifano, who took a swing at him, smashing his heavy Speed Graphic camera. Maggio reacted out of instinct, retaliating with a right cross that nailed Caifano flush on the chin, knocking him cold.

"I'm not a fighter," Maggio said in a 1991 interview. "It was just a natural reflex. If I had used my head, I sure wouldn't have done it."

Most of Caifano's fights ended differently.

Although charges were never filed, Caifano was a prime suspect in the June 17, 1960, fire that consumed the original El Rancho Vegas casino resort on the Strip, the section of Las Vegas Boulevard south of Sahara. County arson investigators ruled the fire accidental, but Ed Becker, who lived in a bungalow behind El Rancho, recalls Caifano making unsuccessful plays for some of the resort's chorus girls. Caifano's boorish behavior and tough-guy routine earned him an "86" from the premises.

El Rancho owner Beldon Katleman booted Caifano from the property just a few hours before the blaze. The rumors only added to Caifano's reputation as the biggest little man in the Chicago Outfit.

31

Caifano's criminal career was far from finished. As Giancana's most prolific hitter, he would be suspected of a string of murders, including the 1973 shotgun murder of corrupt former Chicago chief investigator Richard Cain and the 1977 car-bombing of Indiana oil millionaire Ray Ryan.

The Ryan murder gave insight into Caifano's frightening personality. In 1964, the high-rolling Ryan had testified in court that Caifano tried to extort $60,000 from him. As a result, Caifano served six years in prison. When he emerged from his jail cell, his Las Vegas days were over. A few years later, so was Ryan's life.

Now that's a definition of a long memory.

By then, however, his old pals Giancana and Rosselli were dead. Giancana caught a bullet on June 19, 1975, in Chicago, and Rosselli was slaughtered and stuffed into an oil drum that was found floating near Miami on August 7, 1976.

Ironically, it was his connection to the theft of thousands of shares of unissued Westinghouse stock that nailed Caifano. This time he received a long federal prison sentence. After his release in December 1991, he lived quietly in Fort Lauderdale, Florida.

When he died of natural causes in September 2003, he was ninety-two. Prison seemed to have lengthened his life expectancy.

Caifano remained in Nevada's Black Book for several weeks after his death and was eulogized in the press as an evil man whose career proved that banishment was possible in the emerging regulated gambling business.

Even Johnny Marshall would have agreed the effects of his being blackballed and Black Booked were preferable to the Siegel-Greenbaum retirement plan, of which he is believed to have been an administrator.

# Dapper Johnny Rosselli

Johnny Rosselli was the consummate Outfit guy in Las Vegas. Where Marshall Caifano lacked negotiation skills and had a hair-trigger temper, Rosselli was a diplomat comfortable at the highest levels of society. He moved with élan through the Hollywood scene, knew enough of California politics to be effective, and put his arms around the growing gambling hot spots of Las Vegas without breaking stride.

True, Rosselli had a checkered past. After serving in World War II, he'd been convicted of labor racketeering in the movie industry and as a result of the turncoat testimony of Willie Bioff, served six years in federal prison. It was during his trial that he said, under oath, that he'd been born in Chicago in 1905. The fact is that he was born in 1905 in Boston.

After his release from prison, Rosselli became the Outfit's go-to guy. He was a capable fixer who could communicate the mob's message at the highest levels of government and on the street. That is what eventually got him the Las Vegas assignment.

"Between 1954 and 1957, Rosselli crisscrossed the country, traveling the seams of the national Syndicate, offering 'juice' and protection in the nether regions where no single crime family had established hegemony," Ed Becker and Charles Rappleye wrote in *All-American Mafioso: The Johnny Rosselli Story.* "There were perhaps a dozen such hot spots around the nation, places that, like Las Vegas, had been declared open territory by the national commission."

Rosselli roamed from Hot Springs, Arkansas, to Miami Beach, out to Las Vegas, and back to Boston. He was well connected with the Dragna crime family of Los Angeles, but continued to maintain his Chicago contacts. Rosselli was a celebrity at Havana casinos and in Hollywood. He was even a player in Guatemalan politics. (It was at about this time that Rosselli's CIA contacts developed.)

Johnny Rosselli's presence in Las Vegas began to take physical shape in 1957 with the construction of the Tropicana by a collective of mob backers led by Meyer Lansky, Frank Costello, and Carlos Marcello. Rosselli monitored the project expenses closely and for a time owned a percentage of the lucrative gift-shop concessions.

Unlike a "cleaned-up" former racket chieftain like Moe Dalitz, Rosselli's reputation for running with a violent crowd prevented him from becoming a licensed casino owner. He understood that his success lay in establishing high-end connections in legitimate American society. The Rosselli who is believed to have ordered the vicious Bioff bombing in 1955 is the same Rosselli who charmed Hollywood socialites and worked clandestinely with the CIA to assassinate Cuban leader Fidel Castro. He was a man of many seasons who had many connections.

Frank Costello's crowd busted out when, on May 2, 1957, rising Genovese family star Vincent "the Chin" Gigante shot the reigning crime boss in the lobby of his Central Park West

34

Manhattan apartment. The .32-caliber slug creased Costello's scalp, but didn't kill him. When police searched his pockets, they found a handwritten document listing the last twenty-four days' worth of profits at the Tropicana.

Costello, true to the Sicilian code of omertà, refused to answer police questions. He recovered from his head wound and slipped quietly into retirement.

Becker and Rappleye wrote, "Despite the collapse of Costello's interest in the casino, Rosselli gained renown as the genius behind the success of the Tropicana. His status as an expert in real estate development and finance was unparalleled, and his position of trust within the leadership of the Chicago syndicate, and as a connection to the other top gangsters around the country, was secure. As Costello commented to a friend years later, 'We were always lucky to have Johnny in Las Vegas.'"

Rosselli was on hand for the largest expansion of gambling the nation had ever experienced, and he helped facilitate loans through the Teamsters Central States Pension Fund. He was on the scene when the Riviera was constructed and its key jobs filled with Chicago Outfit personnel.

As the Cuban Revolution consolidated its position in Cuba, Rosselli was a major player in the CIA's unsuccessful assassination attempts on Fidel Castro. Rosselli would later become an intriguing subject for the Church committee's mid-seventies attempt to resolve troubling questions of conspiracy surrounding the plot to kill President John F. Kennedy.

There are some indications that Rosselli really believed that one day he would make the full transition from gangster to corporate boss. He longed to leave the racket world inhabited by the likes of Marshall Caifano. But, of course, that wasn't part of the deal he'd made so many years before in Chicago. It was probable that Rosselli's heart was too full of larceny to make such a transformation possible.

By the mid-1960s, Rosselli and his brethren had their hooks into eccentric Howard Hughes. The bashful billionaire's midnight arrival by train in Las Vegas on Thanksgiving weekend has become the stuff of legends. Hughes went on a buying spree of a string of mob casinos. At times he paid twice what they were worth and reportedly stood by unaware that they were being robbed dry by associates of the men from whom he'd made the purchases.

For example, at one hotel on the graveyard shift, three craps tables were open for action. Only two were reported. As far as the third table was concerned, its drop (the money and markers dropped into the locked metal box that hung beneath the craps table) never made it to the counting room. At the end of the shift, it was opened with a mysterious duplicate key and the proceeds divided among the shift bosses and dealers. This went undetected for several months.

Las Vegas was losing its mobbed-up image and affecting a corporate veil, but Rosselli, a mob man, remained a major player.

He operated with a high profile in Las Vegas. Too high, perhaps. When word got around in December 1966 that Rosselli was associating with—and probably extorting from—some of the city's key casino licensees, Clark County Sheriff Ralph Lamb made him a priority.

Like the sheriffs before him, Lamb maintained a live-and-let-live philosophy with the Outfit men as long as they broke no laws and maintained low profiles. Their safety net was lifted if they did anything to embarrass Las Vegas and endanger its bread-and-butter industry.

On this particular evening, Lamb was told that Rosselli was at the Desert Inn with its owner, Moe Dalitz. Lamb found them in the coffee shop with longtime mob go-between Nicholas "Peanuts" Danolfo.

The sheriff sent in a rookie deputy with specific instructions: Approach and inform him that the sheriff wanted to see him downtown, as all felons who came to Las Vegas had to register their status.

"He told my guy to get lost, which he shouldn't have done," Lamb recalled years later. "I went in and helped him brush up on his manners."

What happened was that Lamb strolled into the coffee shop, grabbed Rosselli by his silk necktie, lifted him out of the booth, and then pulled him across the table and cuffed him about the head and shoulders all the way back to the patrol car. After handcuffs were snapped on, Lamb slammed Rosselli into the backseat.

At the sheriff's office, Rosselli was soaked with a delousing agent like an oversized rat. Whether he fully appreciated the moment remains unclear, but Rosselli was being sent a clear message: His star in Las Vegas was in steep descent. He could no longer hang out in the resorts for he attracted too much heat—and that heat could cause big problems for the casino operators.

From that mortifying day in December, Johnny Rosselli's Las Vegas profile changed. His decline in Las Vegas didn't slow his criminal activity, but it did marginalize it. The man who had been an integral player in the growth of gambling in Las Vegas and was involved in the plot to assassinate Fidel Castro was convicted in February 1969 of rigging a card game at the Friar's Club in Los Angeles. How the mighty had fallen! He was given a five-year prison sentence. When he emerged from behind bars, he was a shadow of his once-dapper self, but he wasn't finished making headlines.

In Washington, the Church committee met to discuss publicly for the first time some of the CIA's clandestine history. Rosselli's testimony about his involvement in the plot to kill Castro figured prominently.

FBI and CIA agents who testified before the committee arrived with elaborate files and working drafts at the ready to relate events as they recalled them. Rosselli worked without props. This clearly impressed Senator Barry Goldwater.

"Mr. Rosselli . . . it's remarkable to me how your testimony dovetails with theirs," Goldwater said. "Tell me, Mr. Rosselli, during the time that all this was going on, were you taking notes?"

"Senator," Rosselli replied dryly, "in my business, we don't take notes."

Rosselli's testimony was more colorful than comprehensive. He gave up none of his mob compatriots. Although he added credibility to what the senators already knew, his presence became a footnote when the committee's focus shifted from the failed Castro assassination plot to the FBI's relentless pursuit of civil rights leader Martin Luther King Jr. and the attempts to destabilize dissident political groups. This program had been confidentially labeled COINTEL-PRO.

Johnny Rosselli returned to his home in Plantation, Florida. He grew bored with each passing day and refused to take seriously warnings from friends.

On August 7, 1976, a fisherman discovered a 55-gallon drum floating off Miami in Dumfounding Bay. Inside the barrel were the remains of once-dapper Johnny Rosselli, who authorities believed had been murdered on orders from Florida Mafia boss Santo Trafficante. The reason: Rosselli gave public testimony without family approval. Others speculated that a hit team dispatched by Castro had paid back Rosselli for his participation in the assassination attempts.

At the time of his death, Rosselli no longer fit in the rapidly changing Las Vegas, but former Hughes aide Robert Maheu still remembers him with affection and awe. Maheu knew both Rosselli and Sam Giancana before the abortive CIA plot to assassinate Fidel Castro. He'd met them through his former business partner, Joe Shimon, when he partnered with Shimon in the investigation business.

With Rosselli gone, the Outfit once again went back to seeking the right man for the tough job of looking after its interests.

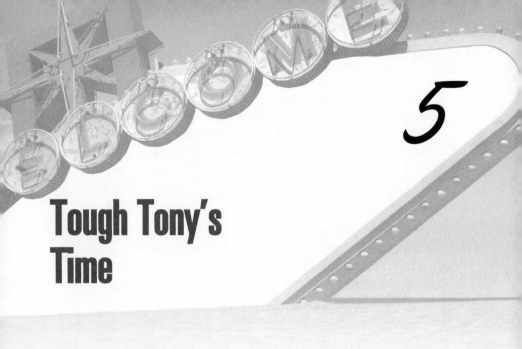

# Tough Tony's Time

**W**hen the Outfit dispatched its new tough guy to Las Vegas as a replacement for Johnny Rosselli and Marshall Caifano, the course of Las Vegas was about to change abruptly.

His name was named Anthony Spilotro.

As an undersized kid who grew up in Chicago, Anthony Spilotro gained an early reputation. He was arrested often for mopery, an extra-constitutional term the Chicago police used when they wanted to get a suspect off the street. Early on, Spilotro developed a penchant for violence. This made him a leader among his peers, future Las Vegans Frank Cullotta and Herbie Blitzstein among them. His activity also caught the attention of the Outfit, which like any large corporation, recruited promising employees.

Spilotro arrived with his wife, Nancy, in Las Vegas in 1971. He immediately obtained a gift-shop concession inside Jay Sarno's Circus Circus casino under the name Anthony Stuart.

(Stuart was his wife's maiden name.) But Spilotro didn't travel to Las Vegas to peddle key chains and souvenir ashtrays. He was there to deliver a message to every half-assed wise guy and loan shark that there was new muscle in town and that tribute would be paid.

Within months of Spilotro's arrival, five local gamblers and loan sharks were murdered. Money lender Jerry Dellman was shot at close range with a small-caliber weapon, likely a silenced .22. Although police initially suspected robbery as a motive, they had to discard this premise when they found a valise with thousands of dollars in the trunk that was untouched.

The murders of Dellman and the others were never solved. Obviously, whoever had come to Southern Nevada meant business. Without a shred of physical evidence, law-enforcement insiders immediately surmised the bloody activist was Tony Spilotro.

Spilotro didn't work alone. His territory was too big. He was being asked to enforce street rackets not only in Las Vegas, but throughout Southern California. He kept trusted childhood pals in his inner circle: Joey Hansen was dispatched to Newport Beach. The crew in Las Vegas included Frank Cullotta and Herbie Blitzstein. Cullotta was a burglar and an occasional hitter. Blitzstein worked bookmaking, money lending, and jewelry acquisitions. There were others, to be sure, but no members of the crew would be closer to Spilotro than these two.

Only days after his arrival, Tony picked up his first task force and FBI tail. Within weeks, there were articles in the press about his place in the underworld pecking order.

Like Caifano before him, Spilotro was short in stature, being 5 feet 5 inches tall. However his reputation for violence made him easily the biggest man on the streets of Las Vegas. He often complained that he needed a ladder to hit a victim in the head. That was his sense of humor.

Frank "Lefty" Rosenthal attracted only slightly less attention when he arrived in town. He had his own reputation in the Outfit, but unlike Tony, he was known as the sports handicapper supreme. He had a head for numbers the boys needed if they were to keep an eye on the skim at their Teamsters Central States Pension Fund-financed casinos. In those days, these included the Tropicana, Stardust, Hacienda, Fremont, and Marina.

Contrary to the impression he gave, Rosenthal was never officially a casino operator. In fact, his battle with the state Gaming Control Board would set precedent in establishing the constitutionality of the state's key employee-licensing and Black Book laws. But even with his innocuous titles of entertainment director, and later food and beverage manager, it was clear at the Stardust that Rosenthal held an uncommon sway over Argent Corporation Chairman Allen Glick.

Glick was a little known San Diego real-estate developer who mysteriously fell into Las Vegas casino ownership. He found willing financial backers in the mob-controlled Teamsters. Although he would be named B'nai B'rith Man of the Year in Las Vegas, Glick was linked to violence. People he did business with, most notably California real-estate partner and Argent investor Tamara Rand, were turning up dead with .22-caliber bullets to their heads. Authorities recognized Tony Spilotro's handiwork—although the little man surely had been assisted by Hansen, Cullotta, and others.

The Spilotro-Rosenthal combination was a setup that should have greatly improved the Outfit's odds of succeeding in Las Vegas where Caifano and Rosselli had failed. With a young bulldog attorney named Oscar Goodman representing them in their never-ending legal entanglements, Spilotro and Rosenthal lived in newspaper headlines even as they defied the authorities at every level.

The Argent casinos were money-churning enterprises, but the high profiles of the two men threatened to expose the boys for good. The state successfully moved to put both men in the casino Black Book. Spilotro's inclusion was hard fought by Goodman, but the decision was inevitable and relatively simple. In Nevada, associations counted, and Spilotro had plenty of

Mafia associates. Rosenthal's inclusion would prove more problematic for he had been more careful in his choice of friends. In the end, it didn't matter, and he, too, was included.

Tony became paranoid—and with good reason. He kept the blankets on his bed pulled up tightly over his head. He was so riddled with anxiety that on some days, he wouldn't get out of bed. Even a man as cagey as Spilotro knew the end was near. Everyone in law enforcement from the FBI to Las Vegas police rough-riding Intelligence Unit wanted to nail him.

The Justice Department's Organized Crime Strike Force was ready to drag him back to trial on charges that would put him away for life. Worst of all, his bosses in Chicago were furious over how badly he had jeopardized their thing in Las Vegas.

There were rumors—in part promoted by law enforcement—that Spilotro was using and selling drugs. (His longtime attorney and friend Goodman called the allegation false, but very damaging in Spilotro's world.)

Spilotro was also having an affair with Rosenthal's estranged wife, Geri. His Hole in the Wall Gang of burglars had been widely written about in the media, giving Spilotro's bosses fits. Most devastating, however, was the fact that the skim operation at the Stardust and the Outfit's Argent Corporation casinos had been exposed. It was this, above all, that doomed Spilotro.

Tough Tony had become a major embarrassment to his bosses. By the early 1980s, it was suggested that Rosenthal and Spilotro depart Las Vegas. It took them awhile to get the hint.

Rosenthal's profile had been so public that for a time he created and starred in his own television program, "The Frank Rosenthal Show." This featured an eclectic variety of guests ranging from Frank Sinatra and O. J. Simpson to bookmakers Joey Boston and Marty Kane. The show was dreadful, but Las Vegas insiders watched it mesmerized as it often disintegrated into Rosenthal ranting at the authorities.

Rosenthal's Chicago bosses were mortified at the high profile of their Mr. Inside.

With a mob-skimming case brewing in Kansas City and the

future of the Civella family at stake, Rosenthal received his retirement suggestion on October 4, 1982, when he turned the ignition of his Cadillac outside Marie Callendar's restaurant on East Sahara Avenue.

The car exploded, and only the heavy metal plating under the floorboard prevented the blast from killing the badly singed, but otherwise unhurt Rosenthal. Rumors immediately circulated, some spread by law enforcement, that Rosenthal's attempted killing was orchestrated by his longtime pal and Las Vegas confidant Spilotro.

From that moment on, Rosenthal's façade of legitimacy was shattered. He withdrew from the public's eye. Eventually he turned up in Fort Lauderdale as the manager, and likely behind-the-scenes owner, of a nightclub called Crocs. He started his own Web site, where he offered odds and handicapping services and occasionally wrote articles about none other than Frank Rosenthal.

Spilotro was more stubborn. He fought on. In truth, he had no choice. There was no safe haven for Tony, and all he could do was slug it out in court at the side of attorney Goodman. He managed to slip and squeeze through the system, winning a hung jury verdict on racketeering charges in the spring of 1986. This related to his Hole in the Wall Gang burglary case. But the government attorneys had determination and infinite resources.

Spilotro faced upcoming wars in the Stardust skimming trial and a retrial in the Hole in the Wall case.

He didn't have a promising future.

Although there was no indication that he might cut a deal with the Organized Crime Strike Force, he faced a life sentence if convicted. Unhappily for him, the mob knew he possessed intimate knowledge of a wide range of their criminal activities in Las Vegas, both within the Outfit's control and without. He knew which resorts were controlled by other mob families, especially those influenced by the incarnation of the Lansky-Genovese combine, which for many years had held a hidden interest in casinos that included Caesars Palace.

When Tony and his loyal brother, Michael, were summoned to Chicago for a sit down with their bosses, they went. They didn't return to Las Vegas. On June 23, 1986, their badly battered bodies were uncovered by a farmer in a wheat field next to the Willow Slough Preserve in Newton County, Indiana. This location was not far from Chicago mob boss Joey Aiuppa's retreat.

The double murder was pinned on Joseph Ferriola's crew, but as of this writing, no one has been charged.

The wheel turns, and in the end, Tony Spilotro died the way he'd lived.

Two of the toughest guys in Las Vegas history weren't soldiers of a Mafia family, but were members of law enforcement. Clark County Sheriff Ralph Lamb, the cowboy lawman who'd taken such pleasure in cuffing around Johnny Rosselli, formed a special task force of bruising linebacker-sized detectives whose primary purpose was to make life miserable for wise guys, thugs, and serial burglars.

They probably violated the constitutional rights of scores of criminals, but they also gained a reputation for ferocity that made even seasoned hit men cringe at their sight. The end of Lamb's career was triggered by a tax-evasion charge, of which he was acquitted. His legal troubles did nothing to diminish his legend among locals.

For years, Las Vegas was considered an elephant graveyard for FBI agents. They came to Sin City to play out the final years of their careers and perhaps to look for work in hotel security. Rarely did they challenge the status quo of the community.

That changed in 1980 with the arrival of an irascible, cigar-smoking former street agent named Joseph Yablonsky. Yablonsky was the federal bureau's first Jewish agent-in-charge and his tenure was marred by controversy, but it was also remarkably successful. His agents, most notably undercover expert Rick Baken, infiltrated Spilotro's Hole-in-the-Wall-

Gang crew and were on their way to putting Tough Tony away for life before his bosses beat them to it.

Yablonsky's undercover sting, Operation Yobo, netted several local politicians and judges. His biggest trophy was the tax-fraud conviction of U.S. District Judge Harry Claiborne, who was later impeached. Although Yablonsky was vilified in the Las Vegas press, and particularly by Hank Greenspun in his *Las Vegas Sun*, by the time he left in 1983, the town would never be the same.

The mob guys who built the Strip and give it its notoriety were shoved off stage by incarceration or internment.

Mob watchers noted that the Carlisi brothers, Sam and Roy, were senior members of both the Chicago and Buffalo families. Reliable sources said that the Carlisis had helped broker a change in Las Vegas in a meeting in Florida attended by members of Buffalo's Joseph Todaro crime family. Although the tough guys still found the city irresistible, for the first time in decades, representatives of the Chicago Outfit were no longer in charge. That duty fell to members and associates of the Buffalo mob.

But it was the same game. And Metro Intelligence Bureau and FBI agents soon had the Buffalo boys mimicking some of the same moves of their predecessors. The twist was clear: They tried to keep a low profile. They appeared to have connections in Nevada's multibillion-dollar telemarketing racket, and they didn't lean as heavily toward violence.

Buffalo's honeymoon in Vegas didn't last long. Its bookmaking and telemarketing operations were riddled with informants. Most of its made guys and associates were known to police. For instance, Big Steve Cino lived in Southern California and Las Vegas. He worked closely with members of the Peter Milano crime group. But the 400-pound bookmaker wasn't cut from the same cloth as Marshall and Spilotro. In fact, lack of menace was a distinguishing feature with the Buffalo mob.

When they finally did muscle up and murder Spilotro's aging lieutenant, Herbie Blitzstein, on January 6, 1997, the hit was telegraphed so loudly that authorities had little difficulty assembling their case. Although in the end, Cino and mobster Bobby Panaro Sr. were acquitted of charges related to ordering Blitzstein's demise, others in their circle were convicted.

Contrary to the contentions of corporate casino moguls and members of the community's unofficial chamber of commerce, there's still an organized crime presence in Southern Nevada. The existence of an endless river of cash makes that a certainty.

But the day of the tough guy in Las Vegas is nearly over. For law enforcement, the greater challenge now is in battling Asian and former Eastern Bloc mob crews. These take advantage of their language differences to slow investigations. Elements of Asian mob presence have been found in the proliferation of the massage-parlor business, which is often just a front for prostitution rings. Increasingly, Russian criminal figures based in Los Angeles have made efforts to establish themselves in Las Vegas.

More calculating and treacherous crews have replaced mobsters. These groups are so efficient that they ran the traditional mob guys off the land.

# Moe Dalitz, Racket Boss Reborn

**I**f modern Las Vegas has a founding father worthy of the title, it isn't Ben Siegel or some ordinary tough guy, but an infinitely savvier fellow named Morris Barney Dalitz.

His friends called him Moe.

Moe Dalitz was an important casino operator, developer, and philanthropist. Although no criminal case against him ever succeeded, mob cops and FBI men perceived him differently. They saw him as a major racket boss, Teamsters Pension Fund conduit, and "first among equals" peer of Meyer Lansky.

At the height of Dalitz's power and influence, he had the endorsement of senators and governors and was worth well in excess of $100 million. Along the way, Dalitz also made multi-millionaires of several devoted apprentices and partners. These were men who gathered their fortunes not on the casino floor, but by building homes and creating hit television series.

Although some preferred to downplay Dalitz's influence due to the notoriety that shadowed him, he was the quintessential patron who understood the strength in diversification. He didn't put all his eggs into one basket unless he owned the eggs and the basket and controlled all the chickens.

Dalitz was a man of complex contradictions. This seemingly gentle, thoughtful little fellow hunted mountain lions for sport from his southern Utah ranch. A loving father and charitable soft touch, he was also a man who was influenced and at times intimidated by the Chicago Outfit.

Moe Dalitz could have afforded a fleet of limousines, but he drove himself around town in an aging canary-yellow Volkswagen Bug.

He was recognized by many members of the Las Vegas Country Club as the elderly gentleman who usually ate alone at his regular table and always had a pleasant word for the staff and the ladies who passed by. New members at the club might never guess that he was one of its founders.

Moe was given to understatement and soft conversation. He liked to laugh and tell a joke although no one ever mistook him for Henny Youngman. By contrast, Moe was also the iron-willed man who encouraged Chicago mob hit man Tony Spilotro to join the country club. From dealing with volatile characters throughout his adult life, Moe knew that the best way to keep an Outfit guy off his back was to throw him a bone and some respect.

Moe was proud of being a Jew. This was never more evident than the time a close friend of builder Del Webb was juiced into the job of manager of the casino at the Sahara by Webb. For the sake of this tale, we'll call the man Jimmy Jacobsen.

From the moment he took charge, Jacobsen strode around the casino floor in ways that produced considerable consternation among the dealers. If he found a worker whose necktie wasn't straight or if he or she smiled in a way Jacobsen didn't like, the staffer was fired on the spot. Fear became so thick, you could cut it with a butter knife. Worse, Jacobsen was known to approach casino dealers to ask, "Are you one of those kikes?" His every third remark was seasoned with anti-Semitism.

Within a few days, news of what was happening reached Moe Dalitz in his office at the Desert Inn. Two men were dispatched to straighten things out.

They found Jacobsen standing at a craps table, berating the stickman. They sidled up to him, one on each side.

"Hi, Jimmy," one said. "Moe Dalitz sent us over to say hello. How are you doing?"

Jacobsen stiffened. He sensed trouble. He glanced first to the speaker on his right and then at the grim-faced man on his left.

"I'm doing okay," he said.

"Good," said the man on his right. There were a few seconds of silence and then, "By the way, Moe sent us with a message for you. He hears you're making nasty remarks about Jews. Moe doesn't like that. In fact, he told us that if you make another one, we're to break your arms and legs."

The man at his left spoke for the first time. "And Jimmy, if you don't believe us, make a remark now."

Jacobsen's cheeks turned pink and then white. He quickly left the table. He packed his personal possessions and was out of Las Vegas by midnight. He never returned.

There was no way for a casual observer to know that Moe Dalitz not only helped to found the country club, but was responsible for much of the growth and prosperity the Las Vegas Valley experienced from the 1960s through the early 1980s. He and his business associates built shopping centers, the first private hospital, and a couple of resort hotels, and his contacts with the men who ran the Teamsters Central States Pension Fund provided the wherewithal to construct almost every major casino property on the Strip.

Moe was born in Boston on December 24, 1899. His father, Barney, was a gambler and businessman who ran an industrial laundry. His father moved the Dalitz family to Michigan when Moe was still in knee pants.

In Ann Arbor, the elder Dalitz opened Varsity Laundry,

which catered to University of Michigan students. It was in these surroundings that Moe expanded his youthful associations not only with the collegiate crowd, but with members and associates of Detroit's notorious Purple Gang.

Although throughout his life he denied he was ever a member, he took advantage of his Purple Gang contacts to expand his business into the dangerous, but lucrative bootlegging racket. It was in those early years that a rising labor leader named James Hoffa befriended Dalitz when an attempt was made to unionize his father's laundry.

During Prohibition, the big money was in booze. Rum-running led Dalitz to Cleveland. There he became an admiral of the Little Jewish Navy of bootleggers who shipped cases and kegs of whiskey from Canada into the United States by boat and barge at night across Lake Erie. Business was so brisk that barges were loaded with trailer trucks filled with illicit alcohol. The crossing was directed by lookouts on shore using a green light/red light system.

"If they didn't get a green light, they'd sink the truck and return later for the booze," Dalitz told a friend. "They'd float a buoy and go after it when the coast was clear."

Repeal doomed the illegal liquor business, but by then Dalitz had amassed a small fortune. He parlayed it into a series of nightclub-sized casinos with names like the Mound Club and Pettibone Club near Cincinnati. He also owned the Lookout Club and the Beverly Hills Club across the Ohio River in Kentucky.

After Prohibition ended, Dalitz and his partners, Lansky and Sam Tucker, kept their hands in liquor production through the Molaska Corporation, which sold powdered molasses to distilleries throughout the Ohio area.

"When I left home, it was during Prohibition in Ann Arbor, Michigan, and I went into the liquor business when it was illegal," he told a reporter in a rare interview. "Then when the repeal came along, we went into the casino business in Kentucky and Ohio where it was legal. I learned everything I know there."

Although none who knew him underrated his toughness, Dalitz was more savvy than savage when it came to resolving disputes. Crime writer Hank Messick observed, "The reaction of Dalitz to a threat was typical of the man and of his methods. Even in those pioneering days of rum-running across Lake Erie, Dalitz and his associates used others to do the dirty work. Caution, not fear, was the basis of their method of operation.

"Even as young men, they understood the value of insulation, of remaining apart from physical violence. A fellow with brains and cash could always find a man with muscle to man the 'rummies,' as the boats carrying illicit booze were known. If necessary, they could also do a little killing."

Dalitz served as a captain during World War II, but this part of his life was almost a nonevent.

Following the war and before Tennessee Senator Estes Kefauver drove the Syndicate boys to Havana and Las Vegas, Dalitz became a powerhouse who owned laundries and gambling halls. In Miami, he co-owned the Frolics Club with New York partners. After Kefauver's Senate Rackets Commission focused on the evils of gambling, the Frolics Club closed down.

Testifying before the Kefauver committee in 1951, Dalitz didn't hesitate to spar with the Tennessee senator.

"As a matter of fact, you have made a great deal of money in recent years, so I suppose from your profits from one investment you would then go ahead and make another investment," Kefauver said. "To get started, you did get yourself a pretty nest egg out of rum-running, didn't you?"

Dalitz replied, "Well, I didn't inherit any money, Senator. If you people wouldn't have drunk it, I wouldn't have bootlegged it."

He used the same logic when questioned by a friend about his early casinos.

"How was I to know those gambling joints were illegal?" he cracked. "There were so many judges and politicians at the tables, I figured they had to be all right."

The heat from the Kefauver committee encouraged Dalitz

to move to Las Vegas, where the gambling activity was legal, and to Cuba, where the mob had a partnership relationship with President Fulgencio Batista. He became an owner of the Hotel Nacional in Havana.

Success in Havana was fleeting, lasting only until 1959 when Fidel Castro's right-hand commander, Ernesto "Che" Guevara's ragtag militia defeated Batista's much-larger army in the battle of Santa Clara and sent the dictator fleeing to Spain.

The Cuban Revolution seized the casinos. It operated them for a year and a half and then closed them.

By then, Moe Dalitz had discovered paradise in the Mojave Desert. Profits swelled in the counting room of the Desert Inn. Now operating legally, he became a respected citizen and a community leader. Only in the eyes of law-enforcement circles did he remain the notorious ex-bootlegger and gambler with mile-deep underworld ties.

Moe wasn't above reminiscing with his few intimate friends about his hair-raising past, but he considered himself someone who had made the break and was deserving of respect for his legitimate casino development and charitable works in Las Vegas.

He tried to limit his encounters with the kind of street guys he'd risen above so many years earlier. When a relative punk like transplanted Boston mob figure Willie Fopiano tried to make contact with his fellow Bostonian, Dalitz gave him the brush.

Fopiano was a gambling addict. He came from a wealthy Boston family and was a former boxer. As a boxer, he was a prolific money-earner for the mob. The mob referred to him as "Thrower" because of his ability to make his boxing losses by knockouts look real.

The mob, of course, always bet on his opponents.

Mob authority Ed Becker helped to get Fopiano's memoir published. It was called *The Godson*, and in it Fopiano wrote of Dalitz, "He tried to act like he was overjoyed to see me when I looked him up, but he didn't want me around at all. Whenever he ran into me he'd give my hand a quick shake and say 'Nice to see you, nice to see you'—and back away even while he was saying it! He got nervous just being in the same room with me.

"After all, Moe was now a legitimate businessman and philanthropist, the owner of casinos and lavish resorts and a pal of politicians like [Governor] Paul Laxalt and celebrities like Bob Hope. I knew too much about him. I knew about the satchels full of cash in the cabanas behind the Fontainebleau. I was an unpleasant reminder of where he came from. Guys like Moe become very selective about their memories."

What Fopiano didn't acknowledge was that someone like Moe Dalitz needed to watch his associations or risk losing his Nevada gaming license. These licenses were the keys that opened the doors to the counting rooms full of casino cash.

Given to bouts of overstatement, Fopiano said he considered trying to shake down Dalitz, but was talked out of it by an associate. In fact, a visiting soldier of Fopiano's stature would have found Dalitz "off limits" even late in the casino man's career. Although Moe was getting along in years, he could still cut his own meat. He was, after all, the man known to have pushed for the hit on Benny Siegel in 1947.

There were still moments when the hard edge from the Cerly days emerged. For example, there was an incident where he was challenged by brutish heavyweight champ Charles "Sonny" Liston.

When Liston raised his hand to hit Dalitz, the diminutive Moe stared him down and said quietly, "If you hit me, nigger, you'd better kill me. Because if you don't, I'll make one phone call, and you'll be a corpse within twenty-four hours!"

Liston couldn't have been more surprised if he'd been hit on the head with a crowbar. The champ lowered his fist, said nothing more, and slumped away.

This prompted local wits to joke about Cassius Clay's "phantom punch" and the fact that Moe Dalitz had knocked out Sonny Liston with no punch at all.

Moe met with Tony Spilotro shortly after that killer arrived in Las Vegas in the early 1970s. Rumors were floated that said that Dalitz paid Spilotro to stay away from him. They weren't true. The two men were quite at ease with each other. Moe offered Spilatro membership in the Country Club if he would buy an apartment in the Regency Towers. Regency Towers, in which Dalitz had a financial interest, was a high-rise apartment building located on the Country Club golf course in which Dalitz had a financial interest. Spilotro paid $67,000 for the apartment. As a Country Club member, he often sat in on the daily poker games.

Moe wasn't afraid to make the argument in the press that he was as good as the next man. In 1962, he told the *Saturday Evening Post*, "Let's say gambling isn't moral. Neither is drinking to excess. I believe Las Vegas has given people lots of fun. Sure, some will get hurt. But listen, they can go to Atlantic City and get into more trouble in a crap game than here, where there's supervision."

Although licensed and legitimate in Las Vegas, Dalitz remained notorious to law enforcement. As late as 1973, his face was featured along with those of Meyer Lansky, Frank Costello, Tony Accardo, and Al Capone on the back cover of a book by Hank Messick and Joseph L. Nellis, titled *The Private Lives of Public Enemies*.

Dalitz received even less respect between the covers. Messick repeated the rumor that Dalitz was an early member of Detroit's Purple Gang and Cleveland's Mayfield Road Gang.

Moe's dilemma was easy to understand: He considered himself a gambler and developer who lived in Nevada where operating casinos was legal. And yet much of the rest of the country saw him as a racketeer who did business behind a veneer of legitimacy.

Dalitz constantly tried to put his past behind him, but the stories wouldn't stop. And yet even in the last years of his life, Mafia representatives from Chicago, Cleveland, Kansas City, and New York listened with respect when he spoke.

Dalitz defied labels. He was a boss unto himself— although

the fact didn't prevent Mafia types from putting pressure on him over the years. He was at heart a relentless entrepreneur. Connected perhaps, but never resting and always investing. His investments included Sunrise Hospital and several shopping centers. He was an original investor in the sparkling La Costa project.

La Costa was a hangout for Allen Dorfman, who was head of the Teamsters Pension Fund from which he financed many Las Vegas hotels and casinos.

After James Hoffa was murdered, Dorfman hired two body-guards to accompany him to La Costa. There he would loudly proclaim to all who would listen that he knew who killed Hoffa.

The proclamation earned Dorfman a bullet in his head when he next visited Chicago.

The La Costa project became controversial when a maga-zine exposé described it as a Teamsters-financed haven for the mob. The 5,600-acre facility was deemed "La Costa: Syndicate in the Sun" by investigative journalists Jeff Gerth and Lowell Bergman. Their article resulted in a half-billion-dollar libel suit against *Penthouse*.

Jimmy "the Weasel" Fratianno told mob authority Ed Becker that around this time he was told to do "a job" on Dalitz. However, a few days later the "hit" was called off.

At the time, the FBI was surveying the Dalitz ranch in Utah. They reported finding cigarette stubs behind a tree over-looking the ranch.

Someone alerted Dalitz that he was being considered a mob "problem." The Desert Inn hired Becker to investigate, but he reported that whatever the problem, it had been cleared up.

Although Dalitz was thin-skinned and rarely missed an opportunity to lament his fate as a man who continued to suf-fer for half-century-old sins, Irwin Molasky and the rest had more to lose. His partners fought on even after Dalitz's claim was dismissed from the lawsuit on the grounds that, like Al Capone, he had no reputation that could be damaged.

During a break in the *Penthouse* trial, Dalitz mused about his fate to Las Vegas advertising executive Marydean Martin. She handled public relations for his Paradise Development.

"Moe almost never complained, but he was feeling down," Martin recalled. "He said, 'I'll bet your grandpa drank whiskey,' and I said that he did. 'I'm the guy who made the whiskey, and I'm considered the bad guy. When does the time ever come that you're forgiven?'"

But by that point in his life, in his heart of hearts, Dalitz knew the answer.

The trial ended with a letter in which neither party admitted wrongdoing, and in the end, a court ruled the article had not damaged La Costa's partners.

In 1950, Dalitz's gaming license had been "grandfathered" in. Although he'd been seen with spiffy hoodlums like Johnny Rosselli and associated with suspected killers Irving Devine and Peanuts Danolfo, he considered himself a legitimate taxpayer who made large charitable donations and was responsible for a long list of building projects.

The publicity surrounding the *Penthouse* trial pressured the Gaming Control Board to open a new investigation into whether the founding father of the modern Strip was suitable to hold a casino license.

The hypocrisy was hero-sandwich thick. Mob killer-turned-informant Aladena "Jimmy the Weasel" Fratianno testified that Dalitz was deeply involved with the Chicago Outfit. New Jersey mob boss Angelo "Gyp" DeCarlo in a recorded conversation expressed awe at Dalitz's power, influence, and independent holdings in Las Vegas.

The Jewish gambler wisely had done what so many of his Italian counterparts had not. He'd paid his taxes and so didn't need to conceal his income, which he then reinvested. DeCarlo noted sagely that Dalitz's voice was often key to who received Teamsters' pension fund loans in Las Vegas. One of his most-devoted friends declared, "If Moe told them to make somebody a loan, they made the loan." And by the 1980s, it didn't take a secret wiretap to understand what that meant.

This didn't prevent him from being honored as the B'nai B'rith Man of the Year.

Molasky recalled, "He tried to be low profile, but he just couldn't swing it. These dime store novels and myths written about him . . . he was tarnished with that all of his life."

Former Stardust General Manager Herb Tobman said, "He never turned me down for any charity. I was in awe of him. As far as I'm concerned, he was a great man. Moe's generosity is legendary. There has never been a greater influence on this city."

After the *Penthouse* trial, Dalitz slid toward retirement. His status in proper Las Vegas society hadn't been helped by the renewed criticism, and so he shrunk his circle of friends, traveled occasionally in his custom RV, ate breakfast at Tobman's Mr. T's café, and lunched at the Las Vegas Country Club.

Every so often, his name would be invoked again in a book on Las Vegas. The view of retired FBI agent-turned-author Bill Roemer was typical of many of his fraternity.

"During his days in Cleveland, Dalitz became close to many of the major mobsters around the country," Roemer wrote in *The Enforcer*. "These included Frank Costello, Longy Zwillman, Meyer Lansky, Bugsy Siegel, Lucky Luciano, Boo Hoff, Angelo Bruno, Joe Bonanno, Carlo Gambino, Albert Anastasia, and many others from the East. He also got close to Frank Nitti, Jake Guzik, Murray Humphries, Paul Ricca, and Tony Accardo in Chicago. They all recognized a keen intellect in Dalitz."

"Some people say Dalitz built Las Vegas," Roemer allowed. "He certainly became one of the town's leading citizens. I can understand the reverence with which some hold him. If you understand how he got there, why he got there, and who he represented when he got there, you might put a different spin on the story."

◆　◆　◆

In Las Vegas history, the Dalitz name would forever be identified with the rise and reign of "Wilbur Clark's Desert Inn."

Clark started to build a hotel and casino, but then lacked the funds to finish them. It was 1949, and Moe Dalitz was feeling pressure to move his gambling clubs to the only state where gambling was legal. So Dalitz and his partners Sam Tucker, Morris Kleinman, and Louie Rothkopf, known in Cleveland as the Mayfield Road Gang, took over the Wilbur Clark project. They used Clark, the affable unofficial mayor of Las Vegas, for their public image. They created the most-posh gambling palace in the burgeoning casino-resort community.

It was Dalitz who was responsible for adding a championship golf course and custom mansionlike homes to go with it at the back of the Desert Inn. He was also responsible for helping to create the Tournament of Champions PGA Tour event in Las Vegas, which gave the city much-needed positive publicity.

By the time the Dalitz group sold the Desert Inn to Howard Hughes in 1967, it had spawned high-end imitators in the Sands, Dunes, Tropicana, Aladdin, and Caesars Palace. Las Vegas was starting to shed its outlaw image although there were still plenty of outlaws left on the casino floor and on the street.

One motivation for the sale of the Desert Inn was increased law-enforcement wiretapping capability that kept uncovering evidence linking casino ownership to members and associates of organized crime.

Dalitz had other concerns. He was indicted on income-tax evasion charges in 1967 in Los Angeles in a case that saw his accountant, Eli Boyer, convicted and fined $1,000. The charges against Dalitz eventually were dropped at the request of the United States Attorney.

Dalitz lamented to friends that no matter how hard he tried to go straight, they kept dragging him back in. Not the mob, but law enforcement and the media.

He insisted throughout his life that he was never a member of Detroit's Purple Gang. His days as an admiral in the Little Jewish Navy of bootleggers were what had made him wealthy. In keeping with his father Barney's philosophy of spreading the money around, Dalitz diversified his business interests into a string of mostly legitimate concerns.

In Las Vegas, Dalitz became something of a hero by helping a number of young entrepreneurs get their starts. His protégés, included Merv Adelson, Irwin Molasky, Allard Roen, and Herb Tobman. These four distinguished themselves in film studios, business, and building development careers.

"Moe was an innovative thinker," said Irwin Molasky. "He said, 'Let's give them something extra. We'll build a golf course.' He was a good thinker. He was a good investor. Moe never bet against the tables. He gambled on people. He was a keen observer of character. It was one of his long suits."

For several years, Dalitz worked out of the Paradise Development office on Maryland Parkway. This was across from Sunrise Hospital, the medical center he was largely responsible for funding and constructing.

His financial backing and philosophical mentoring led to a variety of business successes including the Rancho La Costa Country Club community near San Diego and Lorimar Productions television and feature-film studio. Although some of Moe's protégés would downplay their benefactor's influence, there was no denying Dalitz had been a big man in the lives of many young businessmen who went on to make their millions in the new Las Vegas.

"When he knew he was dying, we would meet at the country club for a drink or two, or sometimes three, with Gen. Charlie Baron," singer Sonny King recalled. "People would approach Moe one after another and say, 'How are you feeling?' And Moe would say, 'I never had a bad day.'"

Near the end of his life, the wheelchair-bound Dalitz became a forgotten man to all but his closest friends. So when a group decided to picnic in the mountains and invited Dalitz, the tough old former rumrunner and casino titan was quick to accept. Marydean Martin wondered to her friend, Herb Tobman, about how long it had been since anyone invited Moe Dalitz to a picnic.

"I'd guess never," Herb Tobman said.

Dalitz stayed for hours and told stories long into the night.

Today, Dalitz's friends continue to guard his memory. "He was fun," Marydean Martin recalled. "He would laugh. It doesn't fit the image some people have of him, but he had a great sense of humor. He was generous and loyal to his friends and family. He was an old-fashioned gentleman. He had old-school manners. He was polite. He didn't swear in front of women, and he treated women like ladies."

By the time of his death at age eighty-nine in 1989, he'd beaten every rap but his own checkered reputation. He was heralded for his accomplishments in business and his life's many charitable works. Outsiders could think what they wished, but in Las Vegas, he would always be remembered as the benevolent godfather.

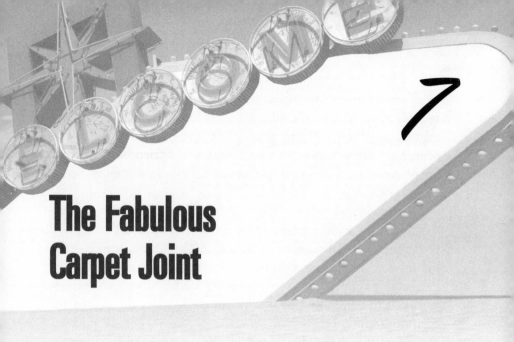

# The Fabulous Carpet Joint

W hen the Dunes Hotel opened its doors in May 1955, a turban-wearing Frank Sinatra rode an elephant into its lobby, and the fabulous carpet joint was heralded as the ultimate in Las Vegas excess.

From its opening night until the night it was imploded on October 27, 1993, to clear the ground for Steve Wynn's Bellagio, the Dunes was the quintessential mob operation. Everything about it was connected.

It offers a swaggering illustration of how brazenly organized crime wove itself into every layer of the Vegas hotel and casino fabric. Although this was clear to all who wanted to see, Nevada's gaming regulators always seemed to look the other way. Only when the mob activity became so brazen that it attracted federal law-enforcement attention did state authorities feel compelled to act.

61

When the Dunes opened, Joe Sullivan was the owner of record. Reporters would play a prank by paging New England crime boss Raymond Patriarca on the house public-address system. This was done so they could enjoy watching Joe Sullivan's antsy reaction, for Patriarca was among the joint's barely concealed owners.

Keep in mind that Las Vegas was still largely a weekend destination in the mid-1950s. Much of its tourist traffic flowed north from California on Friday nights. The Dunes stood on the opposite side of the road on which the traffic flowed into the city. Doomsday prophets said it was on the wrong side of the boulevard and that gamblers of that era would stay on the side of the Strip that housed the Flamingo, Sands, Riviera, and Tropicana.

The critics seemed to be right. For a time, the Dunes struggled and then was forced to close. Then it was leased to the operators of the Sands. This group fronted for the mob, but included the highly respected Carl Cohen and former New York bookmaker Sandy Waterman, manager Charles Turner, and former Arnold Rothstein enforcer Charles "Toolie" Kandell. They quickly tired of its problems, and it was sold to Bill Miller and Chicago oilman Major Riddle. These two had "friends" on both sides of the law.

However it wasn't until 1962 when Riddle sold 15 percent of the Dunes to George Duckworth and Midwest bookmakers Charles "Kewpie" Rich and Sid Wyman that the Dunes became really profitable.

Rich and Wyman catered to the nation of wise guys, and the casino got a big shot in the arm thanks to a development by Julius Weintraub. Weintraub may not have originated the junket business, but he honed it to perfection. Weintraub, known far and wide as "Big Julie," was a character straight out of the pages of *Guys and Dolls*.

Businessmen would book themselves for the "free" junket" at Big Julie's jewelry counter in a shop in the heart of New York's diamond market on Manhattan's Forty-seventh Street between Fifth and Sixth avenues.

They would board a large commercial plane, usually booked in its entirety by the Dunes. Then Big Julie would swing into action. He would peddle his jewelry from seat to seat. Then he'd hold a raffle and insist everybody participate. Then he'd ask everyone to kick in anywhere from $20 to $50 toward tips for the airline staff.

Once checked into the hotel, room, food, and beverage were complimentary ("comped") for the junketeers. Each junketeer would have his table action carefully monitored. It didn't matter so much whether you won or lost. What counted was the size of your wagers and how long you played. If you didn't give the Dunes enough action, you were scratched from future junket lists.

The Dunes was a major skim operation and was a haven for the hoodlum element. For a time, it was a kind of Times Square of Las Vegas as it filled with customers on its corner of Flamingo Road and Las Vegas Boulevard.

Junkets brought hundreds of players and millions of dollars to feed the Las Vegas cash cow each week. The experience introduced newcomers to the gambling experience and choreographed it so that the losses were as painless as possible.

Co-owner Sid Wyman was revered by his workers for his generosity and fatherly—or was it godfatherly?—advice.

Dunes telephone operator Laurie McCutchen echoed the sentiments of many when she said, "If you had a personal problem, you could go to that man and he'd help. If there was a complaint and the employee didn't deserve the criticism, Mr. Wyman would talk to that customer and straighten him out."

Longtime casino man and author Barney Vinson observed, "Today, no one knows who the casino owners are. It's all hidden through corporate structuring. But at the Dunes, the owners were right on the casino floor. They'd greet the players and slap them on the back like they were long-lost friends. Customers got that personal touch so lacking in the business today.

"Wyman had more points than all the rest of them put together. When you passed him in the hall, you gave him one of your children. He was a great man to work for, though."

The owners added the Miracle Mile golf course, and the throbbing, rather phallic eighteen-story neon sign was added in 1965 prior to the completion of the posh Teamsters Pension Fund creation Caesars Palace nearby. At last, the Dunes would be competitive.

With a production cost estimated at $5 million, the Casino de Paris topless floor show was an immediate hit.

The Dunes' twenty-two-story tower was part of the mob's reinvestment in the Strip, largely through its access to Teamsters Central States Pension Fund loans. But nothing was ever as it seemed in a mob hotel. The high-rise was riddled with structural flaws. Not all the sewer lines worked, and patrons who arrived late sometimes found themselves in rooms that lacked toilets. They were forced to use the restroom in the lobby.

In the casino's counting room, a different game was played. It was called skimming. This meant someone was grabbing bundles of the profits before they were declared and became taxable. These were delivered on a regular basis in suitcases to the hidden owners.

Big Julie's junkets were successful, but not all the markers were collectible. It was his job to negotiate settlements with those of his customers who had signed large markers. Weintraub, a heavy gambler himself, was almost beaten to death in the parking lot of Kennedy Airport when he forgot whose money he was collecting. Although he spoke no Italian, he knew the Mafia code of omertà and kept his mouth sealed when lawmen questioned him about the Colombo crime family members who attacked him. He learned his lesson in that single session. After that, every dollar he collected was delivered without discounts.

Colombo crime family capo Michael Franzese professed to making a major score courtesy of the limber operators of the Dunes. Robert Amira, whom Franzese described as a relative through marriage to Dunes owner Morris Shenker and a pal of Anthony "Tony Pro" Provenzano, was particularly accommodating.

"Anything I wanted—the best suites, the most beautiful women—Amira provided," he wrote in *Quitting the Mob*, co-authored with Dary Matera. "He also provided a $50,000 credit line. Instead of gambling the money away, Champagne Larry [Carrozza] and I would make a conspicuous show at gambling by whooping it up, flashing expensive jewelry around our necks and knockout women on our arms, betting heavy, and frequently switching tables and games to give the illusion that we were dropping tens of thousands."

Franzese also made a killing brokering stolen airline tickets for Las Vegas junkets.

"Between the credit line write-offs and the ticket scams, Champagne Larry and I became $500,000 richer thanks to the Dunes Hotel."

In 1975, an entirely new crew took over control of the Dunes. This gang was led by Morris Shenker, Teamster boss Jimmy Hoffa's St. Louis attorney. Shenker received a casino license despite his evident ties to notorious people. Investigators, for example, observed him in a heated conversation with Chicago Outfit underboss Joseph "Joey the Clown" Lombardo, a man intimately familiar with the Las Vegas-Teamsters connection.

Shenker played the role of the "see no evil" monkey when Chicago's representative Tony Spilotro simply took over the Dunes poker room. The Dunes played gracious host to many other organized crime figures, including Kansas City boss Nick Civella, St. Louis mobster Anthony Giordano, and a contingent of Genovese crime family members led by "Matty the Horse" Ianniello.

Civella was listed in Nevada's casino Black Book. He registered at the Dunes as John P. Sanders and sported a hat and fake beard. When his presence was discovered, it could have cost Shenker his gaming license. Instead, and in keeping with tradition, Shenker pleaded ignorance, and the hotel was ordered to pay a tiny fine even while publicly, Nevada's tough-on-the-mob façade remained intact.

Incidents like this did, however, force the Teamsters to withdraw their plan to funnel $40 million into the Dunes. Shenker sued the labor organization for breach of contract, but his case was thrown out of court.

Some of the leading citizens of Las Vegas remained below the radar. E. Parry Thomas was one example. Thomas, a founder of Valley Bank, was for more than a generation a central mover in the growth and development of Las Vegas. It was his bank that facilitated the Teamsters' investments in the gaming industry. He played a controversial, but seldom publicized, role in the Dunes.

Although Shenker was listed as the official licensee, for a time in the 1970s, the Dunes was owned by the Thomas-influenced Continental Connector Corporation. Notable within Thomas's inner circle were mob-connected financial men and attorneys that included Shenker as well as Del Coleman, Al Parvin, and the ubiquitous Beverly Hills attorney, Sidney Korshak.

The Dunes in those years was constantly bugged by the FBI, which knew that organized-crime elements were skimming the Strip casino resorts in a big way—especially those owned by Howard Hughes.

By 1979, Nevada's laissez-faire approach to the mob proved an embarrassment. The FBI announced it had discovered the mob's hidden interest in a number of Strip casinos, including the Dunes. The FBI charged that Kansas City's Civella family headed a group of off-the-books investors in the Dunes. Shenker feigned outrage and ignorance, but this time few believed his act.

Gaming regulators moved swiftly to force changes. However in one move, they outraged federal strike force veterans when they licensed Stuart and Clifford Perlman to manage the troubled property. The Perlman brothers were a duet whose ties to Meyer Lansky and the Genovese crime family had long been documented. A few years later, in an about-face, the Perlmans, who'd served as Caesars Palace executives, were rejected for casino licenses in Atlantic City because of their supposed mob associations.

Deprived of the anticipated additional Teamsters loans, Shenker filed personal bankruptcy. He claimed he was in debt for $34 million, but this didn't stop him from being the target of federal investigators until his death ten years later. The man who at one time enjoyed carte blanche with the Teamsters Pension Fund was indicted for tax evasion just one week before he died.

Although Shenker and wife Lillian were generous with employees, they saved the lion's share of the pretaxed skim for themselves and at one point infuriated the hidden owners in the Outfit. Both husband and wife were known to help themselves to bundles of $100 bills for their personal use.

"Shenker certainly was not committed to maintaining and reinvesting in the property," casino industry veteran Richard Goeglein said. "He milked it dry. Shenker was primarily interested in hauling money out."

After wealthy California farmer and gambler John Anderson failed to return the Dunes to its fleeting past glory, in 1987, Japanese billionaire Masao Nangaku bought the property for an incredible $155 million—nearly twice what it was worth at the time.

Nangaku's Las Vegas experience included a multimillion-dollar background investigation, the hiring of a team of high-priced attorneys to secure his license, and the acquisition of a variety of highly paid consultants.

The Japanese billionaire was soaked like a carnival rube by his new friends in Las Vegas. Although he was eventually licensed despite his association with the pachinko-parlor industry—a racket traditionally controlled by the Yakuza—Japan's counterpart to the Mafia. Nangaku's big plans for the Dunes and a downtown office building to be named the Minami Tower never materialized. When the mile-high Tokyo real-estate market tumbled, so did Nangaku and his fortune.

The Dunes remained a careworn grind joint, and construction on the office high-rise was halted after a foundation was dug. Local wags christened the business project the "Minami Hole."

67

Nangaku sold the Dunes and its massive surrounding real estate and immense water rights in 1992 to Steve Wynn for $75 million. By anyone's measure, this was a bargain price and helped cement Wynn's reputation as a brilliant dealmaker. Wynn made no secret of his plan to erase the Dunes and build his own palace in its place.

The Dunes implosion made international news, and its image was used by Martin Scorsese in the movie, *Casino*, to symbolize the end of hidden mob ownership in Las Vegas.

♦ ♦ ♦

The removal of the Dunes had a touching epilogue. Hundreds of former Dunes employees gathered at a reunion to reminisce about the casino and the incredible clientele it attracted.

Geno Munari, who was a baccarat dealer and also worked in the poker room, remembered one dramatic incident in his career. It happened while he was getting a shoeshine in a casino bathroom. A fight broke out between two Dunes bosses. One pulled a gun on the other. Later, the unarmed Munari was reprimanded for not trying to break up the fight. This was a duty not spelled out in his job description.

Others shared nostalgic memories. In its heyday, the Dunes was a magnet for celebrities. Cocktail waitress Roz Porter recalled regularly pouring copious amounts of white wine for Judy Garland. Porter used to watch Hollywood stars Betty Grable and Lucille Ball at the craps tables, throwing dice like professionals.

"Some of the best years of my life were working at the Dunes," Roz Porter declared.

The legendary Nick the Greek played poker there. Dealers remembered other celebrity gamblers including Dan Rowan, Pat Boone, Elizabeth Taylor, Telly Savalas, and Redd Foxx.

Cary Grant cut quite a swath through the place, causing heads everywhere to turn, and room-service employees who dealt with Laurence Olivier were impressed with his common touch. "We just delivered a beer to Sir Laurence," they said.

One room-service waiter remembered how angry some junketeers became when they lost a lot of money at the tables. He remembered how one unlucky junketeer, knowing everything was comped, ordered room service to deliver a case of expensive champagne to his suite. He then got some sort of sick satisfaction by pouring it all into the toilet, bottle by bottle.

Who would have thought the fabulous, funky carpet joint would engender such loyalty and so many fond memories?

# Howard Comes to Las Vegas

ow Howard Hughes slipped into Las Vegas one November night in 1966 and in less than four years became the most-powerful man in Nevada is a Las Vegas legend. It is as intriguing as any of the other myths that have become the city's trademark.

That Hughes-the-corporate giant consumed so much in so little time, like a glutton at an all-you-can-eat buffet, is not in question. Whether Hughes-the-man was at the helm of the vast buying spree has been a point of dispute between his allies, most of whom grew wealthy, and authors and investigative reporters, who sometimes painted a brutal portrait.

Elements of truth about Hughes have been blended with fanciful fiction and outright deception. We're not talking about Hughes the aviator, or Hughes the Hollywood producer, or Hughes the wealthy playboy of the Western world. No, we're talking about the Howard Hughes who in fact and fantasy is credited with driving the mob from Las Vegas within months of his arrival.

This eccentric rich man came along at a fortuitous time in Las Vegas history. The mob needed him. Desperately.

The fairy-tale view is contradicted by facts, but the Hughes hotel acquisitions did remake the image of Las Vegas into a tourist haven free from organized crime. And in Las Vegas, image has always been more important than truth.

Howard Robard Hughes was born on Christmas Eve in 1905 with a golden spoon in his mouth. He was three years old when his flamboyant father took time out from being an oil wildcatter to invent the drill bit that revolutionized the oil industry. In time, thanks to his shrewdness in licensing rather than selling the drill bit, the elder Hughes became immensely wealthy.

Young Howard was put in charge of his father's company in 1924 and by 1932 had expanded its holdings to include Hughes Aircraft as Howard made headlines by setting world flying records.

A plane crash in 1946 almost killed him. Some physicians would contend that it was the head injuries he suffered in this accident that led to his mania and eccentric behavior in later years.

The Hughes legend, as rendered by some journalists and press agents who sell the gaming industry to the gullible public, mentions Hughes's reclusive nature and his fondness for banana-nut ice cream. However, they rarely refer to his germ phobias, his drug addiction, his virulent hatred of Blacks, his vast contacts within the CIA and the military-industrial complex, and his direct ties to the Nixon White House and the Watergate break-in. Also, his intolerance for any development in Nevada that he didn't control.

Did Howard Hughes clean up Las Vegas and release Nevada from the grip of the gangsters?

His former lieutenant, Robert Maheu, says the answer is emphatically yes.

Robert Aime Maheu, a man who "arranged things" for scores of wealthy clients, became a rich man himself while working for Hughes. Indeed, it was Maheu who later negotiated with the mob behind the scenes and out front in Washington so the Hughes organizations could acquire covertly mob-owned hotels and casinos.

"We didn't make the new Las Vegas," Maheu said in a 2004 interview. "I like to say we got it ready."

And yet, the argument can be made that Hughes contaminated the city with his dictatorial need to destroy everything that he couldn't corrupt or control. Despite the best efforts of the public-relations revisionists, Hughes was a flawed hero.

But what a juicy story he made.

Howard Hughes arrived in downtown Las Vegas by private rail car before sunrise on Thanksgiving Day, 1966. He was carried on a medical gurney to a waiting ambulance and driven directly to the Desert Inn.

The heavily sedated Hughes was deposited neatly into a ninth-floor penthouse suite like a sack of gold.

Hughes had reserved the entire penthouse floor. The first thing his aides did was to shutter and then blacken all the windows in the rooms he occupied.

Hughes had been persuaded to come to Nevada by Southern Nevada's greatest imagemaker, *Las Vegas Sun* publisher Hank Greenspun. Greenspun had extolled the state's tax benefits (no income tax), but what Hughes liked to hear the most was Greenspun's assurance that a man with money could buy land in Nevada in big, brazen chunks.

Howard chose Las Vegas as his headquarters only after rejecting Lake Tahoe at the last minute. Although Hughes was known as a wily and wildly successful business tycoon who made hundreds of millions from the sale of airline stock and the acquisition of federal contracts, it's as if he'd lost at least some of his ability to reason when he settled in at the Desert Inn.

Hughes quickly became Citizen No. 1 in the eyes of Gov. Paul Laxalt, who was faced with governing a state whose major "industry" was now fighting off federal investigators and inquiring journalists.

Hughes had total loyalty from Laxalt and Nevada's tiny congressional delegation. From his Nevada base, Hughes perfected a model of political influence, corruption, and domination that enabled him to secure more than $6 billion in federal military contracts and subsidies.

Robert Maheu insists, "Howard said he came here to buy properties. He didn't have any desire to become involved in gaming. He felt this was going to be his last stand. In Los Angeles, he was one of many, many people who were big. But in Nevada, he could be the biggest fish in a small pond."

That changed when he was given an eviction notice by Moe Dalitz. Dalitz sent word upstairs that the Hughes party would have to vacate the penthouse floor because the casino needed the rooms for high-rolling gamblers. Not wanting to be inconvenienced by having to move, Hughes gave orders to Maheu to buy the hotel.

Circumstance suddenly smiled on Hughes, as it often did. Desert Inn owner Moe Dalitz would ordinarily have deep-sixed any offer for his hotel and casino. Now he was under indictment for tax evasion. Despite his juice with governors and U.S. senators, he knew there was a real risk that a conviction would cause him to lose his gaming license. It was a ripe moment. Dalitz agreed to sell his Desert Inn to Hughes.

Dalitz was later acquitted of the tax-evasion charges.

Now Howard Hughes needed a license.

Laxalt pushed through Hughes's casino license without Howard even having to make the required appearance before the Gaming Commission. If Nevada could license someone with the shady pedigree of a Moe Dalitz, it could grant small favors to the new brightest star in the financial heavens.

In *The Money and the Power: The Making of Las Vegas and Its Hold on America: (1947-2000)*, Sally Denton and Roger Morris observed: "Laxalt instantly recognized that substituting Hughes for Dalitz would provide an improved national image over Teamster-financed property."

Laxalt was rewarded for his efforts. After leaving the governor's office, he participated in one of the sweetest casino deals in Nevada's history. He and a brother were able to build and operate the Ormsby House hotel and casino in Nevada's capital, Carson City. They received loans enough to do this and risked just $1,851 of their own money.

With license in hand, Hughes understood the immense profits possible with casino ownership. He began his casino-buying spree. Over the next three years, he bought and overpaid for the Sands, Desert Inn, Frontier, Landmark, and Silver Slipper. He also bought Harold's Club in Reno. He was as badly taken as any greenhorn who bought the Brooklyn Bridge from a stranger on the street.

Mafia lieutenant-turned-informant Aladena "Jimmy the Weasel" Fratianno said that Maheu's friend, John Rosselli, told him Hughes was "roped into buying the D.I." and the widely circulated story about the billionaire's impending eviction from the hotel was nothing more than a puff of public relations. Rosselli added, "Now it looks like he wants to buy the whole town, if we let him. He's just what we need, especially with Maheu running the show."

Traditional mob control of the Hughes casinos continued. Hughes became a running joke in some Strip circles as the gambling baron whose casinos had a unique quality: They lost money consistently.

How much?

An IRS confidential investigation determined that mob people skimmed Hughes properties for in excess of $50 million. Five of his seven casinos lost money.

Hughes seemed oblivious. Despite his germ phobia, paranoid delusions, and narcotics addiction, he managed to put in a full day pushing the buttons of his empire from his penthouse bedroom.

By the time the Justice Department stepped in to halt

Hughes's buying spree, he already owned 25 percent of the hotel-room capacity in Las Vegas. Hughes also bought hundreds of gold-mine leases and thousands of acres in Nevada.

# Howard Buys Nevada

Volumes of handwritten memos portray him as a microman-ager, but Howard Hughes was clearly unaware that the casinos he owned were being systematically looted of pre-taxed millions. (This is a view Maheu adamantly rejects.) In short, Hughes was as much a sucker as a savior.

In one of the flood of memos to Maheu, Hughes wrote, "I do not indulge in sports, nightclubs or other recreational activi-ties. In fact, I do not do much of anything else at all, except my work. I work around the clock. Holidays mean very little to me since I work just about all the time."

Maheu was a former FBI agent whose network of contacts ranged from top CIA operatives to John Rosselli, the Chicago Outfit's representative in Las Vegas and Hollywood. Hughes refusal to meet new people because of his obsessive fear of germs resulted in a strange relationship with Maheu. The man in charge of all his Nevada interests could communicate with Hughes only by memo and a rare telephone call. The joke that went around was that at his salary of $500,000 a year plus perks, Bob Maheu was willing to risk writer's cramp.

Hundreds of memos were exchanged by the two men, but in the seventeen years that Maheu worked for Hughes, the two men never had a single face-to-face meeting.

In *Citizen Hughes*, Michael Drosnin captured the literary interaction between Maheu and his boss. Drosnin surmised that by the time he reached Las Vegas, Howard Hughes was more smoke than sanity.

"In fact," wrote Drosnin, "Hughes may have been far more of a 'Patsy' than he ever realized. Las Vegas seemed to be changing hands, from the mobsters who created it, to Hughes; but the billionaire may have been only an unwitting front man for the Mob. His arrival could not have been more timely for organized crime. After two decades of lucrative skimming, the heat was on.

"A massive FBI wiretap operation had become public, revealing that the hidden owners of the casinos routinely took their profits off the top, shipping the hot cash down to Miami, where the mastermind Meyer Lansky counted the take in his condo on Collins Avenue and made the split for his Mafia cohorts across the country. Just when it looked like the jig was up, Hughes arrived. A mark with an unlimited bankroll."

The fact that a book like *Citizen Hughes* could be freely published was in itself a reversal of fortune. Early in his life, Hughes developed an obsessive antipathy to publicity. He was particularly afraid of books that might spell out his somewhat peculiar dealings with women. He wasn't concerned about the Katharine Hepburns or Jane Russells, but rather with the many other Hollywood starlets as well as the beautiful ladies he met through Johnny Meyer, the public-relations man who acted as his procurer.

The result had been a windfall for some book publishers. All a publisher needed to do was to announce a forthcoming biography of Howard Hughes and Hollywood attorney Greg

Bautzer would be at his doorstep asking what it would cost to "delay" publication.

Deciding to break this blackout, publisher Lyle Stuart signed a contract with former *Time* magazine writer Ezra Goodman to write a Hughes biography. In 1968, Hughes had been out of the news for years, and Stuart felt a Hughes biography would have strong commercial possibilities.

Bautzer sprang into action. The Hughes organization leased the East Side Manhattan townhouse of model Faye Emerson, who, by then, had married and divorced Elliot Roosevelt, son of former President Franklin D. Roosevelt.

Conferences were held in the townhouse first with Stuart and then with Stuart; his attorney, Martin J. Scheiman; and author Goodman.

Bautzer said that all Hughes wanted was to have the biography postponed until the United States Supreme Court rendered its verdict in the TWA case. Two hundred thousand dollars would be placed in escrow bank accounts for both publisher and author. This money would be returned to Hughes after the verdict at which time the two could go ahead with the book. As a reward for their cooperation, Hughes would answer written questions and follow-up questions, as well. But there were to be no questions about his affairs with women.

The Hughes offer fell apart when Ezra Goodman agreed to postpone the book indefinitely if he could keep the $200,000. Stuart was appalled. "I intend to publish a Howard Hughes biography," he declared. "If Ezra doesn't write this book for us, we'll find someone who will."

Goodman reluctantly agreed to go ahead with the writing.

Shortly after the townhouse meetings, the Hughes people made a secret deal with Goodman. They paid him an outright $67,250 to sign an agreement giving them "editorial supervision." The terms were that Goodman would not turn in any part of the book to Stuart's company before the Hughes people "edited" it. This would allow Hughes to control every word said about him, and he could censor what he didn't like.

A Stuart admirer tipped him off about the secret deal. The publisher was able to smoke it out, and Goodman was told he was off the project. Stuart then sued Goodman for the return of his $10,000 advance and won.

The publisher met with another writer of prominence. But when he mentioned that the writer probably would be approached by the Hughes people, Stuart became uncomfortable with the way the writer's eyes lit up. So he turned to a friend who was a Philadelphia attorney. Stuart knew this man wasn't a great writer, but he also knew he couldn't be bought off. His name was Albert B. Gerber. Like Stuart, he was an active defender of the First Amendment.

It was the first time Bautzer failed in his mission to suppress. *Bashful Billionaire* was published under the Lyle Stuart imprint. The biography sold well enough to make it onto the *New York Times* national bestseller list. From that point on, Hughes gave up on trying to prevent books about himself. A trickle, starting with *Howard Hughes in Las Vegas* by Omar Garrison, was soon followed by a steady stream. Today there are dozens of books devoted to the life and times of Howard Hughes.

Journalist-author Sergio Lalli observed, "Hughes may have had a warped soul for all we know. His body, we know for sure, was wasting away. And narcotics certainly numbed his sensibilities. But during his Las Vegas years at least, the intellect of Howard Hughes functioned well enough to carry on an elaborate and coherent correspondence that would have been impossible if Hughes were merely a raving idiot. He could still think—in his own peculiar manner."

At one point, it was estimated the Hughes machine was spending $367,000 a day on acquisitions in Nevada. From 1966-69, he also made more than $800,000 in political contributions through the Silver Slipper. The casino offered an illegal delivery system for Richard Nixon's presidential campaign coffers. One can only guess how many of the dollars reached their destination.

◆　◆　◆

Less than a year after he set up quarters in the Desert Inn,

Hughes issued a statement to Southern Nevadans. He was going to improve the face of the Silver State. He promised to help diversify the economy by creating industry of the sort that had made him richer and famous.

Hughes painted a future in which Las Vegas would become a clean, bright, shining city in the sun. "We can make a really super environment: no smog, no contamination, efficient local government, where the taxpayers pay as little as possible and get something for their money," Hughes wrote in a memo.

Hughes gave himself wiggle room in the form of an uncertain time frame: "To be completely fair, I should warn you that I am not noted for getting things done in a hurry. I promise one thing: It won't be on as favorable a schedule as you expect, or as favorable a schedule as you would like it to be, or as favorable a schedule as I would like it to be."

As with many promises that he made, Hughes failed to keep that one. He saw Las Vegas as his banana republic, not his reconstruction project.

For example, Hughes wrote to Maheu: "Ever since I arrived here, I have been fighting attempts to downgrade the Strip into some kind of freak show. If one of these sideshows is allowed, there will be three or four or more and then we will have a real avenue of merry-go-rounds and roller coasters."

But Maheu couldn't persuade him to do anything to improve that landscape.

The fact that Hughes didn't build anything and had no intention of creating industry to diversify the local economy did nothing to cool the ardor of his biggest supporter, Laxalt. The governor gushed to reporters, "Anything this man does from the gaming industry all the way down the line will be good for Nevada."

Drosnin observed, "The only thing Hughes would ever build in Nevada was Maheu's new mansion, and indeed he would do his best to block all new hotels, all industry, and all 'competition.' But as each day brought some fresh report of Hughes's intended good works, nobody seemed ready to refuse him a couple of more mere gambling casinos."

"Employees and associates, including senior government officials, exploited his illness," Denton and Morris wrote. "No one lifted a hand to give him obviously needed help. Even to acknowledge his suffering was to endanger the image of a 'competent' Hughes, an image imperative to those around him with their own purposes, the managers and bureaucrats to retain their places in the far-reaching business empire he gave them, his lesser personal aides for mere perquisites."

Something of the private Hughes has been revealed in his handwritten memos. It is through those that the tortured soul of the man emerges.

He was on top of his world, and yet, he felt seriously threatened by Negroes.

Hughes was such a bigot that he not only opposed integration, not an uncommon political stance in that day, but he was also against low-rent housing for the poor. This because he felt so many Blacks would qualify for it. He was very upset when KLAS-TV, the Las Vegas CBS affiliate, announced that it would air Black Heritage programming.

His racism was so deeply imbedded that he actually canceled a championship tennis match at the Desert Inn because the Black star Arthur Ashe was slated to play.

Hughes wrote in a memo to Maheu, "Now, I have never made my views known on this subject. And I certainly would not say these things in public. However, I can summarize my attitude about employing more Negroes very simply—I think it is a wonderful idea for somebody else, somewhere else.

"I know this is not a very praiseworthy point of view, but I feel the Negroes have already made enough progress to last the next 100 years, and there is such a thing as overdoing it."

Hughes, in a fit of paranoia, decided that Maheu was robbing him. He called Maheu a thief and fired him. Maheu responded with a philosophical observation. "Howard Hughes wants total power," he said. "I don't think he feels he has enough power. He wants power over everyone. He craves power. There is no doubt in my mind that he feels he is more powerful than the president of the United States. He wishes to control history."

After he fired Maheu, and jilted Greenspun and others who'd benefited so much from his bankroll, Hughes left Las Vegas in the middle of the night in 1970 aboard a jet borrowed from high-rolling arms dealer Adnan Khashoggi.

He was flown to the Bahamas, where he settled Desert Inn-style in the penthouse of the Britannia Beach Hotel. He could afford the room rate, no matter the tourist-season charge, for by then his operations were earning nearly $2 million a day from the federal government. For those who understood the corrupt system of contract procurement within the military-industrial complex, Hughes seemed a one-man cartel who managed to balance intimate contacts both with the White House and CIA.

James B. Steele and Donald L. Bartlett wrote in their award-winning 1975 series for the *Philadelphia Inquirer:* "Howard Hughes has become almost a clandestine branch of the federal government, operating in total secrecy, guaranteed secret profits, checked or monitored by no outside force whatsoever."

Hughes had an army of ex-FBI agents and Defense Department officials on his payroll in activities that served as a template for procurement of defense contracts in the American military conflict in Iraq during the administration of President George W. Bush. The Hughes cartel practiced influence peddling at the highest levels.

Bartlett and Steele observed: "All this takes place against a shadowy backdrop of occurrences that include: secret political contributions; business dealings punctuated by suicides; stated campaigns to buy and control politicians; sharply inflated markups on government contracts; and the failure of both the Watergate special prosecutor's office and the Senate Watergate Committee to investigate the full range of Hughes' ties to the administration and associates of former President Richard M. Nixon."

Hughes's system of cash political payoffs was entangled with the Watergate burglary, which eventually brought down Nixon.

By the end of his life, Hughes had gone from savior of Las Vegas to a Mafia unto himself with allegations of fraud, government kickbacks, phony charitable organizations, and political corruption.

Whether he was lucid enough to understand any of it is a mystery for the ages.

Howard Hughes broke all his promises to the people of Nevada. He built no manufacturing plants. He built no medical school. Although the tremulous local media uttered few words of criticism of him during his Las Vegas tenure, outside investigative reporters gradually began to ferret out the truth about the man and his vastly corrupt machine.

By the time he left Las Vegas, Hughes controlled a $300-million Nevada empire. Although the federal government had prevented him from buying the Stardust, Caesars Palace, Riviera, Dunes, and Harrah's casinos in Reno and Lake Tahoe, he still owned 17 percent of Nevada's gaming industry. He owned 2,700 mining claims and had acquired tens of thousands of acres of raw real estate.

The boss few people ever glimpsed was the largest employer in the state.

Albert B. Gerber summed him up well in his *Bashful Billionaire*. He wrote: "Probably no man epitomizes our neurotic century better than Howard Hughes."

One of the ironies of Hughes's extended Vegas vacation and reign was his utter lack of imagination when it came to making his mark either on the Strip or downtown. (It was a factor that fueled speculation that he was not his own man.)

In the new century, the citizens of Nevada have few reminders of their one-time king. Among his holding was a vast undeveloped desert tract around Las Vegas that took the name of his grandmother, Jean Amelia Summerlin.

Today, it is the name Summerlin, not Hughes, that is synonymous with planned residential and commercial development in Southern Nevada.

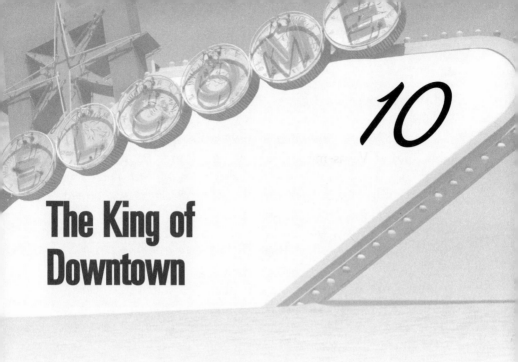

# The King of Downtown

T he elderly man ambled through the El Cortez, one of downtown's oldest casinos, and greeted porters and change girls by
their first names. He stopped to chat with a slot player. Then
he smiled as he bent over to pick up an empty cocktail glass.

He wore no uniform, just a simple sports coat and slacks.
Before his walking tour was finished, he'd emptied an ashtray
and bantered with the casino's venerable shoeshine man about
the man's plans for retirement.

It isn't often in the new corporate Las Vegas that you'll see
a casino's owner picking up in his own joint, but this was a daily
sight at the El Cortez. The gaming industry is a breeding
ground for big egos, but John Davis "Jackie" Gaughan wasn't
above getting his hands dirty. If Gaughan had an ego, he kept it
well hidden, and this wasn't because he didn't have a lot of success to crow about. With the half-dozen moneymaking casinos

that he either owned alone or in private partnership, he could lay claim to the unofficial title of King of Downtown.

Steve Wynn generated more headlines, and Kirk Kerkorian had bigger hotels, but Jackie Gaughan figured he had both men beat when it came to low overhead and profit percentages. What's more, he didn't have a board of directors or a crowd of finicky shareholders breathing down his neck.

Gaughan was the last of a generation of casino men who made their bones when Bugsy Siegel was still alive. And there was a time in the mid-1980s when old friendships and associations haunted him when he applied for a gaming license in Atlantic City. But in Las Vegas, Gaughan remained a pivotal character in the development of the casino business and continued to play an active role in casino operations at the El Cortez, Jackie Gaughan's Plaza, Las Vegas Club, and several slot joints on Fremont Street. He also owned percentages of other casinos. At various times, he held a large number of points in the Golden Nugget and sat on the board of directors of Showboat International.

He was most comfortable downtown and after 1986, appeared content to remain there while his eldest son, Michael Gaughan, expanded the family name in casinos on and off the Strip.

Jackie Gaughan was born in Omaha, Nebraska, on October 24, 1920. The Omaha Gaughan grew up in what was a wide-open town that wasn't restricted much by either Prohibition or its antivice laws.

The Capone mob held substantial sway in Omaha, which was considered a safe town for hoodlums on the lam to cool their heels. With wealthy cattlemen and farmers coming to Omaha for a good time, it produced a steady cash flow for gamblers and bootleggers.

As a young man, Jackie Gaughan saw his uncle, Patrick Gaughan, work as a bookmaker and bootlegger. (Patrick died after being shot during a bootlegging skirmish.) Jackie was sixteen when he took his first job as a bookmaker at the Bell Cigar

Store. True to his nature, he went from clerk to owner in a few years. He also became acquainted with fellow bookmaker Eddie Barrick, who by then had gained a national reputation.

Gaughan took bets and worked a racket that was tolerated by the local authorities. (He would eventually attend Creighton University before being drafted into the Army Air Corps, where he continued to make book.) With Barrick as his partner, Gaughan opened a storefront race and sports book called the Baseball Headquarters.

Outside Omaha, Barrick opened the Chez Paree, which in the late 1930s was considered the largest gambling hall between Chicago and Las Vegas. It operated with minimal scrutiny from law enforcement.

In the late 1930s, Omaha was a volatile place for gamblers. Gaughan's partners, Sam Ziegman and Casey Gaughan, were nearly killed while trying to take over the city's lucrative race-wire services. Their plan was aborted after some of their customers' operations were bombed. This violence inspired the state attorney general to call for a clean up of Omaha.

In 1942, Gaughan found himself in the Army Air Corps stationed in Tonopah, Nevada, where he remained until 1946. He was a frequent Las Vegas visitor, and by the time he left the service, he'd purchased a 3-percent stake in the Boulder Club downtown. Although he sold his interest in the Boulder Club a short time later, in the process he gained valuable friendship with downtown casino man, John Kell Houssels Sr.

At that time, he might have made his mark in Las Vegas, but, instead, Gaughan returned to Omaha where he earned his Bachelor of Science degree at Creighton. He opened a small bookmaking operation inside the Park Avenue Cigar Store and worked part time at the Stork Club in Council Bluffs, Iowa. One of the operators of the Stork Club was Costello mob associate Chickie Berman, whose brother Dave Berman would become a percentage owner of Ben Siegel's Flamingo. Gaughan also was a member of a short-lived partnership that operated a craps game in an Omaha suburb.

Gaughan was arrested four times on minor gambling-related charges and booked under variations of his given name. Whatever the charge, whether "vagrancy" or "keeping a disorderly house," each allegation was eventually dismissed.

His story might have ended in Omaha, but in 1951, Barrick was given an opportunity to acquire a percentage of the Flamingo in Las Vegas. Dave Berman, Gus Greenbaum, and Willie Alderman were the operators of record, and Barrick bought 5.5 percent. Ziegman bought 2.5 percent. Gaughan paid $60,000 (most of it borrowed) to buy 2 percentage points.

His "working points" included working a shift as a casino floorman. Although his college education might have made him an outsider in a world full of men schooled in back-alley dice games, in his early thirties, Gaughan was a gambling business veteran with more than fifteen years experience.

Gaughan retained his interest in the Flamingo, eventually increasing his ownership percentage to 3 percent. He held these points until principal operators Sam Cohen and Morris Lansburgh were pressured into selling the resort to Kirk Kerkorian in 1967 in the midst of a federal investigation into casino skimming.

The investigation established direct links to Meyer Lansky, and the IRS surmised that $2 million in pretaxed profits was being raked off the Flamingo's drop each year.

Jerry Gordon, a Flamingo executive, was a cooperating witness in the investigation.

"Chester Simms told us that when we count, we were to put aside $1,100 from each shift, or $3,300 a day, and not report this amount on the casino game work sheets," Gordon told New Jersey gaming investigators years later during Gaughan's Atlantic City licensing attempt.

Gordon testified that the cash was transferred through Flamingo insider Chester Simms to Lansburgh and Cohen, then directly to the principal owners.

Former Flamingo casino insider Steve Delmont, who was convicted in the skim scandal, gave further insight into the way it worked. Although Delmont swore he never received compensation for his role in moving the money, he said he knew with certainty that Gaughan's close friends and fellow point owners, Sam Ziegman and Eddie Barrick, had direct knowledge of the maneuver.

Delmont's relationship with the Flamingo was due in large part to his longtime friendship with Cohen. Prior to 1960, Delmont worked for Sam Cohen at the Deauville Hotel in Miami Beach. Delmont also worked at Kirk Kerkorian's International (later called the Las Vegas Hilton), as well as for the Taylor Construction Company and mob resort insiders Al Parvin and Al Sachs.

But despite pressure to do so, Delmont didn't implicate Gaughan in the skim and later went to work for the Gaughan family as a purchasing executive at the Barbary Coast casino on the Strip. The Barbary Coast was located next door to the Flamingo and was largely owned by Jackie's eldest son, Michael Gaughan. Delmont also received a pardon for his skimming conviction thanks in part to an assist from then-United States Sen. Chic Hecht of Nevada.

Jackie Gaughan wasn't implicated in the Flamingo skim and insisted to a series of investigators that he was unaware of any criminal activity going on in the casino counting room. It was a denial New Jersey Casino Commission investigators scoffed at when they did their background check as part of Gaughan's unsuccessful attempt to be licensed in Atlantic City.

In a 1978 deposition as part of an IRS inquiry, Gaughan recalled how he became a part owner of the Flamingo.

"Well, I bought the Flamingo Hotel, you know, like in 1951, and I bought my interest from a fellow by the name of Rosen who was from New York," Gaughan said. "The Rosen interest was probably ... the Siegel interest. Siegel got killed in 1947 and he really didn't—Rosen inherited his interest, or something. And at that time he sold all his interest out, and myself, Chester Simms, Ed Barrick ... and there was some fellow by the name Kapri bought this interest; bought this interest that this Rosen had sold. I really, you know, am not really—it's a long time ago, and I wasn't too familiar, but I actually might have bought my interest from—from the—head man in that organization was from Phoenix, and his name was—oh, Gus Greenbaum."

On Gaughan's return to Las Vegas in 1951, he bought several struggling sports books in partnership with transplanted Brooklyn gambler and ex-salesman Mel Exber. Exber had operated the race book at the Pioneer Club and Desert Inn before a change in Nevada law pushed such operations into stand-alone buildings outside the casinos.

In 1952, Gaughan and Exber took over the Saratoga. Two years later, they moved the operation and renamed it the Derby Sports Book. They later opened another sports book they called the Saratoga, which they sold in 1959.

Gaughan was part of an investment group led by Al Parvin that bought a percentage of the Flamingo in 1954. Other owners included Edward Levinson, Michael Shapiro, Chester Simms, along with Barrick, Ziegman, and Morris Baker. Almost every man had direct ties to Meyer Lansky. Levinson and Simms had come to Las Vegas from Havana.

Gaughan's sports-book interests and points in the Flamingo didn't keep him from attempting to expand his business activity into Lake Tahoe. In 1956, nearby Squaw Valley was being considered as the site of the 1960 Winter Olympics, and that meant big possibilities for tourism around the lake. With that in mind, Gaughan invested in the Tahoe Biltmore, a small casino located in Incline Village on Lake Tahoe's north shore. The trouble was that business at Tahoe was seasonal with most visitors coming between Memorial Day and Labor Day. A long summer wasn't enough time to make a casino profitable, and the Biltmore went bankrupt—but not before Gaughan recouped his $30,000 investment.

Gaughan, Exber, and Larry Hezlewood partnered with Kell Houssels Sr. in 1961 to reopen the Las Vegas Club on Fremont Street. They later bought the building outright from Houssels. The Gaughan group then acquired a percentage of the Club

Bingo, another downtown sawdust joint, and in 1962, they added the El Cortez to their Fremont Street holdings. The El Cortez became Gaughan's primary operation, morning headquarters, and substantial moneymaker.

Although he's considered downtown's dominant casino owner, Gaughan continued to expand outside of Fremont Street with mixed success. True to his nature, he was forever on the lookout for a bargain. Strip operators might dream of catering to high rollers and attracting corporate investment, but Gaughan stuck to what had been a winning formula for him: inexpensive rooms, food, and beverages and an eye for cash players and regular customers.

His investment with sons Michael and John D., as well as Frank Toti and Deen Williams, in the Royal Inn on Convention Center Drive from 1972-1979 put the Gaughen group close to the Strip. By then, Michael Gaughan and Frank Toti had taken a controlling interest in the operation. Jackie made himself available to promote the property and consult where needed. Williams had a few minor gambling arrests in the 1950s and later broke away from the group.

The Royal's off-Strip location made it a challenge to run. Jackie Gaughan raised his investment to $250,000. This was approximately 50 percent of the group's total investment, and in 1979, Gaughan sold his interest in the company for $1.1 million.

While the Royal struggled, the Golden Nugget on Fremont Street was on a roll under the guidance of banker E. Parry Thomas and the youthful leadership of Steve Wynn. From 1973-1977, Gaughan was a member of the board of directors of Golden Nugget and was part of an investment group that included mob resort hotel insider Al Parvin, brothers Edward and Fred Doumani, Mel Wolzinger, and Earl E. Wilson. Gradually, however, Gaughan realized that despite experience, Wynn had no intention of allowing him to exert any influence on the budding corporation.

The Doumani brothers later ran afoul of Gaming Control authorities over their controversial partial ownership of the

Tropicana, which was heavily skimmed by Midwestern organized crime families in the late 1970s. In November 1976, Jackie Gaughan sold his 102,000 shares of Golden Nugget and realized a gain on his investment of approximately $1 million.

He was a millionaire several times over, but like other sportsmen of his generation, Jackie Gaughan wasn't ready to quit. Gaughan and Exber held the mortgage to the Nevada Hotel on Main Street downtown from 1974-78 before its operator, former gubernatorial candidate Ed Fike, entered bankruptcy. Gaughan continued to hold title to the property for years.

In Nevada, Jackie Gaughan was a respected and licensed casino man whose character was above reproach. He contributed substantially to charity. His name could be found etched on plaques acknowledging his generosity in assisting in the construction of the community's ballet theater. He was a Las Vegas icon and the undisputed ruler of Fremont Street.

But that status earned him no respect in New Jersey, whose investigators and casino regulatory officials took a jaundiced view of Nevada's system of gaming control as well as many of its licensed operators. In November 1986, New Jersey Casino Control director Anthony Parrillo strongly recommended that Gaughan's license application as a member of the board of directors of Showboat Inc. be rejected due to his historical associations, friendship with Benny Binion, and link to the Flamingo's scandalous years.

Back in July 1978, Gaughan had joined the board of directors of the Showboat, a venerable hotel and casino located on Boulder Highway just off East Fremont Street. Although he didn't participate in the daily operations of the Showboat, his relationship as a member of the casino's in-house audit committee became a point of controversy when the company attempted to expand operations into Atlantic City.

Gaughan's friendship and business relationship with Benny Binion provides insight into the intriguing subculture of Las Vegas. Its importance to New Jersey investigators highlights the contrast between Atlantic City and Las Vegas.

Men considered not only notorious but deadly in other communities had evolved into colorful characters in Las Vegas. Binion admitted killing three men, was suspected of ordering several other murders, and had maintained a decades-long relationship with organized crime, but on Fremont Street, he was a gregarious cowboy gambler who allowed customers to play with as much cash as they could carry into the Horseshoe.

A unique rule at Binion's Horseshoe was that a player could set his maximum bet limit with his first wager up to $1 million.

When Benny's son, Jack, was in charge, he received a phone call asking if this rule was true. He said it was. A few hours later, a cowboy walked into the casino carrying two shopping bags. They were packed with currency. Dealers counted it out on an inactive craps table. It totaled $175,000.

"I want to make one bet with this," the cowboy said.

"No problem," Jack Binion told him, "just as long as it's your first bet."

He was given a single chip.

"That represents your $175,000," Binion said.

The cowboy walked to an active craps table. The shooter was about to come out.

"Place this chip on Don't Pass," the cowboy told a dealer.

The shooter threw a six.

"Six is the point," the stickman announced.

The shooter threw three more numbers before he sevened out.

"Cash or check?" Binion asked.

The cowboy didn't hesitate. "I came in with cash, I want to go home with cash."

Jack Binion ordered the man paid in bundles of $100 bills. There were seventy packets in all. These were packed for him in a new suitcase, a gift from the casino. Security and a limo were provided to escort him home.

As he was on his way out, a gaping observer asked, "How could you bet so much on one bet?"

The cowboy replied, "Well, I was watchin' inflation eatin' up my savings, so I decided to go for double or nothin'."

Although Benny Binion wasn't a licensee at the Horseshoe, Nevada gaming investigators never hassled him, and it was clear that while his sons, Jack and Ted, and wife Teddy Jane supervised the daily operation, Benny was the man in charge.

When New Jersey regulators took after Gaughan, United States senators Harry Reid and Chic Hecht hurried to his side. Former governors Grant Sawyer and Mike O'Callaghan flew to Atlantic City to appear on Gaughan's behalf. They'd not only been on the receiving end of his generosity during their political careers, but they also knew how important Gaughan was to downtown and to Nevada's economy generally. No matter the facts of the Flamingo skim, Gaughan had been on the square, at least by Nevada standards.

Rising star Steve Wynn, whose Atlantic City Golden Nugget also had trouble with New Jersey gaming authorities, vouched for Gaughan's good character, as well.

Atlantic City officials were moved, but Jackie Gaughan would remain in Las Vegas

◆　　◆　　◆

At the time of life when most men contemplated retirement, Gaughan wasn't finished downtown. In 1980, he purchased the struggling Union Plaza for $6.6 million from principal owner Frank Scott and renamed it Jackie Gaughan's Plaza. He'd owned an interest in the Plaza since 1971 when he teamed with Scott and Sam Boyd to build the casino. (The Union Pacific Corporation constructed the high-rise hotel.)

As ever, the race and sports-book wire business was close to Gaughan. A company owned by Scott called Nevada Electronic Wire Services provided race information and telecasts to local sports books for a fee.

With 22 stories, 504 rooms, and a 66,000 square-foot-casino, the Union Plaza broke records when it opened. Its cocktail waitresses wore skimpy overalls, and in an era of hot pants, theirs were considered the hottest. The Plaza offered a pool and

94

a gourmet room in an attempt to lure players from the Strip.

The Plaza was the tallest building downtown. It contained nearly twice the number of rooms of its biggest competitor and featured the largest casino floor space in Las Vegas.

In keeping with a long Las Vegas tradition, critics inside and outside the casino game groused that it had been overbuilt and couldn't turn a profit. Although the Strip established casino dominance with the 1966 opening of Caesars Palace and the debut of Circus Circus two years later, the Plaza offered something downright innovative in the early 1970s: ample space for meetings and conventions.

Thirty years later, Las Vegas would be the nation's convention capital, but the Plaza was considered a strange bird when it added events planning to its overall marketing strategy.

It was obvious to many observers that Gaughan was no longer in business merely for the money, but because he enjoyed the interaction with customers and employees. Although a multimillionaire for many years, he refused to dress like a manicured casino prince. In fact, Nancy Houssels, Kell Jr.'s wife, would recall that for many years Gaughan wore his late uncle's old suits.

He was a casino man, not a dude, and managed to keep his personal life in check despite Las Vegas' many hedonistic distractions. While within his family, Gaughan is famously absent-minded—his son, Michael, once recalled his father failing to cash a $300,000 check—Jackie retained his knack for remembering the names of customers, employees, the house bottom line, and point spreads.

In some ways, Gaughan was a sentimental man in a cut-throat business. Out of a sense of nostalgia and an inability to quit the game he'd grown up in, he held onto his downtown casino properties long after they'd been profitable enough to be salable.

If he hadn't owned them outright, or in partnership with Exber, their relatively meager returns wouldn't have justified keeping them open. He was always reluctant to sell.

In 2003, there was an offer to buy the Plaza, which was

almost as valuable for its real estate as for its aging hotel and casino. Jackie Gaughan wondered what he would do with himself. With that in mind, a deal was structured to allow Gaughan to stay on as a consultant, host, dice instructor, and all-around colorful character.

After Barrick Gaming took over the Plaza, Gaughan's grip on daily operations began to loosen.

His time had passed, and he knew it. But he'd made his mark and built a fortune. Jackie Gaughan could rest easy knowing there would never be another casino man like him.

# Mel Exber's Sporting Life

O ne of the ironies of the sporting life is that so few bookmakers and big bettors appear to enjoy the games on which their fortunes rise and fall. They like winning and hate losing, but rarely show much affection for the spirit of sport.

They reduce great athletic events to mere numbers. Their routine bears a closer resemblance to the toil of accountants than that of pennant-waving fans. Most bookies are as joyless as a bean counter in a Dickens novel.

Bookmaker-turned-casino man Mel Exber was one sweet exception.

He retained his stickball-playing Brooklyn street kid's love of the game throughout his seventy-eight years. When he died in May 2002, some of those who gathered to bid him farewell half believed he'd go out wearing a Dodgers jersey. Such was his unabashed enthusiasm for the game.

Exber was among the last holdouts from a time when men who'd made their mark in gambling back rooms could ease into Nevada, become licensed and respectable, and never look back. Exber lacked the tenacity of old scholars like Moe Dalitz or corporate sharks of the Steve Wynn breed.

He was more a character than a cutthroat. On paper, Exber was equally partnered with downtown casino king Jackie Gaughan in the Las Vegas Club at the corner of Fremont and Main streets. In reality, the casino was pure Mel. Visitors caught their first clue from the outside where the place was designed to resemble Ebbet's Field, home of Exber's beloved Brooklyn Dodgers. Inside, the sports theme was dizzying. It delighted gamblers and fans in the pre-megaresort era when downtown Las Vegas was still considered a tourist destination. No casino better reflected its owner's personality.

The Las Vegas Club featured restaurants called the Dugout, Upper Deck, and Great Moments Room. Exber's friendship with Dodgers' base-stealing champ Maury Wills was reflected throughout the casino's Hall of Fame where photographs and autographed bats and balls lined the walls.

Exber's effusive, cigar-smoking nature paid off in 1962 when he troubled Wills for an autograph in Los Angeles just before game time. Wills rarely gave autographs so close to the first pitch, but he took one look at Exber, an oversized kid, and signed a baseball. Exber, of course, invited Wills to the Las Vegas Club the next time he was in the neighborhood. When the season ended, Wills accompanied Duke Snider, Sandy Koufax, Don Drysdale, and Willie Davis to Las Vegas and looked up Exber at his downtown shrine to the Dodgers.

Wills later mused, "I don't know why I stopped to sign that ball for him. I didn't know who he was. We became friends, but it went further than just friendship. We were brothers. We were like brothers who were friends."

The friendship would have raised eyebrows in the commissioner of baseball's office had the relationship been known. A key player on a major league team hanging out and taking vacations with a professional bookmaker might have caused a scandal.

When his playing days ended, Wills became a sports radio commentator, and Exber accompanied him to All-Star games and the World Series. One night at Yankee Stadium, Wills was having trouble getting the night's batting star, Graig Nettles, to do an interview when Exber intervened. He'd watched the game, so he stepped in and pretended to be Nettles for the interview. Radio listeners back in California were none the wiser.

During the Red Sox-Reds Series in 1975, the two men were finishing dinner on a rainy night when they noticed baseball Commissioner Bowie Kuhn and his entourage entering the restaurant. A moment later, Wills and Exber were outside. There was no taxi in sight. However, the commissioner's limousine was parked at the curb. Exber strolled up to the chauffeur, introduced his friend, Maury Wills, to the wide-eyed driver, and commandeered the limousine. Exber wasn't shy and didn't mind traveling first class.

Exber loved sports and betting and was a daily fixture behind the counter at the Las Vegas Club's sports book. He stood like a cigar-smoking sentry, chalking in new lines and moving the point spreads himself.

He also kept a sharp eye on his competition.

Although Jimmy the Greek Snyder became known for his handicapping prowess, in truth, he had more personality than ability. When he opened the Vegas Turf Club downtown, he would send a runner over to Mel's place to copy the morning betting line.

Exber recognized the spy and soon was feeding him wildly inaccurate numbers. Exber then sent his own men to bet against the Greek's suicidal spread. After losing a large chunk of his bankroll, Snyder learned his lesson. Thereafter, he steered clear of Exber's betting board.

As the years passed, Exber's sports book was eclipsed by the superstores, which featured enormous television screens and oversized reader boards. Exber recognized the trend, but refused to change with the times. He was comfortable inside his little casino, but the club's survival depended on his willingness to change.

The Las Vegas Club's history dated to the town's earliest days. It was one of the city's first casinos. However, no town shows less respect for its history than Las Vegas.

The club was the site of the Overland Hotel, which opened in 1905, the year Las Vegas was established. The hotel and casino eventually expanded to slightly more than 200 rooms. Exber seemed satisfied to keep it that way, but, in the early 1990s at the insistence of his son, Brady, embarked on a major expansion effort.

In September 1995, the Las Vegas Club's sixteen-story tower and Ebbet's Field expansion was completed. The hotel offered 410 rooms, including eight suites, and 40,000 square feet of casino space. (By comparison, the MGM Grand offered 5,000 rooms and 125,000 square feet of casino.) Truth told, the lobbies of the Strip's megaresorts could hold the Las Vegas Club casino with room leftover for the Dugout Restaurant.

Exber was born in Brooklyn in 1923, the son of a tailor. He shared every neighborhood boy's dream of playing for the Dodgers. The closest he ever came to realizing his dream was to befriend some of the Dodgers and booking bets on their games.

"When I was a kid, the game was more important than anything," he said. "We never played a game without making a bet. I don't care whether it was baseball, softball, punchball, stickball, we bet on everything. This was dog eat dog. We pitched pennies, matched coins. Whatever we did, we bet. It's the way it was."

After serving as an airplane mechanic in the Army Air Corps in World War II, Exber wandered out to Las Vegas with a $3,000 bankroll and some acquaintances in the bookmaking trade, which in those days wasn't allowed inside the casinos due to its reputation as being directly connected to the mob. Benny Siegel, you may recall, had first come to Las Vegas as a bookmaking and race-wire organizer, not as a casino developer.

The story Exber told had him losing his $3,000 bankroll to a gambling itch. Instead of returning to Brooklyn, he took a job writing tickets in the earliest stand-alone sports books at the Las Vegas Club, Pioneer Club, and Golden Nugget.

Mel Exber was content to keep under the radar. His likable, apolitical public persona was the early Las Vegas model. He made small donations to political campaigns, served as president of Temple Beth Shalom, the community's first synagogue, and was one of the last downtown property owners to serve as president of the Nevada Resort Association.

He lived a quiet life while more flamboyant and less circumspect operators fell to drink, drugs, and mob association.

In 1953, Exber partnered with Jackie Gaughan in the foundering Derby Sports Book and also bought a piece of Sammy Cohen's Saratoga Sports Book on South First Street. The two made a profit and fought together to prevent the federal government from raising the tax on sports-betting to an exorbitant 10 percent.

With assistance from U.S. Senator Pat McCarran, this tax eventually was reduced to .25 percent. Jimmy the Greek generated the headlines, but Mel Exber was credited with introducing lucrative teaser football cards, with their staggering house advantage, into the Las Vegas sports betting mix in the early 1950s.

In 1960, Exber and Gaughan embarked on an effort to reclaim the old Las Vegas Club from what appeared to be hopeless disrepair. It eventually became known as the casino with the city's most-liberal blackjack rules at a time such marketing pitches were novel.

Exber had not only helped develop the popularity of the parlay card, he'd also been considered a marketing maven back when an owner's personality was considered the greatest marketing tool.

In one of his last interviews at the Las Vegas Club before he was stricken with a brain tumor, Exber said, "I'd go nuts if I didn't have this place to come to. It's the game. It's a helluva game, and that's why I do it. I don't ever want to grow up as far as sports is concerned."

Although Las Vegas changed on him, Mel Exber played the game of his youth until the final out.

# Under the Big Top

12

Contrary to the myth that circulated throughout the early corporate casino era, not all the successful Las Vegas gambling operators were weaned on the rackets. It was true that the casinos' business attracted an endless line of hustlers and confidence men. It was also true that outsiders, usually in the form of hotel-management veterans or Howard Hughes, had been plucked clean by mob accountants and professional skimming teams. And so the accepted philosophy was that outsiders to the green felt were destined to fail.

It sounded true, but it wasn't.

William Bennett and Ralph Engelstad proved dazzling exceptions. They built enormous fortunes for themselves on the Strip, and neither was a gambling man by calling, but both were tenacious. They possessed the ability to micromanage a variety of business interests. They kept a hawk's eye on the counting room and an iron grip on decision making.

Born November 16, 1924, Bennett was the son of an Arizona rancher. Bennett was a Navy bomber pilot in World War II. After the war, Bennett left the family ranch and opened a chain of furniture stores, which he eventually sold at a handsome profit. Then he invested most of his bankroll in a fraudulent financial scheme and lost all of his money even faster than his reputation.

Bennett's bust out had one upside: He managed to groom a friendship with Del Webb Corporation President L.C. Jacobsen. That corporation owned the Mint in downtown Las Vegas, the Sahara on the Strip, and the Sahara Tahoe at South Shore. It recruited ambitious junior executives whose portfolios didn't include gambling-related convictions or connections to the illegal dice and card rooms made notorious in the early 1960s by Attorney General Robert Kennedy.

Bennett was obsessed with mending his name, so he took the first job Jacobsen offered, a casino-host position at the Sahara Tahoe.

Within a few months, his work ethic and his drive moved him ahead of the less motivated, and he went from night casino manager at the Lake Tahoe property to the head of operations at the foundering Mint in downtown Las Vegas. The Mint was awash in red ink, but Bennett rescued the property in less than two years and turned a $4.5-million-a-year loser into a $9-million winner.

He realized then that the immense cash flow even in small casinos helped set them apart from traditional businesses. Because the money was so easily separated from the players, they expected value in exchange for their patronage. The hotel and restaurant functions of many properties were inefficiently run. With few exceptions, the so-called old-school operators were living on borrowed time, and it was men like Bennett who sped their extinction.

Jay Sarno was another example of a man with big ideas whose vision was unmatched, but whose lack of business savvy fated him to fail. Sarno followed up his Teamsters-financed creation of Caesars Palace in 1966 with his magnificent pink, over-stated Circus Circus in 1968.

Sarno's Circus Circus would be the Strip's first family-themed casino with the ground floor wide open for gambling. The second floor was lined with pinball machines and a carnival midway. Circus acts performed on schedule above the green felt. Trapeze artists, high-wire walkers, and even a man who made a living diving from the ceiling onto a small cushion made Circus Circus far and away a unique casino.

Sarno was possessed of an almost savantlike brilliance, but lacked the follow-through to make his dreams work. He opened the casino without rooms, and within months, Circus Circus was hopelessly debt laden. (It also boasted its share of organized crime associates operating gift shops and arcades.)

When Sarno stumbled, Bennett and his business partner, Bill Pennington, saw their chance and took it. They picked up the equivalent of a long-term lease with an option to buy Circus Circus. Sarno barely escaped conviction on charges that he tried to bribe an IRS agent. He could no longer remain in the front office.

Sarno, who died in 1984, eventually admitted knowing well the notorious men who controlled the Teamsters pension fund loans and often demanded a hidden piece of the action on the Strip.

As the Strip was being scrutinized for vestiges of organized crime, Bennett and Pennington cast a clean, corporate image at Circus Circus. The partners gained access to the corporation first by leasing novelty gambling machines. Beginning in 1974, the Bennett-Pennington combination swiftly turned Circus Circus profitable when they built a 395-room tower. Subsequent additions would place the big top among the world's largest hotels—and every room was a bare-bones bargain.

While other casino operators focused on tinsel and flash, Hollywood glamour, and high rollers, Bennett focused on efficiency, cheap buffets, an ocean of liberal slot machines, blanket radio advertising to the hugely important Southern California market, and not a nickel's worth of credit extended in the casino.

While other casinos occasionally showed flat earnings due to unforeseen economic forces or just plain bad luck at the baccarat tables, Bennett's Circus Circus piled up the profits. Bennett and Pennington took the company public in 1983 and kept 76 percent of the stock for themselves.

Under Bennett, Circus Circus became the butt of jokes for its "plate of plenty" buffets and its plain pipe-racks rooms, but it attracted bargain-hunting gamblers and weekenders by the score. With buckets of nickels and quarters, a generation of players cut their teeth under the gaudy big top. Circus Circus reminded all the carpet joints that the masses didn't travel to Las Vegas to see Frank Sinatra, but rather to gamble, eat, and drink on the cheap. The competition could laugh at the awful pink façade and goofy monkey acts, but the property's lusty bottom line quickly silenced most critics.

With Bennett in full control, Circus Circus continued to add rooms. He opened value-focused hotel-casinos in Reno and two casinos in Laughlin. Bennett didn't invent the bargain game, but he came close to perfecting it.

Perhaps it was the embarrassment of his earlier business bankruptcy. Or perhaps it was his inability to control his workaholic personality. It became clear as the 1980s drew to a close, that Bennett was incapable of relinquishing control of the company he'd built. While he privately seethed, less successful operators, like flamboyant Steve Wynn, received most of the publicity in the media and praise in the financial community,

Bennett rarely ventured into the public eye. He steered reporters away from stories about himself to those that made Circus Circus look good. He rarely courted casino celebrity even after it became plain that his 4,000-room, $290-million Arthurian-legend and castle-themed resort called Excalibur would be an enormous moneymaker.

Bennett, local wags would joke, had spared all expense in creating the castle. Nevertheless, the casino was filled with quarter slot-machine players and T-shirt-buyers, and his public loved it.

Bennett was stung by snide comments from Wynn and others who referred to the big, cheaply made cinder-block castle as "Chuck E. Cheese on steroids." Wynn, meanwhile, was being praised for the design of the $700-million Mirage, which unlike Bennett's castle, was financed almost exclusively by high-interest junk bonds arranged through Wynn's friend, Michael Milken.

With an ever-increasing cash flow, Bennett embarked on his next project: a Vegas version of the great Sphinx in the form of the $390-million Luxor, an Egyptian-themed project casino industry cynics privately dubbed "the Curse of the Pyramid."

The pyramid's construction, with added pressure from Bennett's insistence on opening ahead of other Strip competitors, was marked by difficulty. Several construction workers died building the pyramid, named for the ancient Egyptian resort city of Luxor, and the angular walls of its hotel rooms were funky and interesting, but not very practical. There were also challenges getting the "inclinator" elevator to work for the throngs of guests who came to gawk and gamble in the Strip's latest novelty home.

Luxor's opening was rattled by comical malfunctions in its expensive rides and attractions, but eventually, the company broke the curse by limiting the rides and adding a pair of hotel towers that fed into the casino.

Performance pressures increased, and Bennett became even more of a taskmaster. But unlike his leadership in the 1980s, by mid-1994, he showed behavior that bordered on paranoia. He groomed, then drove away talented executives Richard Banis, an accountant who'd played an integral role in the company's growth, and Glenn Schaeffer, a financial wiz with a degree from the famed Iowa Writers' Workshop and a superior understanding of the dynamic directions the gaming market was taking.

Bennett's mercurial style manifested itself in other ways. He alienated even those executives who had been fiercely loyal and genuinely admired him. One of those was Bill Paulos, whom he accused of using drugs. Bennett demanded, with a witness in the office, that Paulos urinate in a cup so he could be tested for drugs. Paulos was furious and confused, but complied. The drama was ignited because Bennett had received an unsigned poison-pen letter.

"I will send you a fucking cup every day if you want it," Paulos told his boss.

Glenn Schaeffer shared the cover of a trade magazine with Steve Wynn, and the article inside its pages credited both men for turning Las Vegas into a family-friendly destination-resort city.

"Mr. Bennett is brooding over that picture," casino executive Mike Sloan told Schaeffer in a story reported in Pete Earley's insightful *Super Casino: Inside the "New" Las Vegas*. "I suspect that he isn't happy about all the publicity you are getting."

When the city of Chicago decided to license a handful of select companies to open casinos in its potential of a multibillion-dollar gambling market, Schaeffer and James Muir led a push to secure one of those licenses for Circus Circus. But, as happens too often in the casino business, politics prevailed and the $2-billion project stalled.

The increasingly testy Bennett exploded at his protégés and accused Schaeffer of scheming behind the scenes to have him removed as chairman. This rift meant a dead end for the careers of Schaeffer and Muir—as long as Bennett was still in control of the company

Schaeffer's friendship with the boss was described as a "father-son relationship," but in the end, both Schaeffer and Paulos were driven from the company by Bennett. Muir, who was essential in the planning and early construction of Luxor, was another casualty of Bennett's unwillingness to slacken the reins.

"I guess I just don't understand people," Bennett said.

Their compensation package: a combined $35 million.

At one point in 1991, Bennett went so far as to announce that he would retire, but it was just talk.

He carried a chip on his shoulder that went back to his days as a failed Arizona businessman. Although he was a resounding success in a town built by men with far more notorious portfolios, Bennett insisted on rewriting his past. After he did this, he was embarrassed by a *Wall Street Journal* account of his insistence on re-creating a personal history that included a glowing write-up in *Life* magazine under the title "The Young Millionaires of Phoenix."

Journal reporter Pauline Yoshihashi wrote in April 1994, "That tale has woven itself into Circus Circus lore. But an inquiry at the *Time-Life* archives fails to produce such a story. A similar piece ran under that headline in the Sept. 30, 1961, *Saturday Evening Post,* and it fits Mr. Bennett's recall in most details save one: He's not in it."

By the time Bennett's conduct caused Wall Street institutional investors to ask for a change at the top of the company, Circus Circus owned eight casinos—all of which followed the boss' hugely successful theme of high volume and solid value. His program generated profits that dwarfed much of the competition: 30-percent return on equity and 30-percent annual growth in earnings per share of stock over a decade. For an industry that couldn't get arrested on Wall Street a decade earlier, Circus Circus was a glowing success story.

Unlike the competition, Bennett never confused his personal tastes with those of the masses to whom he marketed. While he owned a yacht and a jet and homes in Las Vegas and La Jolla, California, Bennett never changed his approach to the market. Critics whispered that he was so focused on the midlevel player and so blindly critical of the enormous and growing convention market that he missed the chance to grow his company and galvanize it against increasing competition.

The industry changed rapidly in the early 1990s as leading companies battled for coveted gaming licenses outside Nevada and Atlantic City. Some pursued agreements with Native American tribes on reservations. Others chased elusive profits with riverboat and barge casinos.

"He was out selling himself," Bennett told the *Wall Street*

*Journal*, speaking of key man Glenn Schaeffer's departure. "He was not out selling the business of this company."

Wall Street, which had paid little attention to Las Vegas casino stocks in general to that point but had shown investor interest in Circus Circus, recoiled. By holding onto his company too tightly, Bennett doomed himself to lose control of it.

From October 1993 through April 1994, the stock price of Circus Circus dropped 35 percent. Even his announcement in early 1994 that he was giving up his chief executive officer's title didn't help. While he remained chairman, the company would remain suspect.

Bennett sold his stock for $230 million. After two decades, he was out of the empire he'd built. After leaving Circus Circus, Bennett continued to turn up in his usual seat at a neighborhood bar.

His addiction to prescription pain medication had gone unreported in the local press, but Circus Circus insiders insisted that it was this drug that made him gradually less accessible to even his top executives. He paid them well, but he refused to give them any day-to-day decision-making power. He complained to whomever would listen about the lack of respect he'd received from the industry despite his incredible success.

Rather than spend more time at his $16-million house in La Jolla or travel the world in style in his $25-million jet, Bennett embarked on a comeback plan that casino observers considered preposterous. He was determined to prove them wrong.

He purchased the careworn Sahara on the northern edge of the Strip for $193 million. He also made a run at purchasing the Hacienda, which stood on the site of what would be the future home of Mandalay Bay, but when Schaeffer and his team blocked Bennett's attempt, the aging gamer focused full time on the Sahara.

His health was failing him, but he remained sensitive about his image in the industry he'd helped develop. For example, he felt slighted when he was not included among the casino devel-

**110**

opers profiled in a 1997 University of Nevada Press book titled *The Players: The Men Who Made Las Vegas.*

No slight was intended, and the exclusion was understandable: By 1997, Bennett's reputation as a captain of the casino industry had been tarnished by his increasingly erratic behavior.

◆　◆　◆

Saving the Sahara was an extraordinarily difficult task. Built in 1952 at a cost of $5.5 million, the Sahara was erected on the site of the old Bingo Club and when it opened enjoyed a prime location across the street from the El Rancho Vegas.

Del Webb picked up 20 percent of the resort as its general building contractor. The Sahara remained a popular spot through the early 1980s, but as Strip development moved south—and casino companies expanded operations into Atlantic City—the resort's prospects faded.

Not only was the Sahara's infrastructure frayed, but the heart of the action on Las Vegas Boulevard had long since moved several miles south to the corners of Flamingo Road. Further south, Tropicana Avenue at the Strip was enjoying a roaring resurgence with the opening of the behemoth, 5005-room MGM Grand, the creation of the New York-New York, and the expansion of the Luxor.

Bennett to the end remained a determined competitor. He poured millions—at least $100 million by one estimate—into the Sahara's sagging interior. He expanded the size of the casino in an attempt to make it more attractive to a younger clientele. He commissioned Speedworld, a NASA-like thrill ride that sweeps riders in loops around the front of the building. He also opened the NASCAR Café in an attempt to cross-market with another investment, the $200-million Las Vegas Motor Speedway, which he constructed in partnership with Imperial Palace owner Ralph Engelstad.

Their partnership, after many years as competitors, was a hand-in-glove match. For very different reasons, the public and professional personas of both men had taken beatings late in their careers, and each appeared to have something to prove to themselves despite amassing vast personal fortunes. Although the speedway would not prove a very lucrative deal, it did generate tens of millions for the local economy by playing host to an annual series of auto races that occasionally drew crowds in excess of 100,000.

Both men noted to friends that, despite their substantial cash investment in a speedway that was generating income for all their competitors, they didn't receive a nickel in marketing assistance from the Las Vegas Convention and Visitors Authority, which they believed was clearly being influenced by the owners of larger Strip properties.

Finally, they sold the speedway.

Bennett gave few interviews, but he did make headlines when he spoke in full-blown support of hundreds of striking Frontier Culinary Workers Union, Local 226, workers. He fed the striking workers hot meals and donated almost $1 million to their cause. This move reflected how close he'd remained to the Chicago-based service workers' union.

Bennett died of diabetic-related problems on December 22, 2002. This was less than a month after the passing of his ornery old friend, Engelstad.

In his lifetime, Bennett had given millions to a variety of charities, but it was that act of generosity to the strikers that helped to positively punctuate his obituary.

A few weeks before Bennett's death, *Forbes* magazine ranked him 368th on its list of the richest Americans. They estimated his worth as $600 million.

If Bill Bennett died without quite completing his comeback, at least he left behind a big bankroll. And in Las Vegas, nothing gets more respect than that.

# The Englestad Enigma

Las Vegas history is riddled with tales of tough guys, but few rival the rise of one of its most unlikely casino operators, Ralph Engelstad.

Engelstad wasn't an Outfit hit man or even the son of a racket boss. He was an irascible, hardheaded Norwegian-American from Thief River Falls, Minnesota, who used a small construction company to start his fortune building. When he died from smoking-related cancer on November 26, 2002, the estimate of his net worth was in excess of $1 billion.

Engelstad's reputation was stained forever by parties he gave at his Imperial Palace Hotel and Casino. They celebrated the birthday of Adolf Hitler. He was subsequently fined by Nevada regulators for embarrassing the casino industry. But the higher price he paid was to become an object of ridicule and scorn.

Yet, despite this insensitivity and bad judgment, his was an amazing personal success story. In an industry full of connected operators who depended upon mob suitcase money, tightly controlled Teamsters pension fund loans, and junk-bond financing, Engelstad was an individualist who bankrolled most of his projects and acquisitions with his own money.

In a city of made men, he was a self-made man.

His business philosophy was based more on his love of hockey than any obsession with Hitler. He played the sport as a boy and became so good as a goalie that his skill became his passport to his higher education.

In Minnesota, where hockey is almost a religion, Engelstad was a skinny kid growing up Catholic in Thief River Falls. Those who remembered him as a boy recall that he wasn't afraid to challenge bigger kids on the ice. He wrapped copies of *Life* magazine around his shins to guard against slap shots, and he took pride in standing steadfast in the crease. At twelve, he worked in a local grocery and also assisted his father, Chris Engelstad, at the AGSCO farm-supply company.

Ralph Engelstad played four years as goalie for Lincoln High School. As a freshman in the state tournament in 1945, he was hit between the eyes with a puck, but went on to finish the game. Years later, in an interview with a Minnesota sportswriter, Engelstad recalled specifics of that game and was animated in recounting what he believed was an improper penalty against his team.

He won a hockey scholarship at the University of North Dakota thanks in large part to a professor named Ben Gustafson. He met Gustafson while working a summer job unloading boxcars. "I didn't have any money to go to school," Engelstad said. "My parents didn't have any money to send me to school. The only reason I got to college was because Professor Gustafson got me that scholarship."

Engelstad took college classes and played goalie for two years. Then he grabbed the chance to play professionally for a minor league team in San Bernardino, California. But San Bernardino was a long way from familiar territory, and he returned to Grand Forks to play semiprofessionally while completing his studies. He graduated in 1954.

He married Betty Stocker and opened a small construction company in the North Dakota town. It was soon profitable, and he and Betty seemed secure. But where other men might have been satisfied with that peaceful life, Engelstad was a driven man.

Leaving his wife and young daughter in Grand Forks, he ventured west once again. This time he was impressed with not only the lights of Las Vegas, but with its potential for growth. He quested for and found opportunities. He started small, building homes on speculation. With profits, he made a land purchase on the edge of a poor neighborhood.

When Engelstad sought his first construction loan, he was turned down at two banks. Then he went to Valley Bank of Grand Forks and was given the $2,500 he needed. It was a lucky loan for both parties because it cemented Engelstad's loyalty to the bank for the next quarter century. He parlayed that loan into a successful home-construction business.

Now he set his sights higher.

Engelstad bought cheap land around the old Thunderbird Airport in North Las Vegas. He sold 145 acres of it to Howard Hughes in 1967 for $2 million. This cash windfall, coupled with his Valley Bank relationship enabled him to bankroll the purchase of the Flamingo Capri motel in 1967. With a reputation as a hard-working, hard-nosed workaholic, he renovated the motel and casino. He also blocked an attempt to unionize his small staff.

Engelstad knew very little about the casinos. This flaw almost always leads to financial disaster for those who invest in them. But he made up for his inexperience by working nonstop, using the cash profits from his successful low-roller marketing program to reinvest in the property. He continued to build tract homes and strip malls, but increasingly, he focused his fortunes on the Flamingo Capri.

Working fourteen-hour days, by the early 1970s he finally

realized that the motel was hopelessly flawed. If he was to prosper on the Strip, he needed to think bigger. And so the concept for his Imperial Palace was born.

The Imperial Palace, with its blue neon and Vegas-meets-Tokyo architecture, gradually grew to 2,700 rooms, which in 1996 was good enough to rank it as the tenth largest hotel in the world.

The Imperial Palace's architecture, thanks to Engelstad's insistence on building with his own bankroll, was a tangle of angles. Nevertheless, its room-occupancy rate was always high. Engelstad knew his low-roller market and catered to it with inexpensive food, a "Legends in Concert" celebrity impersonator show, and his $200-million classic car collection. The car collection was the third largest in the country.

While the rest of the Strip was being swallowed up by large corporations, Engelstad was an iconoclast who bucked long odds to become an industry success.

Engelstad collected Nazi memorabilia. He was also an extensive collector of the papers of U.S. Army Gen. George S. Patton. But it wasn't the Patton memorabilia that got him in trouble.

Engelstad's reputation would be ruined by an act of absurdly bad taste: He held two Hitler-themed birthday celebrations inside the Imperial Palace auto museum. Amid the vintage, million-dollar Duesenbergs and original Third Reich military vehicles, he staged parties complete with a giant-sized picture of Hitler signed "To Ralphie from Adolf."

A cake with a swastika on its whipped cream top completed the scenes. The private parties were attended by hotel executives and Engelstad's circle of friends, which, incredibly, included a few Jews.

It wasn't a Jewish guest, but rather a disgruntled employee who blew the whistle on the parties with their Nazi theme. When the local press broke the story, the Gaming Control Board was moved to investigate Engelstad's suitability to continue to hold his casino license.

"The barrage of local, national, and even international articles about the Hitler parties prompted the Gaming Control Board and the state attorney general's office in December 1988 to hand the commission a two-count complaint against Engelstad, citing state gaming Regulation 5.011, enacted in 1969," Jeff Burbank observed in *License to Steal: Nevada's Gaming Control System in the Megaresort Age*.

"Regulation 5.011 gave the commission full authority to fine and to condition, restrict, revoke, or suspend the gaming license of any licensee who conducted an 'unsuitable method of operation.' Acts deemed unsuitable included 'failure to exercise discretion and sound judgment to prevent incidents which might reflect on the repute of the State of Nevada and act as a detriment to the development of the industry.'"

The Gaming Commission concluded that Engelstad had indeed hosted Hitler-themed parties in 1986 and 1988. It ordered Engelstad to appear before it. The hearing was heated, but ended with Engelstad apologizing for his insensitivity and agreeing to pay a record $1.5-million fine to save his gaming license.

Historically, Las Vegas had an image inseparable from organized crime, prostitution, money laundering, and casino skimming. The state tended to look the other way on these, but it had to draw the line at Hitler-themed birthday parties.

"There was a great deal of outcry over that, especially from the Jewish community," former Gaming Control Board member Jerry Cunningham added. "They wanted his license revoked. There were several thousand jobs at stake. It was a very serious situation. Mr. Engelstad runs a very profitable business. It's good for the economy."

And that was the way things were balanced. Engelstad may have discouraged his employees from cooperating with the investigation, and his actions surely had offended anyone sensitive to the terrible history of the Holocaust. However, he was an "earner" whose casino employed thousands and paid millions in taxes to a state whose fortunes rose and fell with the casinos' bottom lines.

Chastened but unbowed, Engelstad retreated more and more into his business affairs. He continued to build and acquire new properties from coast to coast. Engelstad told friends he believed the intense media coverage continued because it was being fueled and encouraged by his enemy, Steve Wynn.

Engelstad wasn't an easy person to know. While other Strip operators basked in media celebrity, Engelstad would never dream of calling himself a gifted businessman. He was simply a working man who never quit.

His beloved, belligerent hockey was rarely far from his thoughts. It's possible that his playing days, many spent with his brother, Richard, were the only times he felt a camaraderie with his fellow man. Much of the balance of his life was spent working almost around the clock to further enlarge his vast empire.

At one point, he owned more than 150 office buildings and a portfolio that included not only casinos and strip malls, but trucking companies, mines, and concrete-manufacturing plants.

When at work, Engelstad would sit behind the oversized desk in his office on the nineteenth floor of the Imperial Palace, chain-smoking cigarettes and reviewing endless business deals as well as the previous night's casino receipts. Behind him were a bank of television monitors recording strategic cash-transaction positions inside his operation. The casino cage, coin-counting room, and even the cocktail waitress stations were on camera.

When he tired of the office, he'd go down to one of the casino's bars, smoke some more, and sip a vodka and Diet Pepsi. He dressed so casually that even some of his veteran employees didn't recognize him. He was fond of cheap boat shoes and wore no socks.

He was so driven to succeed that his family life suffered, but he remained married, and it was that relationship that tethered him despite his 9 A.M.-to-midnight schedule and hard living. His home and office in the Cayman Islands were said to be identical to his headquarters in Las Vegas. He could step from one world to another with nothing out of place.

He trusted few people outside his family and a small inner circle of friends. The latter included his attorney, Owen Nitz, and dermatologist, Dr. Ken Landow.

Engelstad was so occupied with his business that he ignored his health problems. He resisted medical treatment, and even when he relented, it was on his own terms. Thus when he finally agreed to surgery for his severe case of hemorrhoids, he not only wouldn't stay in the hospital overnight, but he refused an anesthetic. He just bent over and had the hemorrhoids cut out. He spent the next weeks wearing a diaper to absorb the bleeding, but no simple pain in the ass was going to slow down Ralph Engelstad.

His stubbornness and unyielding ways proved unsuccessful with lung cancer. The long-time cigarette smoker developed a nagging cough. When he finally sought treatment, he learned the bad news. He didn't share this with even his closest friends for the grim prognosis was a death sentence.

In December 2002, *BusinessWeek* published a cover story titled "The New Face of Philanthropy." Microsoft founder Bill Gates and wife Melinda led the list of charitable contributors from the business world by a wide margin. Ralph and Betty Engelstad ranked thirty-ninth on the list with their contributions exceeding $100 million. The magazine estimated Engelstad's net worth at that time as approximately $500 million, making their donation 22 percent of the family's total wealth. This ranked well ahead of Kirk Kerkorian, the only other major casino owner in the Top 50.

For all the criticism he suffered, it was Engelstad whose casino won a presidential citation as National Employer of the Year for hiring the handicapped. And it was Engelstad who quietly fed seniors during the holidays and provided hundreds of wheelchairs for the infirm.

Crusty old Ralph Engelstad, it seemed, had a heart after all.

After his death, one alumni association executive from the university described Engelstad as "the most outstanding and successful entrepreneur to graduate from the University of

North Dakota in its entire history."

Although he was an object of ridicule in Las Vegas, he was looked upon warmly at the university. Its alumni association commissioned a bronze statue of the no-nonsense businessman following his $103-million gift to create a new hockey arena.

True to the man, the bronze depicted an unsmiling, square-shouldered fellow in a simple sport shirt and slacks. The likeness was sockless. Etched near the entrance of the arena was its namesake's credo: "My learning experiences and my dedication to the Fighting Sioux tradition provided the format for the road to achievement which I often express in my mottos, 'No dream comes true until you get up and go to work' and 'The harder I work, the luckier I get.'"

At Engelstad's memorial service, former University of North Dakota President Tom Clifford said, "No matter what our experiences with Ralph, he was a man of conviction. He had a passion for detail. He worked fourteen hours a day. He followed his goals tirelessly. He accomplished them."

Work defined Engelstad's life. He worked with the kind of hunger common to the Depression generation.

Just hours after Engelstad's funeral, the sharks of Las Vegas began to circle. The Strip buzzed with speculation that his family would rush to sell the Imperial Palace. On its face, this seemed logical: Betty Engelstad was in her seventies and had never been a regular at the hotel. Although daughter Kris McGarry was familiar with the company's operations and had once worked with her father, in recent years she devoted herself to caring for her two young children.

Offers were received from many sources. Some were speculative exercises, but others appeared legitimate. Engelstad's holdings were so vast and diverse that keeping track of them would frazzle a crew of accountants.

But Betty Engelstad was no pushover. She'd lived forty-eight years with her hard-driven husband and endured his shortcomings and eccentricities to be taken advantage of in a time of mourning. She dispatched family attorney Owen Nitz to inform Nevada gaming regulators that the Imperial Palace properties on the Strip and in Biloxi were not for sale.

The sharks, it seemed, would have to wait.

# Closing Time for a Vegas Guy

I t was closing time at Fellini's, the popular Las Vegas restaurant, and the bar crowd had finally thinned out. In one corner, through the haze of cigarette smoke, sat maverick casino man Bob Stupak and his companion, Las Vegas City Councilwoman Janet Moncrief.

Stupak had not-so-secretly assisted Moncrief's upset victory over an embattled incumbent, who like so many local politicians, was under FBI surveillance in a political corruption investigation.

On most nights, Stupak wasn't above swallowing his fill of booze and singing a few slightly slurred standards accompanied by the restaurant's piano player. But on this night, he was strangely quiet, like a salesman whose best deals were behind him. The Vegas Guy remained in the shadows.

"The days of characters are gone," Stupak told a reporter. "There's no more Jay Sarnos around. There are no more me's around. It's over."

He was correct. The time had passed when an individualist with some money, some savvy and a few contacts could score big if he played his cards right. Those days were gone, swept away by a bottom-line-obsessed corporate culture that had endeared itself to Wall Street, even while making long-time Las Vegas visitors pine for the days "when the mob ran the town."

There wasn't much room for an aging huckster like Stupak.

Bob Stupak was born in Pittsburgh on April 6, 1942, to Florence and Chester Stupak. From the time he was in knee pants, Bob appreciated the importance of making friends and influencing people. When he wasn't hustling a buck or hanging out on the street corner, taking in movies or getting kicked out of school, Bob Stupak studied his father's every move.

Chester Stupak was king of the South Side gambling rackets at a time when the mob muscled the action. In Pittsburgh in those days, it took a relatively few bucks to persuade most cops and politicians to look the other way. Little Chester Stupak remained a big man on the streets of the South Side from just after World War II to the early 1980s. His dice games were so open that every cop in the precinct knew the names of every player.

Stupak learned his gift of gab at the heels of his father. The Pittsburgh gambling boss was diminutive in stature, but big on experience. His son brought his schtick to Las Vegas, bet against heavy odds, and beat them for a long time.

He took the worst piece of real estate on Las Vegas Boulevard, a site fit only for a used-car lot, and, against everyone's advice, built a casino there and succeeded. As gaudy as it was, Bob Stupak's Vegas World was big time among the casino moneymakers.

Here is a man who constructed his dream project, the Stratosphere Tower, and, in so doing, won the admiration of many of his former critics. For the first time, everyone agreed that Bob Stupak was a winner with his 1,049-foot tower with the rooftop roller-coaster and the NASA-like rocket ride.

Naturally, it went bankrupt.

On the way down, Stupak's personal stock holdings lost more than $100 million in value. He also lost the trust of his hundreds of investors.

Somehow, he managed to retain his sense of humor. He would need it on the rocky highway ahead.

After leaving school, Bob Stupak pursued several interests simultaneously. He found gamblers and ran his own illegal card games, bought and sold watches, raced motorcycles, became a nightclub singer and cut several singles while under a brief recording contract as "Bobby Star." He served in the National Guard and created a thriving business selling two-for-one coupon books. The coupon books took him all the way to Australia, where he developed a lucrative telemarketing operation.

"I never had a steady job," Stupak once said. "All the jobs I had were self-inflicted."

With his own cash and dollars raised from his father's friends, Stupak bought a homely 1.5-acre parcel north of Sahara Avenue at Las Vegas Boulevard South that could have served as the community junkyard.

What he built and opened on March 31, 1974, was a small slot joint absurdly named Bob Stupak's World Famous Historic Gambling Museum.

"The name was about 10 feet longer than the casino," Stupak recalled years later.

On May 21, an air conditioner caught fire, and the joint burned down. Arson was suspected, but not being able to prove anything, the insurance company eventually settled the claim.

Stupak was on his way to creating Vegas World, a testament to his persistence. By the late 1970s, Las Vegas casino culture was peopled with college graduates and experienced hoteliers who dressed more like bankers than pit bosses. With his wild sport coats and nonstop patter, Stupak was a brother from another planet. Yet he managed to persuade Valley Bank legends Ken Sullivan and E. Parry Thomas to lend him more than $1 million to complete his 20-story tower.

Vegas World opened on a Friday the 13th, 1979. It suffered

from its mediocre location and Stupak's scrawny bankroll. Vegas World was neither downtown nor on the Strip. Construction had eaten his reserve funds. The only thing strikingly different that his club offered was the unique personality of Bob Stupak and his tremendous talent for promotion.

Somehow he survived. During the next decade, Stupak developed quirky and original rules for traditional games. He offered crapless craps where a shooter who threw 2, 3, or 12 on his come-out roll wouldn't lose his pass line wager, but instead that number would be his point.

Double Exposure 21 was a blackjack variation where the dealer exposed both his cards. The catch to this player advantage was that on "pushes" (when dealer and player have the same total), the dealer would win. There were other original games like Experto and Polish Roulette.

He also accepted high-limit wagers at the tables and in his sports book, where he sometimes recklessly shifted the odds in order to attract action.

His motto was plastered across the building: "The Sky's the Limit."

"Don't come to the big place with the small bankroll," Stupak was fond of saying, as he echoed Horseshoe patriarch Benny Binion. "Come to the small place with the big bankroll."

What set him apart and made Vegas World famous was its direct-mail coupon promotions. He flooded the mails with these, and they worked. For $369, one could buy "a Vegas vacation." This included three nights at the hotel for two people plus breakfast and a dinner plus a coupon book that gave its holder free slot play, souvenirs, match-play coupons at the gambling tables, a guaranteed surprise gift, and on and on.

True, Vegas World rooms weren't exactly fit for a king. The clothes closets lacked doors. The bathroom drinking cups were plastic. But the casino excitement was real, and all the promised chances, gifts, and discounts were delivered. The by-mail offers drew customers to Vegas World by the thousands.

Stupak constantly promoted himself, believing that in so

doing, he was also promoting Vegas World. He appeared in movies and on television and once starred in a 1987 episode of "Crime Story."

He also used politics as a promotional tool. He ran for mayor in 1987, survived the primary with 33 percent of the vote, but lost to the incumbent. His next big political push took place four years later when he ran his daughter, Nicole, for City Council against Frank Hawkins. Despite plenty of dirty tricks and thousands of dollars spent, Hawkins pulled out the victory. Stupak also financed his son's Nevada's 1999 campaign to unseat incumbent Councilman Gary Reese in Ward 3. Reese won by a handful of votes.

Many of these campaigns appear to have been made as much for publicity reasons as for political office. He played no-limit poker for $500,000 against the ORAC computer on a national television program. He made a $1-million bet on Super Bowl XXIII and made regular appearances at the World Series of Poker.

He won many of his wagers, but the value of his winnings was overshadowed by the wide free advertising Vegas World and its owner received.

At its peak, Bob Stupak's Vegas World generated more than $100 million in annual gambling revenues. Ever the gambler, in the late 1980s, Stupak devised a way to make an even-bigger mark in Las Vegas.

All he had to do was risk everything he owned.

The idea for the Stratosphere Tower began after a heavy windstorm blew down the sign in front of Vegas World. With hyperbole running through his veins, Stupak figured that the best way to attract business for his casino was to erect the world's tallest sign. This idea was refined after a journey to Australia to see his daughter, Nicole. While there, he saw the Sydney Tower. It intrigued and inspired him.

When he returned to Las Vegas, Stupak did research on observation towers. He found that, throughout history, they not only had redefined the skyline, but attracted crowds.

True, they weren't cheap to construct.

Stupak began building his dream tower with the cash flow from Vegas World. At the same time, he tried to round up investors and make an initial public offering of stock in the Stratosphere Corp.

But persuading a skeptical public to trust the same Bob Stupak who gave it Vegas World, and who gave the voters fits with his outrageous campaigns, and who gave the Gaming Control Board headaches with his complaint-generating two-for-one coupon vacations wasn't easy.

By late August 1993, the tower was a half-completed stumpy but not unsubstantial 510 feet high. The offering was similarly situated. With a deadline looming, there were still millions of dollars to raise.

A fire on August 29 ruined Stupak's chances. Although no structural damage was reported, few were the people eager to invest in a project already labeled a "towering inferno" by the press.

When the fire happened, Stupak was in Minnesota trying to carve out a partnership in the project with Lyle Berman of Grand Casinos Inc. At that moment, Berman was on the hottest roll in the casino industry. His agreement to take on the project meant two things: First, Stupak would finally see his dream tower completed; and second, Stupak would no longer be in charge. He would become just another investor, albeit a major one.

And that's the way things went until the night of March 31, 1995, when Bob Stupak and his son, Nevada, were involved in a devastating accident. He crashed his Harley-Davidson motorcycle going more than 60 mph. While Nevada only suffered a broken leg, Bob Stupak broke every bone in his face. Emergency-room physicians were sure he wouldn't live. If he did, they were sure he'd remain a vegetable for the rest of his life.

Bob Stupak confounded all the medical experts. He emerged from his coma weeks later and in the months that followed, he regained his health. When he was back on the street, Stupak sold some of his stock holdings and with the proceeds, cut checks to charity. The huckster was clearly grateful to be alive.

He continued his rehabilitation as his Stratosphere moved toward completion.

Its costs mounted. Its debts skyrocketed.

Although Stupak was assessed fines totaling $2.9 million for gaming violations linked to his vacation programs, these were settled for a much smaller sum.

Then, a discouraging reality set in.

When the Stratosphere opened at the end of April, it was touted as a $550-million project, the third most-expensive hotel casino in the history of Las Vegas. It attracted crowds of tourists, but not enough of them gambled, ate, or shopped in the hotel.

Stratosphere's stock price slumped from $17 a share to a few bucks in a matter of weeks

The Stratosphere went bankrupt, changed management hands, and was later gobbled up by takeover magnate Carl Icahn.

After that, Stupak rarely set foot in the place.

In the spring of 1999, the Las Vegas City Council rejected his plan to build a 280-foot time-share, shaped like the Titanic ocean liner. As quickly as that plan was rejected, he announced his intentions to buy the Moulin Rouge on Bonanza Road.

But could he make a comeback in the casino game?

"The big problem Bob has is you can't enter the industry as easily as you could in the old days," author and poker expert David Sklansky said. "If you don't have $100 million to throw around, it's hard to get into the game."

Singer Phyllis McGuire, his then-current romance, had a different perspective. "He's not really down," she said. "He saw his dream realized. The dream is that the tower should be finished. I've never seen him as happy as the night it opened. He's already survived the biggest challenge of his life."

She later dumped him.

♦　♦　♦

To be sure Stupak had managed to keep his name in the news. He always showed a knack for self-promotion—even if it did sometimes make him the butt of jokes.

He was still a dangerous poker player, but when he finagled his way into a head-to-head match, he played as much for the camaraderie as for the cash. As if to illustrate the adage about idle hands, Stupak often found himself in the news for his odd-ball behavior. For instance, he was involved in a brief scuffle with 80-year-old reputed hit man R.D. Matthews at Piero's Ristorante, an incident connected with his running feud with Binion's Horseshoe owners Nick and Becky Behnen. (He later mended fences with the Behnens and played cards in their poker room and ate breakfast in their coffee shop.)

Stupak had a cameo in the forgettable straight-to-video movie *Angel Blade* with Margot Kidder and was involved in a lawsuit over the rightful ownership of genuine moon rocks that had been an attraction at his long-since-demolished Vegas World.

In early 2003, Stupak worked behind the scenes to promote the candidacy of his girlfriend, hospital trauma nurse Janet Moncrief, for a City Council seat held by a controversial ex-cop named Michael McDonald. McDonald's name was linked to a pair of public corruption investigations associated with the community's infamous topless bar racket. Although he was not indicted when other local elected officials fell later that year, the bad publicity made him vulnerable.

Moncrief initially denied any direct association with Stupak, but it was clear to reporters who'd followed Stupak's career that neither the candidate nor the casino rebel were being entirely candid.

On election night, Moncrief blew McDonald out of office. Stupak arrived late to her victory party, having deliberately waited until the television cameras were gone. A few weeks later, Moncrief sported a large diamond engagement ring from Stupak.

She later dumped him.

◆　　◆　　◆

Stupak would appear to make an ideal boxing promoter. Although his history of problems with the Gaming Control Board and various states' attorneys general defined him as a loose cannon in the now buttoned-down casino industry, his antics were ideally suited for the fight business. That racket was colorfully defined by flamboyant convicted felon and Las Vegas denizen Don King.

Stupak told an associate, "This fucking boxing business was made for me. I'm out of the box. I'm off the wall."

And so Stupak, a carnival pitchman at heart, distanced himself from the casino business and moved into the fight game by acquiring promotional rights to several boxers and putting together mid-sized cards. He even planned to promote a heavyweight title contender. All he had to do was find one.

"I'm going to retire five years after I die," he said, laughing and lighting up another cigarette.

If he's become more a character than a competitor, he did alter Nevada gaming regulations and the Las Vegas skyline forever. And now he's out to change the boxing business.

For better and worse, Bob Stupak's name would always scream "Vegas Guy."

# 15

# The Unlucky Horseshoe

L uck has been a powerful lady in the Las Vegas mythology. Tales of good and bad fortune proliferate in the casino culture from the crap tables to the sports book.

Some Las Vegans even today wonder whether Binion's Horseshoe owner Becky Binion Behnen traded away her good fortune the day she decided to sell the casino's legendary million-dollar display. This consisted of one hundred mint $10,000 bills mounted underneath a glass frame. For decades, the impressive display drew thousands of tourists to the downtown casino for a free photograph of themselves standing in front of the million dollars. Nor was the appeal limited to the average Jane and Joe. Famous movie stars and other major entertainers also made it a point to be photographed with the million-dollar display. These included Jack Benny, the Marx Brothers, and singer Vic Damone.

In time, the photo became a destination point, and many

gamblers who otherwise would never have left their plush Strip hotels made it a habit to get one of those pictures on every visit to Vegas.

Its sale suggested that the new owners of the Horseshoe were in serious financial trouble. Why else would they dismantle such a successful attraction?

The Behnens had gained control of the casino from Jack Binion in one of the nastiest family fights in the city's history. Jack retained a 1-percent stake in the Horseshoe in order to maintain his Nevada gaming license, but he joined Ted Binion and Barbara Binion in selling out their remaining interest to sister Becky in 1998.

Not that Becky ever admitted her club was in trouble. On the contrary, she and her husband, Nick Behnen, assured skeptics that their management strategy was in the process of returning Binion's Horseshoe to its glory days. For starters, Behnens' limited bankroll wouldn't allow the Horseshoe to take the big bets that had made it famous. And, said *Las Vegas Advisor* publisher Anthony Curtis, "They sweat even the bets they do take."

Gamblers remembered those times when the downtown casino accepted the highest action in Las Vegas. You could set your own maximum up to $1 million with the size of your first wager. Saying this policy was returning was a colorful story line, that evoked images of Benny Binion and old Las Vegas, but it was a fantasy.

The setbacks started even before Becky won her gaming license. Racks of $5,000 casino chips mysteriously disappeared at about the time her wild brother, Ted Binion, was being expelled from the industry because of his drug use and mob contacts.

When she couldn't offer proof that they were stolen, Becky was forced to make good on the chips.

Becky had no experience running a casino. Husband Nick was another matter. His background included running illegal card games, and there was an occasion when he was suspected of attempting to murder a man by placing a pistol in his mouth and pulling the trigger.

The man survived, and Behnen wasn't convicted, but the incident fueled his reputation as a fellow capable of anything.

Throughout Becky Behnen's stormy ownership of the Horseshoe, husband Nick was believed to be assisting the show from behind the scenes. He denied abusing help and firing veteran employees he perceived as being loyal to the previous regime in violation of his wife's licensing agreement.

The Behnens were also suspected of giving damaging information about Jack Binion to gaming authorities in an effort to cause him licensing trouble in other casino jurisdictions. (Licensing probes in Illinois and Indiana discouraged Jack Binion and played a role in his decision to sell his immensely profitable casinos in late 2003 to Harrah's Entertainment for $1.45 billion.)

Without any high-end marketing, and with only 360 rooms, Becky had to cater to walk-in customers. But she wasn't big on advertising or smart about publicity. The casino known for its widely popular $2 steak dinners and 50-cent whiskey drinks cut back on this successful marketing feature.

Some table games were removed, and more slots were installed. Becky's denials to the contrary, Binion's had turned into a grind joint. What emerged was a sawdust joint in tatters running as a cheapskate machine that alienated long-time customers.

Top poker players stayed clear of the Horseshoe out of loyalty to Jack Binion, and even its reputation as the center of the Texas hold'em universe began to tarnish.

The Behnens announced their decision to deduct 3-percent of the prize money from the World Series of Poker pot and divide it among casino personnel. This not only infuriated poker dealers and irritated players, but sparked a Gaming Control Board investigation.

Those who groused about management's acumen—poker professional Paul Phillips, for instance—were barred from the casino. The Horseshoe hired and fired poker-room managers and fumbled away every marketing opportunity for its famous

World Series of Poker. This at a time when unlimited Texas hold'em had become a television spectator sport watched by millions, making it the hottest game in the nation.

Meanwhile, bills for electricity, food, linens, and sundries went unpaid. Outstanding, too, was an estimated $1.5-million assessment for the casino's maintenance share of the Fremont Street Experience pedestrian mall. Other Fremont Street casino operators managed to pay their dues to maintain the light show, but the Behnens said the Fremont Street Experience didn't benefit their casino. Becky stopped contributing shortly after she took control of the property.

"We've tried for over a year to collect the overdue amount," attorney Stephen Peek told reporter Jeff Simpson in August 2001. Eventually a judge ordered Behnen to pay the debt, but by then she was confronted by even bigger concerns: $5 million in unpaid payroll taxes, employee health insurance lapses, and worse. By August 2002, Horseshoe employees faced the prospect of losing their medical insurance.

Weeks later, the Gaming Control Board forced Behnen to unplug approximately 500 of its 1,300 slot machines due to the Horseshoe's insufficient cash reserves. Comically, a Horseshoe executive claimed the lack of greenbacks on hand was because so many employees cashed their paychecks at the casino cage. What he didn't say was that those employees did so because they feared their checks wouldn't be honored at local banks.

And with huge waves washing over its bow, the Behnens still denied the ship was sinking. "The Horseshoe is a great place to gamble and have fun," Becky Behnen assured a skeptic, "and we'll now be able to provide more slot machines."

She poured millions of her own inherited dollars into the casino in an effort to keep it afloat. Gaming authorities monitored the club's slide, and the National Labor Relations Board notified the owners that they were in violation of their obligation to contribute to the Culinary employees' health and welfare plan.

Gaming authorities faced a difficult question. It was one that illustrated the strength and weakness of casino licensing in

Nevada. Should they move in, as was their right, and shut down the shabby property due to its violations? Or should they allow the Horseshoe to sputter along and, by doing so, keep its 900 workers employed?

The answer was slow in coming, but in early 2004, U.S. marshals and state gaming regulators closed the Horseshoe and seized its assets. The excuse was its failure to pay millions into the union employees' health and welfare fund as mandated by federal law.

Gaming investigators found conditions inside the cage worse than they'd suspected. Within days of the raid, an announcement was made that the Horseshoe was being sold to Harrah's, which had little interest in the careworn property except to acquire the Horseshoe brand name and its rights to the World Series of Poker.

The board also appeared concerned that, as during the previous management changeover, a large quantity of gaming chips might turn up for redemption by the new owner from players who claimed to have been stashing them.

It doubled the amount of cash to be reserved by Behnen to $3 million.

While gaming observers noted the oddity of the hastily assembled meeting, it was clear the Control Board and commission had encouraged the trouble at the Horseshoe by failing to act on dozens of complaints of mismanagement.

Angry critics focused their ire on Nick Behnen, but the buck stopped at Becky's desk for it was her responsibility to keep the casino functioning at a standard that did not bring embarrassment and disrepute to the rest of the industry. She fell far short of that mark.

Although Gaming Control Board member Bobby Siller said his agency was "shocked" by its findings during the investigation that followed the Horseshoe's closure, he chose not to air a lengthy list of concerns on the public record. This spared the previous owners embarrassment and protected the image of the industry and its regulatory apparatus.

Regulators were so motivated to end the Horseshoe embarrassment that on March 3, 2004, they voted to permit a highly unorthodox transfer of ownership from the giant Harrah's Entertainment to the diminutive MTR Gaming Group of West Virginia. The total sale price was $50 million, but most of that money was used to pay off the crippling debts Behnen's management team had accumulated in just fifty months.

The MTR deal was made swiftly. Harrah's agreed to manage the Horseshoe for one year before abandoning it to the smaller player.

Mayor Oscar Goodman, meanwhile, confronted a different problem. If, as was becoming clear, Harrah's had every intention of yanking the popular World Series of Poker from a struggling Fremont Street after a quarter century, downtown casinos were sure to lose one of their best weeks of the year for traffic flow. An unabashed booster of downtown redevelopment, Goodman immediately began rattling sabers about what the city might be forced to do to prevent such a calamity from occurring.

He intimated that the new owners might have difficulty transferring their liquor license—a potential catastrophe for a gambling operator, for liquor is the motor oil of the casino machine—but those who knew the applicable laws and regulations realized Goodman was merely puffing. All he could actually do was to watch the once-mighty casino change hands and become an also-ran.

Veteran attorney Bob Faiss represented Behnen on the last day before both tiers of the state's casino regulatory structure, which noted the oddity of the Harrah's-MTR arrangement, but also appeared relieved that the troubling previous management was out.

"The Horseshoe Club has always been the passion of Becky Behnen's life," Faiss told a reporter. "It was her dream, but today marks the end of that dream."

As Las Vegas approached its centennial in 2005, it would do

so with one of downtown's flagships only a shadow of its former self. The hell-roaring casino's collapse would have brought tears even to tough old Benny Binion's eyes.

# Searching for the
# New Frontier

Visitors to Las Vegas would be hard-pressed to believe it now, but there was a time when the Frontier was the most popular casino in town. The Hotel Last Frontier might have reinvented itself and evolved along with the Strip, or, like other early operations such as the El Rancho and Bonanza Club, faded into the postcard memories of Vegas past. It did neither.

Neither thriving nor expired, the Frontier exists in a netherworld and is not defined by its quaint and colorful history, its short-time ownership by Howard Hughes, or as the former home of illusionists Siegfried & Roy. Rather, it is best known for its 2,325-day strike by Culinary Union service workers. The strike crippled business and turned its owners into pariahs.

The place was jinxed.

When it opened in October 1942, the Hotel Last Frontier

defined the Las Vegas casino experience. Theater magnate R.E. Griffith and his nephew, William J. Moore, visited Thomas Hull's El Rancho a year earlier and came away convinced that Las Vegas had potential.

The Last Frontier was influenced by the El Rancho's Western theme, but Griffith and Moore paid closer attention to detail. At a time when, due to World War II, construction materials and skilled tradesmen were scarce, Moore managed to design and build a resort that raised the bar in bustling Las Vegas.

Although the Last Frontier's low-rise, motor-inn design and 107 rooms would be considered simplistic compared to current day tastes defined by pirate-ship battles and 3,000-room megaresorts, Moore gave his resort a Hollywood Western dude-ranch feeling that tourists loved. Security guards dressed as sheriffs and carried six-shooters. With its wagon wheel-shaped chandeliers, decorative bullhorns, and authentic back bar, the Last Frontier was as close as most folks would ever come to the Wild West.

When Moore adorned the walls with some of "Doby Doc" Caudill's amazing mountain of Western memorabilia, the Last Frontier was unsurpassed in its theme.

Moore sold the place in 1951 to well-connected trucking and brewery-company owner Jake Kozloff. Kozloff's contacts included many of the city's underworld benefactors. By 1955, the Last Frontier had emerged as the Hotel New Frontier. History would note that Kozloff's Frontier was not only associated with organized crime, but was being brutally skimmed.

For a time, German actress Vera Krupp became an owner of record, and Kozloff was suspected of robbing her interests. Then Kozloff sold his interest. He invested sale proceeds in the mob's latest casino creation, the Dunes. Meanwhile, the New Frontier was losing its edge at the tables with each successive casino that opened.

The Western theme became stale, and the motor inns on the Strip were being overshadowed and being made obsolete by new high-rises such as the Sands, Riviera, and Dunes. Warren Bayley, creator of the Hacienda, tried his hand with the Frontier, and a collection of characters led by Maurice Friedman, T. W. Richardson, and Detroit mafia figures Anthony Zerilli and Michael Polizzi, took over the property on paper and behind the scenes.

One of the owners of the Frontier in 1967 was Steve Wynn, a cocky twenty-five-year-old son of an East Coast bingo-hall operator. Although the FBI investigation would find hidden ownership and organized crime connections, Wynn wasn't among those charged.

For publicity-sensitive Las Vegas, the scandal ended in July 1967 when Howard Hughes emerged as a man on a white horse and cut a check for the careworn, cash-strapped Frontier.

Margaret Elardi took possession of the Frontier by buying it from the Hughes' Summa Corporation after Hughes died. It was a niche property with a reputation for introducing, but rarely keeping, popular Las Vegas entertainment. For example, in addition to Siegfried & Roy, headliners included Robert Goulet andou Newton.

Margaret Elardi had, for a time, owned the Pioneer Club downtown. She was an unpretentious woman who spent much of her time in the resort's gift shop while her sons supervised the casino. The Elardi family gaming interests eventually spread to Laughlin, where they operated the successful Pioneer Club on the Colorado River.

The Elardis weren't dynamic operators nor did they have big ambitions. In the land of behemoth egos, they were content to grind out a profit and keep low profiles. This ended when they reached an impasse in contract negotiations with Culinary Local 226.

The Elardis felt they couldn't afford to provide the same wage and benefits package that the larger, more successful Strip resorts agreed to. Although downtown casinos received modified contracts, and in future years the Culinary Union would get absolutely cozy with a variety of employers, the financially anemic Frontier had become a test case of the labor organization's strength. If it couldn't prevail over the Elardis and their relatively tiny property, the theory went, what hope did it have in the long run against the megaresorts?

On September 21, 1991, workers voted 464 to 7 to walk out. They took to the sidewalks, and the die was cast. For the union, the Frontier was a natural flash point that attracted national media attention—most of it unfavorable for the tight-knit Elardi clan.

In one respect, the family was in excellent shape to fight off a protracted dispute: They had their own money and no stockholders to appease. But it was also true that every day saw less action at the tables. Over the course of the next six years, the Frontier received little walk-up traffic and less support from gamblers who had empathy for the maids, waiters, cocktail servers, and bartenders who were striking for what amounted to a few extra pennies per hour.

Eventually, the strike became part of the Strip landscape. With the exception of the occasional fistfight, made-for-TV rally, or an appearance by casino man Bill Bennett's meals-on-wheels brigade, the picket line was quiet. Replacement workers entered through a guarded side entrance, and the Elardis managed to pay the light bill.

Many of the original strikers found new jobs in the booming Las Vegas service-employee market. Others averaged a few hours on the line each day in exchange for subsistence strike pay.

Labor-backed politicians from Nevada and across the country made a pilgrimage to the Frontier picket line to pay their respects to the strikers. Missouri Congressman Richard Gephardt captured the image that organized labor wanted to project. "You are winning this thing for the unions of America, not just unions in Las Vegas," he declared.

Although the strike was costly to the Culinary Union, it was critical to win or face the probability that other resorts would try to slip from the fold.

Nevada Gov. Bob Miller, heavily supportive of the union,

made unsuccessful attempts to bring the warring parties together. Federal arbitration specialists were also ineffective. The Elardis had assumed a bunker mentality that bordered on paranoia.

The media marked each anniversary and covered major rallies featuring labor-friendly congressmen from across the map as well as chief supporter, the Rev. Jesse Jackson.

On occasion, the Culinary's detractors reminded the media of the union's historic ties to organized crime, most notably to the Chicago Outfit through the friendship of international president Edward Hanley and mafia boss Tony Accardo. Locals in New York, Atlantic City and Las Vegas were known to be saddled with mob influence and corruption.

No man better exemplified the Culinary's Las Vegas ties to the underworld than Al Bramlet. He was the revered and reviled Local 226 executive secretary who came to Nevada from Arkansas in 1946 and had watched the growth of the casino business.

It would have been folly to attempt to gain power on the pit floor, but Bramlet understood the clout inherent in the large number of service employees who kept the hotels running smoothly. Some called him "a caricature of the autocratic and corrupt union boss."

Bramlet was a cutthroat political player, but he won the admiration of thousands of working people. He operated in Democratic Party politics throughout the 1960s and early 1970s at a time when some politicians were known to enter casino count rooms to fill their pockets with cash contributions.

Bramlet fired up his members and helped get commissioners, legislators, governors, and senators elected, always keeping in contact with his Chicago benefactors.

Authors Sally Denton and Roger Morris observed: "From the beginning of his dominance, he had given the Syndicate casinos almost unbroken labor stability, while steadily adding to the ranks of his local. At the same time he joined in the plunder of kickbacks and inside dealing, owning on the side operations

145

that did business with casinos, some in services that competed with his own members."

Bramlet slipped off his leash when he tried to organize local restaurants through pure intimidation. This attracted the attention not only of federal investigators, but from the Outfit, which then dispatched a new representative, Anthony Spilotro, to act as its cleanup man.

By 1977, Las Vegas all but ceased to be an "open city." The Chicago mob had taken over and, in exchange, agreed to stay out of the newly legalized gambling scene in Atlantic City. But Bramlet now considered himself a boss unto himself, and something had to be done about this defiance.

The solution came when Spilotro, using father-and-son contract killers Tom and Andy Hanley, took care of the Outfit's union problem. Bramlet's body was found in February 1977 in the desert near Mount Potosi in the far southwestern end of the valley.

The Hanleys were convicted of the killing, but refused to implicate Spilotro.

The Culinary Union would enter into and emerge from a federal stewardship designed to rehabilitate its credibility. This convinced most skeptics that the mob influence had been flushed out.

Years later in 1997, it was neither the mob nor the feds who were responsible for finally ending the record-setting six-and-a-half-year strike. The peacemaker was a quiet Kansas businessman named Phil Ruffin, who was encouraged by Strip operators to look at the careworn Frontier—but found himself more intrigued by the substantial tracts of undeveloped land adjacent to the hotel. He saw what others had lacked the imagination to see.

Ruffin was cut from tough cloth. He owned a dozen Marriott hotels, the Crystal Palace casino in the Bahamas, and a truck-dolly factory in Wichita. When he looked at the Frontier's twenty-six acres, he liked what he saw and acted quickly. Then he picked up the option on the adjacent sixteen-and-a-half-acre parcel also owned by the Elardis.

The Frontier had potential, but big problems. The hotel tower needed retrofitting, and the 41,325-square-foot casino floor was one of the smallest on the Strip. The hotel had few restaurants and suffered from its terminally seventies design. During the six-and-a-half-year standoff, its cash flow had shrunk to half its pre-strike size.

In short, the Frontier could have been renamed the Wreck.

But Ruffin was a man whose business was running a chain of service stations rather than a group of craps tables. He paid the Elardis $167 million and settled the strike with the Culinary Union.

His Nevada gaming license received expedited treatment, and he was unanimously approved after only a fifteen-minute hearing. Ruffin even received an ovation from those present in the hearing room after his license was granted.

"Tonight, this is a real expression of power to the people," the Rev. Jesse Jackson proclaimed as the hotel reopened. "It's about American democracy. It's about the American dream."

It was also about finding a wealthy man with a Vegas itch so great that he was willing to scratch it at the woefully out-of-step, 986-room Frontier.

The Frontier's marquee shouted, "EVERYONE WELCOME. STRIKE'S OVER!"

But the crowds didn't come. The strike had crippled the Frontier, but it was also true that Las Vegas had changed during the six-plus years of labor strife. Two gaming analysts put the Frontier's problem in perspective for reporter Dave Berns. Said CIBC Oppenheimer Corporation's David Wolfe, "It's a C-type property at best in a B-setting, and it's going to need quite a reshaping of its image. If you frequented Las Vegas, you went out of your way to avoid that side of the street if you were walking."

Salomon Smith Barney's Bruce Turner added, "Let me put something into perspective for the new owners. If they believe the only reason their cash flow was cut in half was because of labor unrest, they are delusional. The market changed dramatically over that time. There are a large number of operators who have seen cash flow change during that time. However, the strike's end will help."

All that would save the Frontier in the future was an entirely new look and the development of the north end of the Strip.

Ruffin announced in January 2000 that he planned to build a $700-million "City by the Bay" San Francisco-themed resort capable of competing with the south Strip's behemoths. The plan drew raised eyebrows and triggered litigation from a man who claimed the concept was his. Five years later, visitors had yet to find a replica of the Golden Gate Bridge on Las Vegas Boulevard.

But the north Strip finally showed signs of life with the development of Steve Wynn's new hotel-casino. Named Wynn Las Vegas, this would be Wynn's monument to conspicuous consumption. In 2005, plans to construct high-rise condominiums were announced by the Soffer family and Hilton Hotels.

It remains uncertain whether Phil Ruffin still had plans to leave his heart and bankroll in a faux San Francisco, but in July of 2004 came the announcement that would change the way tourists and locals perceived the Frontier.

Donald Trump, whose Atlantic City casinos are always in deep financial trouble, announced that he would team up with Ruffin and the pair would build a sixty-four-story, $300-million hotel with condominium apartments just west of Las Vegas Boulevard behind the Frontier. Trump, who'll do anything to get his name in the newspapers, announced that if Michael Jackson was acquitted of child molestation charges, Trump would welcome him as a resident in the new complex.

After so many years of turmoil, had the Frontier's jinx finally been broken?

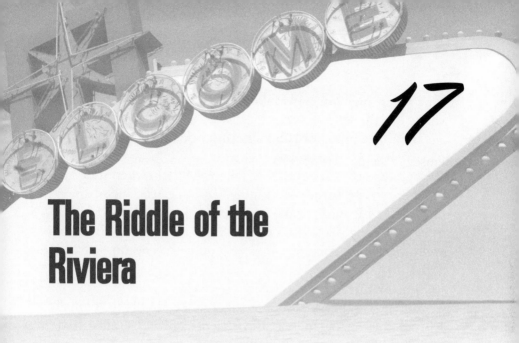

# The Riddle of the Riviera

L ike an aging showgirl battling the ravages of time, the Riviera has had endless facelifts.

It's no longer that hot, handsome dame that once captured the imagination and money of a generation of steady gamblers, but it still has its place in the massive Las Vegas visitors market. It's a survivor. And how it survived is nothing short of amazing, given the competition on the Strip.

While the Dunes, Sands, Landmark, and Hacienda have imploded back to desert sand and rock, the Riviera stands tall with a lot of brass, not much class, and an acceptance of the reality that now it is a niche player.

It's difficult to imagine, given the opulence of the Bellagio, Venetian, MGM Grand, and Mandalay Bay, that there was a time when high rollers wouldn't have considered staying anywhere but the Riviera.

Built by a group of Miami businessmen who met weekly to play high-stakes poker and backed by the Chicago Outfit, the Riviera was only the seventh hotel on the Strip when it opened its doors in the spring of 1955. Headlining was star-spangled pianist Lee Liberace, who was paid an unprecedented $50,000 a week. An early publicity photo of Elvis clowning at the piano and Liberace strumming a six-string guitar has become a classic Vegas image.

The men who ran the Riviera were classic, too.

But first things first. See if this sounds familiar: Originally scheduled to cost $6 million, the Riviera came in $4 million over budget. By the time the last nail was hammered into the roof of the new nine-story palace, the original investors were tapped out.

In what has become the equivalent of a Las Vegas version of Kabuki theater, the fanfare of the Riviera's opening was followed by convenient bankruptcy filings. These wiped out the early investors with the effect of seasoning the casino. Like the Flamingo and Desert Inn before it, the Riviera emerged from its early glitch as a slick money machine thanks in no small part to the presence of the Outfit's insiders, Gus Greenbaum, Dave Berman, and Willie Alderman.

Although Greenbaum's personal life was fast coming apart in the prime Vegas fashion (drug abuse, rapacious sexual behavior, alcoholism, and thievery), the casino rolled right along. Contrary to some theories, he hadn't taken any trade secrets with him when he left the Flamingo after seven years and was "persuaded" to run the Riviera by Outfit rising star Tony Accardo and its financial expert, Jake Guzik.

What got Greenbaum in trouble were his sticky fingers and his big mouth. His substance abuse grew to where he no longer kept his own counsel, and when he fell hopelessly in debt—more than $1 million by one estimate—he became Mr. Expendable.

His grisly murder in 1958 was a clear confirmation of who really ran the Riviera.

Notable among the owners who survived Greenbaum's demise was Chicago Outfit bookmaker and gambler Ross Miller. He was a 4-percent owner who would be best known in later years as the father of Nevada Gov. Bob Miller.

The Riviera possessed two defining traits: constant construction and expansion and a suspiciously close relationship with men who historically had mob ties.

No one associated with operating the Riviera embodied the old school more than Ed Torres. He emerged as a Las Vegas casino executive after supervising the casino floor of the Havana Riviera in Cuba for Meyer Lansky, dictator Fulgencio Batista, and a cartel of organized crime figures. Most notable of these was Vincent "Jimmy Blue Eyes" Alo of New York's Genovese crime family.

Torres was granted a casino license even though he admitted social relationships with Gerardo Catena and other mobsters. He had been an original owner of the Sands and a part owner of the Fremont Hotel downtown when both were mob controlled. His name was on the Justice Department's Organized Crime Principal Subject list.

It was known to police authorities that he'd attended a 1964 meeting at a Holiday Inn in Marion, Ohio. Among those present were Meyer Lansky and at least one other Las Vegas casino owner. At that time, Lansky was believed to be the biggest behind-the-scenes force in Las Vegas.

In November 1966, a federal grand jury convened to interview witnesses and weigh evidence of mob influence at the Riviera. Michael DeFeo, then the special assistant U.S. Attorney in Las Vegas, spearheaded the investigation and would spend the next two decades arguing that Nevada's casinos were riddled with mob influence.

The Riviera grand jury marked one of the first times the FBI investigated the goings-on in Las Vegas. For many years, the bureau failed to focus on traditional mob activity despite Justice Department knowledge that casino floors and front offices were abundantly sprinkled with men of notorious repute.

At the time, FBI Director J. Edgar Hoover, himself no stranger to gambling at racetracks, said Nevada's legalized casino industry "occupies a position of major importance in the scheme of organized crime and racketeering."

Within a year, a suddenly "enlightened" Nevada would begin forging the transition toward corporate ownership of its casinos. This move initially failed to flush out the mob. Instead it had the effect of making it more difficult to investigate its operations.

Torres barely made headlines in Las Vegas where many of the casino men had similar pedigrees. He received absolution from the Gaming Control Board and Gaming Commission. In November 1968, Dean Martin's name splashed on the front page when it was announced that the singer was moving to the Riviera as a percentage owner.

Torres was never far from the thoughts of local FBI agents, who knew his historical ties to some of the biggest names in organized crime. But in February 1973, Torres, Harvey Silbert, Harry Goldman, and others sold the Riviera for $60 million to Meshulam Riklis and his travel company American International Travel Service Corporation (AITS) of Chestnut Hill, Massachusetts.

In a twist appreciated by those who knew the shadows of Las Vegas best, Torres didn't miss a beat. He remained with the new company for several years.

Riklis controlled the Riviera through his debt-laden umbrella company, Rapid-American, which at one time employed 65,000 people and owned the Lerner women's clothing chain, Faberge, Schenley liquors, Zodys, and McCrory's among others. Riklis was a classic practitioner of the use of high-interest junk-bond financing to take over companies. His strategies inspired future bond king Michael Milken.

Riklis expanded the hotel. He added a pair of towers, and then he doubled the casino space. But he made the Riviera's impressive entertainment parade a thing of the past when he insisted on headlining his wife, Pia Zadora.

While the Riviera kept expanding and sucking in millions, the Justice Department looked for a prosecutable case. The Riviera was part of a sweeping investigation into hidden ownership by the mob. Other casinos under scrutiny included the Dunes, Stardust, Aladdin, and Tropicana. A quarter-century after it opened, the Riviera was still believed to be controlled by the Chicago Outfit through legendary mob lawyer Sidney Korshak working with Torres. Others believed to have a piece of the action were Anthony Salerno and a collective of other Genovese family members.

No matter. Despite evidence of relationships with major criminal figures, Torres was a colorful and effective manager who kept the Riviera operating. It was business as usual. The resort's Delmonico gourmet room was redone, and a new casino pit was added.

Crisis, what crisis?

Riklis was no stranger to notoriety. He was licensed despite historical ties to controversial Miami attorney Alvin Malnik, a Meyer Lansky associate.

Riklis borrowed $150,000 from Malnik and kept mob mouthpiece Sidney Korshak on the Riviera payroll. Even exposure of his business ties to men linked to the Colombo crime family failed to slow him down.

While the FBI was investigating the resort, Riklis was negotiating with operators of Nevada's Public Employee Retirement System (PERS) for a long-term loan. The decision to deal with Riklis marked the first time the state had invested pension-fund dollars in a casino project.

It was a less-than-auspicious debut.

First, Riklis clipped the retirement system for $25 million at 12-percent interest. Then he borrowed $15 million at 16 percent. Then he squeezed an additional $17 million at 17 percent, for a total of $57 million at typical high junk-bond interest rates.

In 1981, the Gaming Control Board was still trying to figure out the riddle of the Riviera. Despite reams of paper indicating ties to suspicious people, Control Board chairman

Richard Bunker found no evidence linking the casino to a broad range of Mafia figures from Chicago to Miami and even Denver's Smaldone crime family.

A grand jury confirmed his conclusion when it failed to indict anyone associated with the casino. The Riviera's run of luck continued. It was on a roll.

It wasn't what might have been going on behind the scenes that made regulators grumble. It was what Riklis was brazenly doing in broad daylight. When, as anticipated, the Riviera couldn't meet its interest payments, Riklis returned to the PERS board to have the interest percentages reduced. When that failed to balance his books, he simply stopped paying interest and slid toward Chapter 11 bankruptcy status. The Riviera filed for Chapter 11 protection in August 1983, from which it emerged two years later.

Robert Vannucci joined the Riviera as its president just as it came out of its second bankruptcy. It was reborn as the publicly traded Riviera Holdings.

Vannucci's background included employment at a restaurant/disco frequented by mobsters Carmine Tramunti and Thomas Mancuso. That link led Vannucci to be temporarily considered a "non-member associate of the Lucchese family," according to Gaming Control Board files.

Meanwhile, Riklis and the Pia Zadora relationship continued to be the butt of jokes up and down the Strip. Riklis worked overtime to promote his wife's career even while the Riviera's prospects darkened by the day.

Reporter Clyde Weiss in a 1983 *Las Vegas Review-Journal* article observed, "If you wanted to find multimillionaire Meshulam Riklis last week, you would have had to look in Paris, where he was reportedly traveling with movie star wife Pia Zadora. And that's what has some Nevada gaming officials worried. Just who—they wonder—is really running the Riviera?"

Riklis was considered reckless in his financing, and he ended up before the Gaming Control Board, which could have revoked his privileged license due to his associations with underworld figures. Instead, and in keeping with a longstanding Nevada tradition, the board gave him a good scolding.

"Our whole purpose is that you take us in a serious vein, more serious than other boards," Control Board Chairman Barton Jacka told Riklis at the hearing. "I think we have your attention here today."

But if Riklis felt any heat, he didn't show it. For instance, when asked about the mob ties of business associate John Maggliocco, Riklis responded, "I couldn't care less."

The Riviera tottered on the edge of insolvency for several years, then gained a foothold in the market again thanks in large part to the efforts of a Riklis accountant named Arthur Waltzman. Balding and spectacled, the understated Waltzman had a flair for promoting.

Once a home for top entertainment, the Riviera now emerged as the venue for the "Gorgeous Ladies of Wrestling" tits-and-ass show. It became home to the first fast-food restaurant on the Strip. "Splash" was a girl-oriented variety show. Then there was "An Evening at La Cage," which featured a bevy of female impersonators. Voyeurs loved "Crazy Girls," which was short on talent, but long on skin.

Waltzman focused on giving customers value, and they responded.

"The trick to this game is pizzazz," he explained to a reporter. "The slots, the tables, they're all the same everywhere. You've got to give people a special reason to come to this place. We want people to go home saying, 'I saw something you're not going to believe.'"

The shows at the Riviera would never be confused with those on Broadway, but they gave tourists thrills at budget prices, and they gave the resort an identity it could market.

Riklis was indefatigable to the end. As late as 1990, he talked of creating a family-friendly resort with an indoor amusement park and Ferris wheel. If only he could raise the $250 million he said would be needed to build the 50-story, 2,000-room hotel tower to accompany his carnival. Nothing happened, and, in time, Riklis's credibility took a beating. Riklis sold and left the difficult work of running the Riviera to more-focused men. Pursuit of the family market was abandoned, and the Riviera's new motto became "The Alternative for Grown-ups."

Vannucci's Gaming Control Board licensing application was in jeopardy briefly due to his background as a nightclub operator in New York, Miami, and Atlanta. His most-celebrated late-1960s association with New York Jets quarterback Joe Namath and former NFL player Ray Abruzzese at the Bachelors III hot spot in New York City was also among his most complicated. The Bachelors III ownership put Namath's nightlife in a national sports spotlight and got him in trouble with NFL officials. It also made Vannucci, then more commonly known as "Bobby Van," an intriguing character in Namath's circle of pals.

In March 1969, the New York Liquor Authority produced a scathing report on Vannucci and his circle of friends, investors, and associates. In blasting him, officials wrote, "The sources of the funds used by Vannucci have not been satisfactorily explained. To the contrary, his finances, financial dealings and explanation are unacceptable to the Authority and are rejected as unworthy of belief."

More than a decade later, when Vannucci was scrutinized by Nevada gaming authorities, the past was forgotten, and he received his license.

The Riviera managed to attract an eclectic circle of entertaining characters, including "Splash" show producer Jeff Kutash, an associate of Colombo crime family capo Michael Franzese. Kutash made headlines when he beat federal charges that he bribed District Judge Gerard Bongiovanni for favorable treatment in a civil case.

Show producer Norbert Aleman was another complicated character who for a time called the Riviera his home. His "Crazy Girls" show was popular, but his circle of pals included mob figure Joey Cusumano, and that brought more heat to the hotel.

And there was entertainment director Steve Schirripa, the

affable former New Yorker who turned a part-time acting career into stardom as rotund Mafioso Bobby Bacala Baccalieri in the HBO hit series "The Sopranos."

"In the early 1980s," Vannucci points out, "the Riviera was one of the largest hotels in the world, and today we're the twenty-first largest hotel on the Las Vegas Strip. It kind of tells you what things have happened in the last twenty years."

If anything, Vannucci is as bullish today as Riklis ever was.

"When I started in this business in 1965, it was the gambling. But it's more than that now. We've got a fairly good product here. We could use a little bit of a facelift, yeah, but the thread core of the theme of the property works."

Today, the publicly traded Riviera Holdings is the owner of record, and the Riviera has carved out a niche as a haven for middle-market gamblers and a venue for smaller-scale conventions and trade shows.

The Riviera continues to struggle to outrun its past as a debt-riddled former star. Its net loss in 2002 was $24.7 million, up from $6.4 million the previous year. Long-term debt was $216.7 million with an overall value placed at $241.3 million.

The Riviera seemed ripe for a buyout, and Chairman William L. Westerman appeared to do little to slow speculation about the company's future. On the heels of record losses, Donald Trump increased his stake in Riviera Holdings by $1.7 million, or 8,000 shares, in January 2003.

This, of course, fueled speculation that the Atlantic City casino mogul was about to enter the Las Vegas casino market for the first time. He'd already announced plans to build a sixty-story condominium project to the south with Frontier owner Phil Ruffin. But Trump's buyout of the Riviera didn't materialize.

Nor did the unsolicited offer made by Fabrizio Boccardi in April 2003. The offer briefly raised the Riviera's troubled stock price on the American Exchange, but Boccardi was no stranger to announcing big plans that failed to materialize. And nothing could conceal the Riviera's leaky bottom line.

The Riviera Holdings Corporation also owned a nickel slot-machine casino on the Strip called Nickel Town, as well as the Black Hawk Casino in Black Hawk, Colorado.

Fifty years had passed since Gus Greenbaum and the boys jump-started the Riviera and made a go of it, only to be disappointed in the end. A shaky financial picture was one thing that hadn't changed in half a century at the Riviera.

And yet, by the third quarter of 2004, laughable Riviera stock rose past the $20-a-share mark. There was serious talk about its bright future.

It was an undeniable sign that the sharks of Las Vegas were near.

# The New Dukes of Downtown

ublicly, no person is a bigger cheerleader for downtown than
Oscar Goodman. The veteran criminal defense lawyer was
a mob mouthpiece who represented notorious clients ranging from Meyer Lansky and Nick Civella and from Tony
Spilotro to Natale Richichi. None of this kept him from being
swept into office as mayor in a landslide in 1998 and reelected
by a record margin four years later.

It was clear that a majority of Las Vegas voters loved their
mayor. What was uncertain was whether those with genuine
working capital bought his vision of a sparkling Fremont Street
and a revitalized downtown where sixty-one acres of undeveloped real estate would be filled with a million-square-foot furniture mall.

Like a pair of poker players with limited bankrolls but
uncommon aggression, Internet millionaires Tom Breitling and
Tim Poster (who grew up in Las Vegas) bought the Golden

Nugget from MGM Mirage in 2004 so they could enter the gaming industry. For $215 million, they picked up the best property on Fremont Street with the Golden Nugget Laughlin thrown in as a pot sweetener.

Gaming industry analysts arched their eyebrows at the deal because the prevailing mantra was that if downtown were a horse, someone would shoot it. However, starting at the very birthplace of legalized gambling was the fastest way for Poster and Breitling to become high-profile operators in what was becoming a billionaires' game.

They might not have fully appreciated the role of savior in which they cast themselves. At stake was the soul of once-prosperous old Las Vegas. It's only a slight overstatement to say those cocky young millionaires, and a few brave characters like them, are all that stand between downtown's casinos becoming a vast parking lot.

Poster and Breitling possessed a mix of the qualities of both the old and new Las Vegas and embraced gambling models to make the Golden Nugget successful and revitalize shabby Fremont Street in the process. Their long-term prosperity depended on achieving both goals. Until Fremont Street experiences a true revival, no downtown casino is safe.

One of the first things they did was to create a national reality-based casino show for television. It was bad beyond imagination. After several weeks, the project sunk into that quagmire that digests the world's worst ideas.

Politicians and historians like to call Fremont Street the place where the great American gambling culture got its start. There's truth in the geography, but the fact is that shortly after World War II, downtown started to be out of step.

Las Vegas history is divided into high rollers and grinders. The high rollers pursued expansive dreams on the Strip while the grinders remained downtown. Although men like Jackie Gaughan and Benny Binion amassed substantial fortunes on Fremont Street, most of the big money and bigger egos were found on Las Vegas Boulevard.

Steve Wynn is the classic example of a man who made the transition from downtown operator to Strip mogul. When Wynn took over the Golden Nugget in 1972, he remodeled it after its sparkling cousins on Las Vegas Boulevard. Within a few years, the Golden Nugget outshone the competition—although it wasn't more profitable than the Horseshoe, which was directly across the street.

While Wynn focused on his Strip developments and Gaughan counted his fortune and grinned about not having any stockholders to listen to, the rest of downtown lost pace.

By the time Breitling and Poster made their offer, the "For Sale" sign had been up at the Golden Nugget for years. Donald Trump had sniffed at it, but as with many of the things the publicity-hungry tycoon does, his was merely a maneuver to get his name into the newspapers.

Benny Binion's son, Jack, had also been offered the operator's keys, the story went, for as little as $2 million in cash if he assumed the long-term debt created by the Wynn administration.

Buy the Golden Nugget and you would have to assume a bundle of obligations. Its 1,907 rooms and suites were considered the equal of those in any Strip hotel. Its 32,000-square foot casino floor was small by Strip standards, but the space was large enough to hold 1,260 slot machines and 58 gaming tables. Too, the Golden Nugget had for years taken advantage of the small convention market with its 29,000-square feet of meeting space. The Golden Nugget Laughlin, meanwhile, offered 300 rooms and a 32,000-square-foot casino floor. It was a pearl in a Colorado River market increasingly battered by competition from the Indian casinos.

At first glance, Breitling and Poster seemed a team straight out of Mutt and Jeff. While Breitling dressed more like an accountant than a casino man, Poster had Vegas Guy written all over him. He was fond of expensive gold blazers that would have made Benny Siegel blush with envy. Like a character from the past, Poster could say, "We love action, there's no question" without any hint of irony.

161

The two new owners were industry neophytes, but as founders of Travelscape.com, they believed they understood the dynamic flow of the Las Vegas hotel market. In 2000, they sold Travelscape to Expedia for approximately $100 million. This allowed them to finance the Golden Nugget purchase with cash and by selling $155 million in secured notes.

Along the way, they took as a high-profile minority partner their longtime friend, tennis star Andre Agassi.

Breitling and Poster were jumping headfirst into the treacherous casino waters. By the time they came up for their Gaming Control Board license hearing, they had experienced the discomfort that comes with the scrutiny necessary for a licensing investigation.

Agassi wasn't their only old friend in Las Vegas. Crazy Horse Too topless-club owner Rick Rizzolo was another. At the time Gaming Control was doing its background check of Poster and Breitling, Rizzolo was the subject of FBI and IRS criminal investigations. There was talk of hidden ownership, tax evasion, and racketeering offenses related to a series of bar customers' beatings.

One of those customers, a Kansas tourist named Kirk Henry, suffered a broken neck after a dispute over a $66 bar bill. Rizzolo's bouncers and bar managers looked more like linebackers than U.N. negotiators. Authorities focused on the presence at the Crazy Horse Too of reputed mob associate Vinny Faraci, the son of Bonanno crime family capo "Johnny Green" Faraci, and Rocky Lombardo, the brother of reputed Chicago Outfit underboss Joseph "Joey the Clown" Lombardo.

Although Rizzolo was infatuated with playing the Vegas wise guy, surrounding himself with sports and Hollywood celebrities as well as mob figures, he also had much in common with Poster and Breitling. He, too, was a local boy who made good in a thriving Las Vegas business.

Poster used Rizzolo's million-dollar casino credit line when the two went out high rolling, and although Poster paid the debt, his companion's notoriety wasn't looked upon kindly by the Gaming Commission.

Gaming Control Board member Bobby Siller, a retired Las Vegas FBI special agent in charge, dressed down Poster and Breitling, whom he considered naïve to the seductive ways of the mob.

"People such as you, very successful, very young, are considered marks," Siller told them. "People in organized crime try to set you up to steal some of your funds. And I think that's what they're trying to do with you."

Rizzolo might have been in no position to cut too deeply into Poster and Breitling had that been his motive, but Siller had a background of historical experience on his side. Las Vegas was filled with stories of fellows who considered themselves smart, but who'd lost fortunes both at the gaming tables and in the front office of the resorts. Using attractive women, such as were at Rizzolo's beck and call, to curry favor with future marks was the second oldest game in town.

A few years earlier, veteran casino man Al Rapuano had been given a rough time by Gaming Control authorities for his relationship with the characters associated with the Crazy Horse Too, one of whom was Rizzolo's pal, Black-Book-listed Joey Cusumano. The reluctant saviors couldn't easily be knocked out of the industry for their associations, but they could be scolded. And so after a two-and-a-half-hour public hearing, the Control Board recommended limiting their gaming license to one year due to the Rizzolo connection. Control Board Chairman Dennis Neilander, perhaps in an attempt to calm concerns, said, "Overall, these guys are a big plus and a positive for downtown Las Vegas."

In addition to the poor judgment issue, Siller was concerned with the duo's questionable stock deals. These had attracted the attention of Securities and Exchange Commission investigators. At least one of the deals appeared to involve Rizzolo.

The Nevada Gaming Commission softened the Control Board's blow by extending their license limitations to four years. This gave the two men time to prove they were up to Nevada's standards of gaming-licensee comportment.

Poster spoke the right words to soothe the commission when he said, "I fully appreciate the consequences of my actions and decisions. A gaming license is a privilege, not a right. I believe a gaming licensee needs to avoid even the appearance of impropriety."

The Poster Financial Group was quick to boast that Lehman Brothers was its financial advisors on the deal, but the Rizzolo association caused Moody's to temporarily downgrade its rating of the company's $155 million in secured notes.

Although most of the Golden Nugget's casino managers remained in place, change was felt on the casino floor where larger wagers were being accepted. Computer Group betting master Billy Walters took his betting action there, and word hit the street that the Golden Nugget was wide open again. For his part, Walters, one of the biggest golf-course developers in the country, was highly complimentary of Breitling and Poster. He described them as "good young men with bright futures."

Casino marketing legend Dan Chandler, who while at Caesars Palace had attracted some of the biggest players in the history of the city, was courted to bring big gamblers to increase the action in the casino. That meant high play from a variety of wealthy sources, and in the gambling world, it didn't hurt that Poster was the nephew of bookmaker "Pittsburgh Jack" Franzi.

Profile writers noted the age similarity between the thirty-four-year-old Poster and Breitling and the Golden Nugget's previous high-profile owner, Steve Wynn, who was thirty when he took over the company in 1972. The level of competition had increased dramatically in three decades, but Poster and Breitling appeared to enjoy comparisons to the one-time Vegas casino king. The comparison was laughable, but Poster beamed.

While other boys dreamt of glory on the athletic field, Poster recalled that as a child growing up in Las Vegas, he fantasized about owning a casino. His parents had roomed at the Sands for six weeks before deciding to settle in the community, and Poster would recall that he first ordered room service at the age of six.

"Tom laughed [at the casino idea]," Poster told *Las Vegas Life* magazine writer Amy Schmidt. "But I figured somewhere over the years, I'd find a way to pull it off. We had to buy our way in, but we did it. We are now in charge of caring for one of the premier landmarks of this city. We are not going to let anyone down.

"Today, almost all of the casinos in Las Vegas are owned and operated by large corporations and many have lost the individual personality that scores of dedicated players, find so attractive and exciting. We want to revive that bygone-Vegas feel and make the Golden Nugget the first choice of visitors who long for that traditional Las Vegas experience."

Poster might have lacked know-how, but he wasn't short on confidence.

◆     ◆     ◆

Poster and Breitling weren't the only new players on the old street. Former Circus Circus executive Terry Caudill, who turned the Magoo's Gaming Group into a wildly successful bar-and-slot company in Southern Nevada, stepped up to purchase the Four Queens. And the Majestic Star Corporation of Michigan, headed by Don Barden, acquired the struggling Fitzgeralds. This made Barden the first African American to own a major Nevada casino.

When Barrick Gaming stepped in to purchase Jackie Gaughan's Plaza, it was another sign that times were changing downtown.

Meanwhile, Mayor Oscar Goodman promised the downtown area Nevada's first academic medical center, a major-league sports stadium, a performing arts center, and restaurants, shops, and upscale urban housing.

Perhaps Goodman was a giddy dreamer, but over time some bought into his vision. When an enormous outlet mall sprang up on the previously fallow land and attracted crowds of customers, it was a sign that downtown still had some life left. When the furniture center broke ground in early 2004 with a completion date of July 2005, the first phase for the Goodman promise was in place.

Privately, Goodman groused about his daunting task, hoping against hope that most of the traditional casino operators would sell out to make way for fresh entrepreneurial blood—or at least a fleet of bulldozers.

For every Boyd Group that bought the Main Street Station out of hock and through strong marketing to Hawaii had made successful ventures out of the Fremont and California Club, there was Jackie Gaughan, whose half-dozen casinos made money largely because their owner understood the importance of nickel players and hadn't had a mortgage on his properties since the Kennedy administration. But it was also true that Gaughan hadn't changed his marketing approach in several decades.

The new dukes represented downtown's future, but the trouble with Fremont Street is its past. One of the greatest challenges was making the $70-million Fremont Street Experience work. This gargantuan light canopy stretched over Fremont Street from Main to Fourth Street. It was designed to attract tourists.

Initially, the Experience was meant to be the staging area for an overhead parade that would feature floats suspended from the ceiling of the canopy. Instead, it evolved into a light show with a pixel pattern that made its computerized images appear more like an oversized child's toy and less like a television screen. In an age of rapidly advancing technology, the Experience was out of date before it was finished. Subsequent cash contributions from city coffers made it even more controversial.

The same was true for the more handsome, but even less successful $90-million Neonopolis shopping mall built in part with taxpayer funds. Neonopolis featured a multiplex movie theater, food court, three restaurants, numerous shops, and almost no business. Like the Experience, Neonopolis was funded during the administration of Jan Jones, mayor from 1991-1999 who left office to accept an executive position with Harrah's Entertainment. Future councils and mayors were left to help prop up those costly projects.

In November 2003, thirty-five-year travel industry veteran Joe Schillaci, a former president of California's Six Flags Magic Mountain theme parks, took over as chief executive officer of the Fremont Street Experience.

It was a good sign for Fremont Street and downtown, the Rodney Dangerfield of Las Vegas's casino world.

Downtown still had potential and energy, but its problems persisted. One emanated from the Golden Nugget as Poster and Breitling appeared to be a couple of ditzy hosts rather than owners trying to make their mark. By November 2004, they sold the Golden Nugget Laughlin, a moneymaking grind operation on the Colorado River, for $31 million.

The Las Vegas Golden Nugget didn't lack high rollers. The trouble was that some appeared to be better than the house—so much so that the casino was having trouble turning a profit despite scads of national publicity generated from the awful reality show, "The Casino." The owners dealt to celebrities and entertained top performers from the music industry, but they were blowing their big chance.

Behind the scenes, Poster appeared to be having trouble living up to his promises to the Gaming Control Board. And local FBI agents were intrigued by the duo's business deal made in such close proximity to the embattled topless club operator Rizzolo.

By February 2005, Poster and Breitling were gone.

The casino soap opera that started a year earlier with such hype, ended with blood in the water. Although they might claim to have been made an offer they couldn't refuse, they were folding in the tradition of all those other moneyed lightweights who came to Las Vegas with big plans and had made big fools of themselves. Jabbed columnist Jane Ann Morrison, "These boys have commitment issues."

Their $295-million sale to the Landry's seafood restaurant chain was interesting because its chairman, Tilman Fertitta, was a relative of Station Casinos' chief operators. Poster had previously worked at Palace Station and had maintained a relationship with the Fertitta family.

Those seeking irony in the sale might smile at the fact Poster and Breitling had sold to a company that specializes in fresh-caught fish.

# Casting Off the Castaways

## 19

The Castaways could never be confused with a Strip megaresort, but it managed to weather rough economic seas for nearly half-a-century before falling victim to the feeding frenzy now taking place in Las Vegas. Originally called the Showboat, its closing in January 2004 was yet another sign that whatever camaraderie had existed in the gambling town built by tough but warm-blooded men no longer exists in the icy waters of the new Las Vegas.

With its paddle-wheel and smokestack facade, when it first opened in the 1950s, the Showboat appeared to be stuck in the sand during a very low tide. Positioned at the far east end of Fremont Street, the paddle-wheel-themed casino was closer to the Stauffer Chemical plant than the lights of Glitter Gulch. It was miles from the expanding Strip. It stood next to the Green Shack, a Boulder Dam-era restaurant that on many days had more customers than the casino.

But with William Moore and J. Kell Houssels Sr. backing it, and Moe Dalitz's Cleveland group supervising the operation, the Showboat gradually found a niche with the nickel-slot and cheap-steak visitors and locals. Years later, it would be considered the first locals-oriented casino.

Moe Dalitz used his clout to book popular entertainers for the place such as comic George Jessel and western-swing legend Bob Wills. But the Showboat, with its out-of-the-way location, would never be able to compete with downtown's lounges and the Strip's showrooms.

When the Dalitz group moved on to other projects, Houssels flipped the property to Joe Kelley. Kelley, who learned the business on a Tony Cornero gambling boat and at the Garden of Allah Club in Seal Beach, California, was a World War II veteran who'd flown interference for Gen. George Patton. He was believed to be just the man to whip the Showboat into shape.

In 1959, Kelley opened a twenty-four-lane bowling center. One year later, the Professional Bowlers Tour added the Showboat as a televised tournament stop. The Showboat was finally on the map.

Kelley expanded the bowling center to 106 lanes. Then for his Showboat Pavilion, he booked boxing events, roller derbys, professional wrestling, old-time rock 'n' roll acts, and even a big band or two. However when Kelley retired in 1988, the Showboat began to sink again.

For a while, it became just another holding on a lengthy list owned by Harrah's Entertainment. Harrah's sold it to casino operator Michael Villamor. He renamed it the Castaways (not to be confused with the Castaways that stood on the Strip across from the Sands), and he ran up $50 million in debt before being forced to seek Chapter 11 bankruptcy status in June 2003.

Joe Kelley died January 7, 2004, and three weeks later mortgage-broker Vestin foreclosed on the Castaways. The business was shuttered after forty-nine years and 800 people on the payroll found themselves unemployed.

The closing on January 29 came so suddenly that dozens of hotel guests were told they had only two hours to pack their bags and clear out.

Cage employees knew that the daily cash drop was being drained from the casino. Management later argued that the withdrawals were necessary to keep daily suppliers paid up, but the workers also noticed that slot machines were being emptied frequently. By the time the place was shuttered, many slots were no longer in service, and Villamor had stopped paying into employees' insurance, retirement, and Social Security accounts. All this was done under the eyes of state gaming regulators and federal labor officials who had been acutely aware of the Castaways' sinking financial status.

Gaming Control Board Chairman Dennis Neilander told reporters the state had ordered Villamor to pay all jackpots and winning sports tickets. The order was largely ignored, and weeks later the Gaming Control Board was still receiving complaints from jilted players.

Vestin moved in like a shark to close the property. But it didn't stop there. Sensing that some of the problems inside the casino had been generated by management in the final weeks of operation, Vestin attorneys went to federal bankruptcy court and filed an emergency motion to compel Villamor to "turn over receivables of cash and collateral." In other words, upward of $1 million that had vanished in the final days before closure.

But Vestin was a high-interest lender. It could easily absorb a $1-million hit.

It was those 800 former employees who truly suffered from the failed management and sudden closing.

While the casino was being bled dry, myriad employee benefits went unpaid. A few days after the foreclosure, the depth of the disaster became clearer: The Internal Revenue Service froze the workers' 401(k) accounts. Social Security contributions had lapsed with tax season approaching. And some employees were left without health insurance.

"The regulators had to have known what was going on,"

fourteen-year veteran employee Pamela Calhoun said. "They had to have seen it. It was no secret. What this man did to us is outrageous. I just hope I get my final paycheck."

Vestin, meanwhile, had gained a once profitable 445-room hotel and casino on 25.9 acres at the bargain price of approximately $20 million. The mortgage broker, known best for its advertisements featuring professional football Hall of Famer Joe Namath, was immediately approached by suitors. They saw in the Castaways what Joe Kelley had seen so many years earlier: an ideal opportunity to cater to locals, snowbirds, and bargain shoppers.

Longhorn and Bighorn casino operators Randy Miller, Richard Gonzales, and Richard Iannone immediately picked up an option on the property, and billionaire Carl Icahn became interested. But while the others were still thinking about it, the local casino giant Fertitta family scooped it up for $33.7 million.

Even if the Castaways would never have the Las Vegas locals market to itself again, it still had potential.

Meanwhile, Castaways issued a letter to employees apologizing for the company's failure. Despite the $50 million in debt that had forced it into bankruptcy, Villamor blamed Vestin for moving so destructively. Then he delivered more bad news.

"I don't know how long it will be before your paychecks arrive," he said. "I know it must be hard on everyone, but we were left with nothing. I agonize deeply for the welfare of you and your families. I am truly sorry this happened."

While details were discussed in bankruptcy court, former Castaways employees were left in the cold.

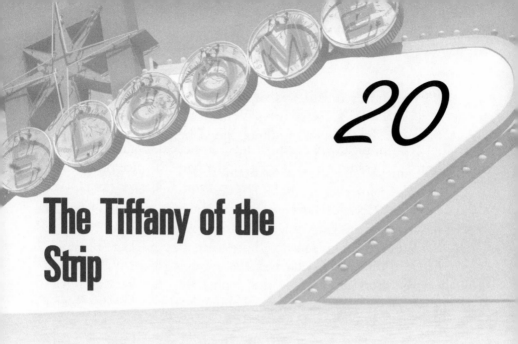

## 20

# The Tiffany of the Strip

Visitors to the Tropicana inevitably find their way into the Casino Legends Hall of Fame. There, Las Vegas history comes alive in displays celebrating high-rolling casino players, hotels and casinos past and present, as well as a parade of the glamorous entertainment stars who put the city on the map.

No visit to the Tropicana is complete without going to the Folies Bergere, a classic from that era when casino owners imported leggy production shows "direct from Paris" in the late 1950s.

If the Tropicana sometimes seems to live in the past, it's understandable for that's where the venerable resort had its most prosperous era. Tropicana was a Syndicate creation from the start, but, as usual, it took a "visionary" to develop its theme. His name was Ben Jaffe, and he was a gambler and owned points in Miami Beach's Fontainebleau Hotel.

Ben Jaffe's dream was heavily influenced by Miami's art-deco look. His Tropicana was destined to set new standards for opulence. In room décor, there would be something for every taste from Asian to French Provincial. Fronting the hotel would be a huge tulip-shaped fountain that, in time, became the resort's identifying symbol. (Jaffe could not have foreseen that Southern Nevada's harsh water would quickly peel the surface of the fountain, making it necessary to repaint it regularly.)

Jaffe was experienced in hotel management, but it was his friend, Phil Kastel, who was the gambling expert. Known as "Dandy Phil" because of the dapper way he dressed, Kastel supervised hundreds of slot machines in Louisiana for Mafia kingpin Frank Costello.

Dandy Phil had a history. In the heart of the Roaring Twenties, he'd been an associate of Arnold "the Big Bankroll" Rothstein. It was Rothstein who fixed the 1919 baseball World Series by bribing its key players on the White Sox team.

Jaffe had so much confidence in the poor eyesight of Nevada's gaming regulators that he audaciously recommended Kastel for licensing. But even Nevada officials read newspapers, and Kastel had been widely identified as a Syndicate man. So Kastel was rejected as an owner of record.

Jaffe opened the Tropicana's doors in April 1957 with Dandy Phil's name nowhere on the books. Not that anyone in the know believed for a Minnesota minute that Kastel and his boss, Frank Costello, had gone elsewhere with their investment.

After Costello was shot in the head and nearly killed in Manhattan by future Genovese crime family boss Vincent "the Chin" Gigante, the police emptied Costello's pockets. They found a slip of paper that tied him directly to the ownership of the Tropicana. "Gross casino wins as of 4/27/57 $651,284," the note began.

With Costello's connection exposed, old, reliable downtown casino man J. Kell Houssels was trotted out like a venerable relief pitcher to lend respectability to the ownership structure. And so the first chapter of the Tropicana's mob story was written.

For the two decades that followed, and while other mob-owned joints showed record-high profits even after the skim, the Tropicana underperformed like a poodle in a vaudeville dog act who forgot why he was on stage.

The Tropicana tottered along on the verge of bankruptcy. Detroit mob junketeers worked marker scams in the casino, and Kansas City's Civella crime family secretly seized a piece of the action. But it wasn't merely the skim and behind-the-scenes gyrations that caused the Tropicana to be so financially rickety.

For one thing, its 300 rooms made it one of the smaller class properties on the Strip. Worse, until the behemoth Excalibur, MGM Grand, and New York-New York casinos were added late in the century, the location of the Tropicana was much too far south to catch the walk-in market.

Its Polynesian theme and Folies Bergere were popular with its guests, but, of course, what visitors didn't see was the Tropicana's true ownership. Styles had changed since 1957, but the Trop was one casino that was owned and controlled by organized crime.

Finally, fourteen years after it opened, "the boys" decided to launder their investment, and the place was sold to Minnesota investment broker and financial scammer Deil Gustafson in 1971.

Superficially the casino known as the "Tiffany of the Strip" cleaned up its act. The trouble was its associates were tied to the Midwestern mob families.

Stauffer Chemical heiress Mitzi Stauffer Briggs, known as "pretty Mitzi" in San Francisco, was conned into becoming a percentage owner in 1975. Her accountant and son had been wined and dined and otherwise entertained by the hotel's people. She was assured her investment would be profitable. It was bad advice.

Immediately after her arrival, the Tropicana's true owners started fleecing not only customers and the Internal Revenue Service, but Mitzi, as well. All kinds of unpaid invoices suddenly surfaced.

Briggs was a certifiable mark. Not only did she come to Las Vegas with $44 million in personal wealth and zero experience in the gaming industry, she also appeared to suffer some emotional instability.

Deil Gustafson encouraged Briggs to invest her fortune in the Tropicana. In the end, he sold her 51 percent of the stock, and, in her innocence, she was puzzled by the inability of the Tropicana to turn a profit. What she didn't know was that Folies manager Joseph Agosto not only ran the show on stage, but operated the casino skim on behalf of Nick Civella and his Kansas City crime family. He seemed just another of several Tropicana employees who flattered Mitzi and soothed her insecurities.

Agosto, an unassuming man of Sicilian heritage, kept a low profile, but was a highly significant figure at the Tropicana. He'd arrived in Las Vegas after multiple convictions in Sicily. His battles with Immigration and Naturalization Services officials started the day he stepped off the boat.

Agosto maintained an office a short distance from the Las Vegas airport so that all messengers for the Kansas City mob could fly to Vegas, take a taxi to the Agosto office, pick up the skim money fom the Tropicana, and taxi back to the airport.

Attorney Oscar Goodman represented Agosto from the time he arrived in Las Vegas in 1975. Twenty-five years later, Goodman expressed surprise that the little man with the black fisherman's cap actually wielded influence.

"He was an extraordinary human being," Goodman said in a biography of him that I wrote called *Of Rats and Men: Oscar Goodman's Life from Mob Mouthpiece to Mayor of Las Vegas*. "The reason I didn't think there was a mob was in large part because of Joe Agosto. He would wear one of those little hats like the guys in the Mario Puzo story, *The Sicilian*, almost like a yarmulke, a rectangular one. A stupid hat with a little brim.

"And he looked like a cab driver."

It wasn't until November 1978 that law enforcement learned some of the truth about the Tropicana's ownership. This happened because they had planted a recording device in the home of Josephine Marlo, a Civella relative, in Kansas City.

The tapes captured the crime bosses, Agosto, and respected

Las Vegas casino executive Carl Thomas discussing the skim at the casino. At that time, Thomas owned the Slots A Fun and Bingo Palace (later the Palace Station).

The Marlo tapes, as they were later called, changed the course of Las Vegas history. Not only did they expose the hidden ownership, but they confirmed what Nevada officials had always been so quick to deny: that the mob still pulled the strings in the casino business a quarter-century after Kefauver. The transcript of the tapes was 600 pages long, and each page was an indictment of the way casino insiders did business.

Thomas had handled the skim at Circus Circus in the late 1960s and later at other Syndicate-influenced operations. At one point, he reminisced about the lack of security in the counting room, where locked boxes rarely stayed locked and the attention of state gaming agents was easily diverted.

"There's two locks needed to open the box. One key's supposed to stay in the cage, and one key stays with the comptroller upstairs. When the count team arrives in the morning, they come get this key and they get the key over there. Now what I've done for the last—I don't know how many umpteen years—when they take those keys, you have a key made that you keep in the palm of your hand, and you go back that night. See, the cashier's with us. You follow me? He's in on it. So you grab the cashier's keys, go into the vault, and snatch the money.

"I remember one night in Circus Circus when we had an obligation to meet. I was young and had some balls, I guess. There were two guys from the state standing outside [the count room], and I was in there on my fucking back, filling my pockets with cash, and those agents weren't as far from me as that refrigerator. Putting money in my pockets. I think if you do things out in the open, you stare the guy right in the face, the guy won't think you're doing nothing."

In November 1979, state gaming officials forced the wily, one-armed Gustafson and the painfully naïve Mitzi Briggs to surrender their casino licenses. Gustafson would eventually be convicted of fraud.

The FBI tapes all but destroyed the Civella family. Only death from cancer in 1983 saved Nick Civella from a prison term. His brother, Carl Civella, Carl DeLuna, and others received long sentences.

Carl Thomas, looking out for himself, agreed to testify against his former partners, as did Joe Agosto. Agosto died of a heart attack shortly after the Tropicana convictions—and after he was debriefed at great length by FBI agents, who learned for the first time of the vast network of confederates the underworld maintained in the city's large casinos.

The Tropicana was sold to the Ramada Corporation in 1979 for $80 million, but a funny thing happened as the former owners were stepping offstage. After making initial payments to the outgoing Tropicana investors, Ramada stopped cutting checks and challenged the sellers to sue them.

Believing that some members of the selling group were so closely tied to the mob that they'd never dare undergo legal depositions, Ramada played hardball until the end. Finally, it was forced to admit it had reneged on its agreement.

An infuriated District Judge Earle White punished the motel giant and, in 1989, awarded Gustafson, Briggs, and the others a total of $34 million. This was the largest award of its kind in Nevada history. Where the money went, who pocketed it, and how the group decided to pay taxes on it would make headlines six years later.

Mitzi Briggs wound up broke even after the Nevada Supreme Court reaffirmed the award. Her stake in the Tropicana had been chewed up, and she later worked as a hostess in the Copper Cart restaurant, where she announced that she was "happy for the first time in years."

After being forced to cough up millions due to its arrogance, Ramada finally had a chance to operate the resort. It pumped millions into building a hotel tower and a new pool, as well as a tropical atrium area. The gardenlike poolside setting was enchanting, and guests could swim up to a bar and blackjack table.

The Tropicana's fortunes should have improved, but there was no accounting for the depth of incompetence of Ramada's executives. The chain is arguably one of America's poorest-run companies.

Marketing heavily to Asian high rollers gave the Tropicana a lucrative niche in the market, but it also exposed the casino to potential losses. What if a few million-dollar gamblers got lucky at the baccarat tables?

That's exactly what happened in 1989. In a business in which net casino profits of 10 percent or more are common, the Tropicana managed to lose $18.6 million in the first quarter of its Ramada Inn management.

Ramada sold its popular motel chain to the Cheng family of Hong Kong for $540 million and spun off its casino holdings under the Aztar name.

◆　　◆　　◆

Despite its size, or perhaps because of it, for several years the Tropicana managed to attract some of the world's heaviest gamblers. Among these whales was businessman Ken Mizuno, undoubtedly one of the most enigmatic men ever to sit at a casino table game.

Mizuno was a professional baseball player who accumulated a billion-dollar fortune selling sporting equipment. Authorities believed he had ties to Tokyo's Yakuza organized crime families.

Mizuno's Teppan Restaurant at the Tropicana was a sign to some that the high-rolling gambler also had a piece of the casino even as he won and lost millions at the tables. Before being convicted in Japan of a billion-dollar golf-course country-club membership swindle in the 1990s, Mizuno was a favorite player at Steve Wynn's Mirage, and he kept a locker at Wynn's posh Shadow Creek golf course.

Handling Asian high rollers is a tenuous high-wire walk for Las Vegas casinos, whose representatives must balance local, national, and international currency laws with the realities of debt collection.

During the Asian economic crisis of the 1990s, Las Vegas marketing representatives found themselves being arrested for money laundering in Korea and elsewhere. Casino hosts such as Laura Choi of the Mirage and Chung Saemiyong of the Tropicana were caught smuggling money out of Korea from high rollers.

Choi was arrested while trying to take out $630,000 she'd collected from players. Chung had been stopped with $81,000. Korean law forbids taking more than $10,000 out of the country without government permission, and such permission was unlikely to be granted in the middle of a deep recession.

Both casino collectors went to jail for a short time, and Choi found herself embroiled in controversy after Mirage officials comically claimed they hardly knew her and she never received debt-collection instructions from them. The trouble led to the ouster of Mirage attorney Bruce Aguilera, who had been caught lying to investigators in the Choi affair, which ended up costing the company $325,000 in fines.

The Tropicana, meanwhile, faced fines of up to $1.3 million. In true Nevada style, it settled quietly with state authorities for $200,000.

Much in Las Vegas had changed in the nineteen years that had passed since Deil Gustafson and his fellow investors were pressured to sell the troubled Tropicana to Ramada. The ensuing lawsuit against Ramada resulted in that $34-million judgment against the motel giant, but in 1995, a thirty-count indictment for bankruptcy fraud was returned against Gustafson, longtime casino investors Edward and Fred Doumani, millionaire oilman Jack Urich, Minnesota attorney John Jagiela, and former Tropicana employee Nicholas Tanno, all of whom had owned the resort through a corporation called Conquistador.

Conquistador attorney Harold Gerwerter also was indicted.

The charges against him were later dismissed. Justice Department attorneys claimed that the defendants had committed fraud and funneled partial proceeds of the sale to organized crime.

Additional pressure was put on the defendants when Gustafson pleaded guilty to bankruptcy fraud and agreed to testify against his former partners in exchange for sentencing consideration. As part of his plea bargain, Gustafson was allowed to write off a $2-million tax debt, reduce his fine, and avoid other tax felonies related to the investigation.

Gustafson had served forty months in prison from 1984 to 1987 for bank fraud and other felonies and, at age sixty-six, had no desire to spend the last years of his life in a penitentiary cell. He would do anything to avoid prison.

At his trial, he was exposed not only as a convicted felon, but a liar as well. Defense attorney Edward Kane said Gustafson had "sold his soul to the devil" and was "a bought-and-paid-for piece of merchandise. He is a hired liar. The only thing that is more despicable than a hired liar is the government that hires him and presents him to you."

In an autobiographical manuscript found during pretrial discovery in the case, Gustafson revealed his inner thoughts about the deal he made. He wrote, "It's put very coldly that if you don't answer the questions the way they want them answered, they will not help. The agents and government attorneys are not interested in what your memory is telling them. They are only interested in whether you memorize the script.... I spoke from memory, but still I am sure that I was affected by their previous rehearsals. It eventually got so that my memory began to blur with the rehearsed statements.

"These agents were not gathering evidence for an impartial trial; they were constructing evidence improperly to gain a conviction.... It's a little like negotiating with a drowning man. What will he say or do to get a life-saving rope thrown to him? I caught myself saying to myself, 'What do they want?' so that I could give the desired answer to maintain their goodwill."

On the witness stand, Gustafson's testimony was torn to shreds by defense attorneys. It was a clear example of the Justice Department cutting a bad deal with a central figure so it could indict the lesser players.

Justice Department trial attorney Lynn Panagakos argued, "Only a person like that is going to give you the inside scoop on a conspiracy."

Unfortunately for the government, the jury didn't accept Gustafson's marginal credibility. The prosecution lost its best chance to convict when it turned on Las Vegas attorney Gerwerter, who'd given statements to the FBI illustrating threats he'd received after the Ramada settlement. Gerwerter had been the government's best friend. Instead of using him and protecting him, he was indicted.

In the upside-down world of federal prosecution, the Justice Department had done exactly the wrong thing in its effort to do the right thing. Prosecutors watched with dismay as United States District Judge Justin Quakenbush dismissed fraud charges against Gerwerter and the jury acquitted the remaining defendants.

By alienating Gerwerter and bedding with Gustafson, law enforcement lost its best opportunity to discover the truth behind what happened to the $34 million.

For Las Vegas, the only positive development to come out of the Conquistador case was the metaphorical line its resolution drew on the calendar. After forty-one years, the ghost of the mob at the Tropicana appeared to have fled.

This made the Casino Legends Hall of Fame with its casual references to "the boys" all the more ironic. About the time Gustafson was receiving probation for his guilty plea in the bankruptcy fraud case, the Tropicana cut the ribbon on curator Steve Cutler's museum that many believed would be the start of something permanent at the resort newly christened "the Island of Las Vegas." (The museum closed in May 2005.)

Gustafson died in Minneapolis one year later at age sixty-seven. He was eulogized as a former Iowa farm boy who'd started his career as a promising young attorney with a background in business and finance. He taught economics at the University of Minnesota and had served as a fund-raiser and deputy director for Hubert Humphrey's losing 1960 presidential campaign. (But one shouldn't forget the years he spent in prison for fraud.)

The newspapers quoted him as saying that when he bought the Tropicana in 1971, it was so rundown that "it was like an old elephant that needed a stab in the rear."

"I'm not going to miss him," Gerwerter told a Las Vegas reporter. "He was a skunk. He was a skunk when he was alive, and just because he died doesn't make him any less of a skunk. The smell doesn't go away when you die. He was a master manipulator and a pathological liar.

"I guarantee you right now Gustafson will find a way to cheat the devil."

◆　　◆　　◆

By the late 1990s, the Tropicana was still fighting for its survival. Corporate politics was something in which Hector Mon held an advanced degree. In more than twenty-four years with Harrah's, Mon had risen to the position of president of the Las Vegas resort. He came to the Tropicana in late 1999 after being dumped by his longtime employer.

He inherited a formidable task when he took charge of the Tropicana. The property was nearly half-a-century old, hadn't been kept in top condition, and suffered from a steady turnover of employees on the casino floor.

"This property had a real casino orientation and was pretty singularly focused on casino and direct marketing," Mon told *Review-Journal* reporter Len Butcher in 2001. "What we've done is to bring a little more intelligence and balance to that, so we've been really able to grow our leisure segment and cash revenues. We've improved our relationships with our wholesalers, and improved the prices they're charging us. If you compare our financials today to two years ago, we show a much more balanced picture between casino and retail. Our growth and profitability last year far exceeded our peer group in the market." Its peer group being the Strip's other survivors.

Today, the Tropicana bustles with activity even though it remains an architectural hodgepodge in need of a wrecking ball and a billion-dollar financial infusion. There has been talk of big changes at the resort, but Aztar's limited financial resources slowed some of those plans. To reinvent the resort, the company negotiated with Chicago's Jaffe family, which continues to own the land beneath the Tropicana.

These days, no one argues that the Tropicana is too far south on the Strip. It stands on Tropicana Avenue just across the street from the MGM Grand, the Western World's largest hotel. Its neighboring casinos are all thriving. The Trop brings tourists through the door with its convention space, tropical theme, Gaming Hall of Fame, and venerable Folies Bergere.

All things considered, that it is still afloat in the Las Vegas's shark-infested ocean is nothing short of a miracle.

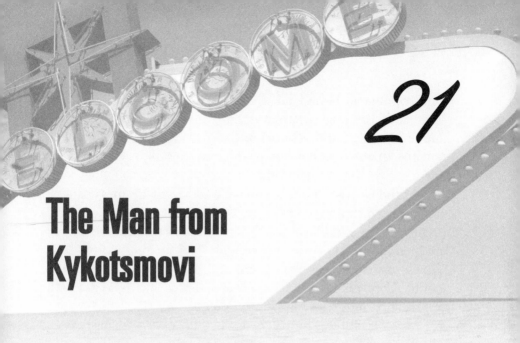

# The Man from Kykotsmovi

## 21

Jacob Coin was neither an ancient mariner from the old Las Vegas nor a rising predator from the new Las Vegas. He wasn't from Las Vegas at all. He grew up in the village of Kykotsmovi, in northeastern Arizona, as a member of the Hopi Indian tribe's Tobacco Clan.

In a nation of rapid reservation-casino expansion, the Hopis don't allow gambling on their land. That made Coin perhaps the casino industry's most unlikely player. As a boy raised on the two-million-acre reservation, Coin heard the elders speak of white society with distrust and disdain. The 12,000-member Hopi had been part of the Indian Reorganization Act of 1936, but until 1961, Hopis had no presence in Washington.

That lack of political sophistication led to the embarrassingly lopsided deal that the tribe cut with Peabody Coal Company. For a few pennies per ton, the tribe allowed the company not

185

only to mine on Hopi land at Black Mesa, but to use millions of gallons of precious groundwater to carry coal more than two hundred miles to the Mojave power plant near Kingman.

The environmental and economic impacts of the arrangement continue to be felt today.

At the University of Arizona, Coin studied business administration while watching the rise of the Native American civil rights movement. He realized that the only way for Indians to progress and secure their sovereignty "for as long as the grass grows and as long as the river flows" was to participate in the political process few understood or believed in. By 1988, with the creation of the Indian Gaming Regulatory Act, which established the legal basis for reservation casinos, the Indians needed all the help they could get.

"The Hopi tribe never had any sort of real presence in Washington, DC," Coin said. "Since the Navajo land dispute of 1882, for more than one hundred years, the Hopis believed that because we won the case at every level, it was beneath us to make an appeal to the political elements in Washington. So we didn't think it important to have a presence in Washington."

By 1989, not even the isolationist Hopi could avoid having a Washington presence. When the tribal chieftain asked Coin to become his people's representative in the nation's capital, Coin agreed.

Some tribal elders remained suspicious. Coin recalled being admonished by the old ones at a gathering of 8,000 tribal members where he was warned that Washington would evade its obligation to the Hopi if it ever had the chance. "They've taken more land, more resources, and more lives from us than they ever could repay," he was told.

"It was like a fist in the gut for me," Coin recalled years later, but the public scolding hardened his resolve.

As executive director of the California Nations Indian Gaming Association, Coin represents more than fifty Indian nations in the state's estimated $18-billion reservation-casino market. He is part of a new generation of tribal members who are better educated and experienced in affairs off the reservation, but whose feet remain planted firmly in the traditions of their people.

Coin's duties are complex. Indian casinos are the fastest-growing segment of the American gaming market and the most controversial. In California, cash-rich tribes have become substantial political players at a time when they are also being looked on as possible tax-revenue sources in the financially foundering state. Their expansion has sent a shock wave through the Nevada casino industry, rippling through larger casino corporations while rattling smaller and older operations to their foundations.

Some casino companies have preached isolationism on the subject of Indian gaming. Others have all but donned headdresses and applied for membership in an attempt to share the riches being mined in the heart of the immensely lucrative California market.

For his part, Coin and other Indian officials like him watched with a mixture of bemusement and disdain as the Las Vegas boys spent millions in their effort to marginalize Indian gaming in California. After those efforts failed, they coughed up more millions in an effort to partner with tribes.

Experienced casino-management teams, generally run by white men with Vegas backgrounds, have become standard operating procedure at the best Indian casinos. That irony has not been lost on critics of reservation casinos, who claim with some justification that many management agreements too heavily favor the outsiders and return too little to tribal members.

Donald Trump on his first visit to the Foxwoods Resort Casino in Connecticut observed, "I didn't see a single dealer who looked like an Indian. Nor did I see any dealers that an Indian would think looked like an Indian."

The stakes are high for Indians and for Nevada's casino industry, as well. Nationwide, reservation casinos won $18 billion in 2004—compare that to the $9.4 billion won by Nevada casinos.

The largest area of growth came from Indian gambling halls in California. While gaming analysts are unsure about the impact on Las Vegas, the threat to older Strip properties, downtown's venerable sawdust joints, and the Colorado River resorts at Laughlin seemed all too clear. The more time small-stakes gamblers spend playing in their own backyards, the less they will contribute to the Nevada gambling machines.

Casino proponents, however, for years had speculated without proof that "minor-league" reservation casinos would create new players who eventually would be curious enough about life in the "big league" to try their luck in Las Vegas. Although this theory was riddled with flaws, it played well with reporters.

It did not, for example, account for the fact that those so-called minor-league operations were rapidly evolving into built-to-scale Las Vegas-style resorts that featured gourmet restaurants, rock concerts, Strip-style entertainment, and championship golf courses.

Reservation casinos were still highly vulnerable to shifting markets, competition, and changes in the law because they were focused far more on gambling than were the new multiplex resorts of Las Vegas. But gone are the days of the dusty Quonset huts with blackjack tables. By 2005, new reservation resorts cost more than $200 million each—and promised to win that much in their first full year of operation.

University of Nevada, Reno professor William Eadington, who heads the system's Institute for the Study of Gambling and Commercial Gaming, offered a candid assessment of the threat to a reporter: "With San Diego and all of the other Southern California markets, there has to be some erosion of the Las Vegas market."

In the end, the convenience of gambling in one's own backyard will outweigh the glitter, flash, and intrigue of Las Vegas—especially with the prospect of crowded Interstate highways, long waits at airports, and rising hotel and food prices.

To some analysts, Reno's experience is a glimpse at the future of the older end of Las Vegas should the reservation casinos continue to proliferate. Once Nevada's largest city, for a generation Reno had steadily lost ground to Las Vegas in the expanding tourism market. The opening of a string of Indian casinos near Interstate 80, the main artery linking Reno to Northern California had the immediate effect of softening the market throughout Northern Nevada. In 2004 alone, reservation gambling resorts put 5,250 slot machines between Bay Area players and the Reno-Lake Tahoe area—a more than 100-percent increase.

In truth, Las Vegas had long since crushed its Northern Nevada neighbor. While Las Vegas attracted thirty-seven million visitors a year, Reno played host to fewer than five million and generated only $534.8 million in gaming revenues.

◆　◆　◆

Pulitzer Prize-winning reporters Donald L. Bartlett and James B. Steele observed in a *Time* magazine series, "At the end of the 1980s, in a frenzy of cost cutting and privatization, Washington perceived gaming on reservations as a cheap way to wean tribes from government handouts, encourage economic development and promote tribal self-sufficiency. Congress enacted the Indian Gaming Regulatory Act in 1988. It was so riddled with loopholes, so poorly written, so discriminatory and subject to conflicting interpretations that 14 years later, armies of high-priced lawyers are still debating the definition of a slot machine.

"Instead of regulating Indian gambling, the act has created chaos and a system tailor-made for abuse."

Coin laughs at such criticism, calling it the typical view that purposefully fails to appreciate that each Indian tribe is a sovereign nation, albeit all nations depend on heaping handouts from the federal government. As with Native Americans in general, Indian gaming has a foot in both worlds.

Who benefited most from Indian gaming?

In part, casino backers such as South African Sol Kerzner, Chinese Lim Goh Tong, and American Lyle Berman. They made substantial fortunes by bankrolling reservation casinos.

**189**

Berman, a major investor in the disastrous Stratosphere tower project in Las Vegas, is involved in many casino deals in California. Berman's Lakes Entertainment owns a majority of the stock of the World Poker Tour, which in 2005 became the hottest and most widely watched series of gambling tournaments in history.

Diana Bennett, CEO of Paragon Gaming and the daughter of the late Circus Circus Chairman William Bennett, cut what was, dollar for dollar, one of the best deals in the California market when she arranged to build a small, 350-slot casino on land near Palm Springs owned by the Augustine band of Cahuilla Mission Indians. Tribal population: one, Maryann Martin.

But while California Indian gaming expansion threatens some Nevada casinos, the fact does nothing to stop Nevada companies from pushing for management agreements of their own. When the tiny Pauma tribe near San Diego solicited partners for a casino, it had no shortage of suitors. Caesars Entertainment, the Hard Rock Hotel, and the ubiquitous Station Casinos forwarded plans for what eventually would become a $250-million casino resort project in the heart of a fifteen-million-person gaming market.

The casino in Pauma Valley would offer 500 rooms—10 percent of the number at the MGM Grand—but would feature a 100,000-square-foot casino including the maximum-allowed 2,000 slot machines.

Although Indian advocates are not shy about discussing their rich heritage and troubled history with the White Man, they are now adept at playing politics. California Congressman George Miller, for example, received substantial political contributions when he sneaked legislation into an enormous spending bill that helped the Lytton band of Pomo Indians of Santa Rosa convert a poker room into a full casino. Although members of Nevada's congressional delegation were embarrassed, and their casino-

190

industry benefactors furious, the move illustrated that the Indians, too, could play Washington-style politics.

For his part, Nevada Sen. Harry Reid was often a critic of the National Indian Gaming Association. He was one of the authors of the 1988 Indian Gaming Regulatory Act, and as a consummate politician, he was willing to work with the native lobbyists. He moved with alacrity to halt a tentatively planned bill in 2003 that would have enabled Alaska native corporations to open casinos anywhere in the continental United States.

Even Indian nations with histories of bitterly fighting became allies to battle the White Man. Tribal chairman Anthony Pico of the Viejas band of Kumeyaay Indians described the struggle in traditional terms. "Make no mistake my friends, we are at war. But this is not a war of guns and bombs. It's a war of words. It's a war of perception, and it's a war for truth.

"Gaming has opened a door for Indian nations. In the long term, my hope is that this door leads to freedom, freedom from oppression, and freedom from poverty, freedom from shame, freedom from the shackles of the past. There is great pressure because we know and we fear that this door may be open to us only for a short time."

California tribes spent nearly $100 million to promote the successful passage of ballot initiatives that effectively expanded the definition of casino gaming while maintaining their monopoly in the state. One tiny tribe, the San Manuel band of Serrano Mission Indians, contributed $34.7 million that, according to a *Time* investigation, averaged nearly $520,000 per adult member.

It is true that Indians contributed so much money so openly to some campaigns that it was impossible not to notice their footprint on the political landscape. California Attorney General Bill Lockyer, for instance, received $800,000 from tribal governments and $175,000 from the Aqua Caliente Indians over a four-year period..

The Indians had learned how to play the game well.

Critics focused on what Coin called "the myth of the rich

Indian." "The notion that all Indians have become millionaires is certainly not evident on many reservations and rancherias in California and throughout the country," he wrote in a pointed essay. "There persists a long backlog of needs in Indian country where, despite a binding trust obligation by the federal government, the nation's First Americans are deprived of basic services and programs readily available to all others."

The games are strong and forever favor the house. The improved location of Indian casinos and the increased sophistication of the operators were hard to beat. National Indian Gaming Association Executive Director Mark Van Norman wondered aloud to reporters whether anyone would have imagined that in just fifteen years, Indian casinos would generate more than the budget for the federal Bureau of Indian Affairs.

The fact was that old-school sharks such as Moe Dalitz and Jackie Gaughan, knowing the odds, could have predicted as much.

## 22

# The Curse of the Tally Ho

The new Aladdin formed a riddle as it pressed up against the boulevard dressed in its Vegas-meets-Arabian-Nights theme. It was at once intriguing and perplexing.

If not quite a mirage, the 2,547-room megaresort offers walk-up customers a mystery in the form of a question: How could a gambling palace that cost $1.1 billion be built without a front door?

In truth, the entrance did exist. Nor did visitors have to shout "open sesame" to access it. It was just that throngs of tourists might have found it easier to make a carpet fly than to step inside the building from the street. Las Vegas megaresorts like to market themselves as exclusive—but not that exclusive.

Such were the troubles of the new Aladdin when it premiered in the year 2000 on property where its namesake and the original Tally Ho casino project had been cursed with everything from bad location to hidden mob ownership.

A smart-aleck columnist christened its tumultuous history "the Curse of the Tally Ho," and within a year of its grand opening, the all-new Aladdin, with its handsome shopping mall and exclusive gambling salon created to attract the world's biggest players, had fallen under the curse.

Insiders talked about restructuring or even dumping the property as late as the day before its financial collapse. It managed to lose money even in the casino and was said to be $725 million in debt. Officials said they wouldn't seek bankruptcy. As the days passed, their denials became less credible.

What most observers did not then appreciate was that the jumbled design and inefficient way the Aladdin had been rebuilt had doomed it from the start. Others blamed its failure on the layered ownership and lack of a vision.

But that came later. What Las Vegas historians noted with arched brows was the almost eerie run of bad luck the property had suffered from its earliest incarnation in 1963. Then it was the Tally Ho, an oversized motel that touted itself as Las Vegas Boulevard's first nongaming luxury resort. It fizzled from the start because few visitors in those days came to Las Vegas for any reason other than gambling.

Investigators smelled the distinct scent of organized crime in the Tally Ho's financial structure, most notably in the razor-faced hit man Aladena "Jimmy the Weasel" Fratianno. He'd risen in mob ranks by eliminating shakedown artist Russian Louie Strauss and sports-book robbers Tony Trombino and Tony Brancato, among others.

But Fratianno couldn't keep in the shadows, and the Tally Ho changed names and ownership, reopening a second time. Now it was called the King's Crown.

In 1965, it was purchased for $16 million by former Sahara owner Milton Prell.

Prell was serious about making the property a winner, and he was responsible for envisioning the Arabian Nights theme. When it reopened as the Aladdin on New Year's Day 1966, Prell had added restaurants, a lounge, and a 500-seat showroom.

Prell had the Vegas idea when it came to design: He knew whatever was worth doing, was worth overdoing. He added the property's signature beacon, a fifteen-story-high Aladdin's lamp.

The curse seemed to be broken.

Prell had gotten his gambling start with a bingo palace in California. When he took possession, he found that, like the competitive bingo games, the big prizes were paid to shills. He was furious and gave orders that the prizes were to be awarded honestly to the players.

"Mr. Prell, if you do that, we'll be out of business in six weeks," an employee told him.

He stared at the balance sheet, awash in red ink. "If we don't, we'll be out of business in eight weeks," he said. "Pay the prizes!"

Almost overnight, word got out that the Prell operation was an honest one. His bingo club thrived. When he needed money to buy the Mint on Fremont Street, his brother-in-law, Gil Gilbert, sold a profitable mattress business so he could lend Prell capital.

"Gil, I'll never forget this. You'll have a job as long as you live."

He was a man of his word, and Gil Gilbert managed the Mint. When the Aladdin opened its doors, Gil Gilbert was at the helm.

Prell parlayed the Mint into his purchase of Tally Ho. He had a publicity break in 1967 when Elvis Presley and his Priscilla were married in an Aladdin suite. But both the marriage and the casino were headed for a rocky road.

Milton Prell suffered a severe stroke, and the Aladdin's fortunes started to fade. A very determined Prell, now confined to a wheelchair, insisted on walking with two canes across the casino floor to his office each morning. Almost unable to speak, he would rehearse the simplest sentences so he could make and respond to phone calls.

He was a gutsy fellow. But even guts couldn't keep the magic lantern burning. The Aladdin was sold to Al Parvin, the mobbed-up financier who operated the Stardust and other casinos from behind the scenes. It had all the signs of a joint destined to fail when it was sold a few years later to a group fronted by Morris Shenker and a list of St. Louis and Detroit investors, some of whom were later tied to a mob skim.

The Aladdin added a twenty-story hotel tower (later found to have a severe structural flaw that made it unsafe to occupy during high winds) and a 10,000-seat Theater for the Performing Arts (with help from the Teamsters Central States Pension Fund). The tower and theater construction was a scandal. Parvin had new carpeting torn and replaced by one of his companies as a way to divert extra money into his pockets.

Even more shifty was the property's true operator, former Detroit resident James "Little Jimmy" Tamer. The slightly built Tamer's official title was entertainment director. His real job was directing the casino skim.

He didn't do a very good job, and he and several of his crew were eventually caught, convicted, and sentenced to prison terms. Tamer was also placed in the state's casino Black Book.

With the mob's frontmen and financial experts out of the picture, new owners were needed. For a brief time, Wayne Newton and Meyer Lansky's old friend, Ed Torres, reopened the place, but found the going too rough. When the Aladdin went into bankruptcy in 1984, the fault couldn't be attributed to its current owners. It was headed that way for years thanks to the forty thieves who'd operated it.

When all else failed, the Aladdin was sold for $51.5 million to Japanese businessman and high-rolling gambler Ginji Yasuda. Yasuda, appeared to be in love with the idea of owning a casino. He certainly was not like the hands-on owners of previous generations. He seemed confident in hiring high-paid executives to run the show for him. Yasuda died in 1989, and the Aladdin was again put on the market.

After slipping in and out of bankruptcy, the Aladdin wound up in the hands of Jack Sommer, the son of Sigmund Sommer. Sigmund, a New York real-estate maven, headed a family who'd been developing properties since 1886.

Jack Sommer liked to talk about his earliest Las Vegas experiences, which included taking Big Julie Weintraub's junkets from New York City to the Dunes. While he had gambled long enough to know casinos from the customer's side, he was totally inexperienced when it came to operating in the exceedingly competitive casino business.

Steve Wynn, who knew Sommer, said aloud to anyone who would listen that the young man was making a mistake keeping the elephantine Theater for the Performing Arts. And why did they cling to the name Aladdin, which had become an albatross of a name with its dusty theme?

Sommer's innocence in gaming was nothing new. Plenty of otherwise smart businessmen had tried it before, and a few had survived and even thrived. But the latter were exceptions. Sommer's challenges were only to build a competitive resort in an era of megastores and to persuade skeptical state gaming officials that he could handle the casino side.

In 1997, Sommer hired gaming industry veteran Richard Goeglein as president of Aladdin Gaming Holdings and Aladdin Gaming LLC. Goeglein had credibility not only with state regulators, but also with institutional investors. Both groups would need to be convinced of the ownership's ability to make the billion-dollar dream become reality.

Goeglein's journey provides a barometer of the difficulties the Aladdin encountered. The *Wall Street Journal* lampooned the Sommer group's ability to get the job done. By 1999, with construction delays mounting and a new contractor on board, Goeglein added crisis manager to his growing list of job descriptions.

The all-new Aladdin boasted 2,500 rooms, a half-million-square-foot shopping mall, and an expansive casino—including the exclusive London Club high-roller salon.

When the resort finally reopened in August 2000, Goeglein was its logical CEO. After all, it could be argued that without him, it never would have been completed.

What it didn't have to Goeglein's astonishment was a computerized customer base. That meant it couldn't measure customers' play and know which people to pamper and which to ignore.

Less than a year after it opened, the Aladdin was once again hemorrhaging on the accounting books. It faced the daunting task of meeting its high-interest bond payments. After September 11, 2001, everything went into a tailspin. Institutional investors grew nervous, and observers believed their suspicions were justified that Sommer had been in over his head from the start.

Although it was clear to many that the Aladdin's design flaws and lack of marketing strategy had hurt it more than the slump following September 11, Goeglein, without whose credibility, expertise, and work ethic the Aladdin might not have opened, was fired on September 21, 2001.

He lost a lucrative buyout package, but, worse, he was being accused of the sort of felonious activity that could cause him to lose his gaming credibility—the very credibility Sommer and Company had used to get past state gaming regulators.

"I have built a reputation over my whole career for high integrity, honesty, and fair dealing," Goeglein told a reporter. "This significantly and negatively impacts my reputation. I'm not letting it stand . . ."

Goeglein hired former Organized Crime Strike Force prosecutor Stan Hunterton to fight the termination. In the end, he had to settle for the comfort of knowing that at least he wasn't the biggest loser when the Aladdin, in keeping with its forty-year tradition, failed again.

Sommer lost his tailored shirt on the deal, and the United Kingdom-based casino company London Clubs International fared even worse. It lost not only its initial $50-million investment in the resort's half-baked plan to attract high rollers to an exclusive "salon" casino within a larger casino, it dropped $128 million more chasing its initial investment in an effort to ride out the early financial fiasco.

The decisions shook up the company and forced the resignation of its chairman, Alan Goodenough, who failed to live up to his name.

Goeglein, the jilted lover, remained unabashedly optimistic about the Aladdin's chances under different leadership.

"I lost my objectivity about the Aladdin a long time ago," he said. "I fell in love with the project and put a lot into it. There's no terminal flaw in the Aladdin's design. What's terminal is the expensive, complex ownership web."

Veteran casino industry consultant Bill Friedman would differ on the design issue. He was adamant that the Aladdin's design made it an odds-on-favorite to repel customers Not only was it shackled by the presence of the Theater for the Performing Arts and its front entrance obscured—visitors generally found their way in through the below-ground valet parking area—the high ceilings in the casino were found to turn off gamblers.

Friedman made this observation in his book, *Designing Casinos to Dominate the Competition*. In short, the Aladdin's casino suffered from what Friedman called the "Barn Factor."

"Obviously, design, from my point of view, plays a key role in the problems that it's having," he said. "I don't think anyone would disagree that the entrance to the Aladdin was weak design. But since we already have a casino that has many people entering it every day, especially since it's the newest on the Strip, attracting more people into it with a low ratio of gambling isn't going to help much. They aren't going to accomplish much by improving the interior.

"The best thing to do is to address the exterior and interior, but it is the interior which will have the effect of dramatically increasing the ratio of people who will gamble. If only one of them can be done, the interior is the most important.

"When the data regarding every competitive situation were combined, they revealed that particular interior design elements substantially influence player counts. I was stunned! I had not anticipated that consumer gambling behavior would be so consistent and quantifiable, or that the simple interior design concepts I was developing could so accurately and mathematically predict a casino's degree of success or failure."

Conceding that some of what he considered weakly designed casinos were still successful, Friedman insisted that none of these lived up to their potential. And the Aladdin foundered in no small part because of its lack of attention to detail in its gambling center.

By July 2003, none of that mattered. The bankrupt Aladdin was auctioned off to an investment group called OpBiz led by Planet Hollywood CEO Robert Earl. The purchase price: $635 million for a resort that cost an estimated $1.1 billion less than three years earlier.

The resort was saved from the scrap heap of Strip history by the efforts of a crisis team led by Aladdin President William Timmins, Chief Financial Officer Tom Lettero, and General Counsel Patricia Becker. Although they were well compensated when the Aladdin changed hands, they also were largely responsible for pumping up the bottom line after it appeared institutional investors and other corporate officers had lost hope.

The Planet Hollywood group, which included Earl, Douglas Teitelbaum, Starwood Hotels and Resorts Worldwide, and Bay Harbour Management company, wisely decided to change the name and theme of the property, investing $90 million for that purpose. They surely would take into account the design flaws and faulty business plan overlooked by the previous owners.

A name and theme change? Now there was an idea whose time had certainly come. It had been ignored years earlier when Jack Sommer first got his hands on the shabby resort.

While the Aladdin's secured creditors limped into a minority net partnership position under the terms of the new purchase agreement, its unsecured creditors took a severe hit—realizing just $7 million from the $70 million they were owed.

Now the Culinary Union appeared and lobbied the new owners to organize the property. When the owners appeared reluctant, the union sent a letter critical of the sale to the state Gaming Control Board. The union alleged the Aladdin sale had been rife with unseemly insider dealing and conflicts of interest. All who knew the history of the property would have called such allegations, even if proven, par for the course.

For his part, Earl's business track record was mixed. Planet Hollywood had experienced its own litany of financial problems, and Earl had been yanked from the board of directors of Star East Holdings for reportedly failing to fulfill his fiduciary responsibilities.

While Earl had his problems, it was also true that the Culinary wouldn't have hunted him had he expressed a friendly attitude toward organized labor.

The Aladdin's expansive Desert Passage shopping mall offered everything available at other Strip properties—and not much else. Trizec Properties, a Chicago real-estate and mall-investment group, poured $250 million into the mall, and the Sommer Family Trust added another $125 million, only to reap slow traffic and disappointing sales.

By the summer of 2004, Earl was approved to reinvent the Aladdin once more. With industry veteran Mike Mecca as president, the new Aladdin group planned to invest $500 million to renovate the old white elephant, $100 million of this would be spent on a new high-rise apartment complex and other millions to transform the Theater for the Performing Arts into a state-of-the-art facility.

This time, they hoped the curse of the Tally Ho could be broken.

# Fathers and Sons I

"Las Vegas is a great place if you have no weaknesses," Horseshoe Club patriarch Benny Binion's eldest son, Jack Binion, often remarked. "If you have a weakness, Las Vegas will find it."

Clover Jewelers owner Mickey Leffert confirmed this with his admonition, "Stay out of Las Vegas if you have a weakness for women, wine, or wagering. Any of those three Achilles' heels will absolutely destroy you in this town."

Binion and Leffert knew of what they spoke. Binion amassed a vast fortune estimated at more than $1 billion by assiduously avoiding the traditional Las Vegas pitfalls of drugs, booze, and fast women. However, he'd watched his own family members fall victim to those same influences.

One of Binion's daughters fought drug addiction and depression before attempting to end her life. She died of injuries resulting from her suicide attempt. But it was his younger brother, Lonnie Ted Binion, whose reckless life and mysterious death proved Jack Binion's adage and scratched the Binion name on Las Vegas' wall of infamy.

The story of fathers and sons is part of the arc of Las Vegas history. The fathers accumulated legal fortunes in Las Vegas after leaving behind their illegal gambling roots. The sons, raised in privilege, sometimes drowned in the excesses of Las Vegas.

On Fremont Street, downtown, there was Jackie Gaughan and his sons, Michael and Jackie Jr. There was Sam Boyd and his son, Bill Boyd. There was J. Kell Houssels Sr. and his son, Kell Jr. And at the Las Vegas Club, there was Mel Exber and his son, Brady Exber. But no family carved a legacy as haunted as Benny Binion and his boys, Jack and Ted.

◆　　◆　　◆

They called Benny Binion "Cowboy Benny," but in his youth, the only thing he roped was trouble. Born in 1904 in Pilot Grove, Texas, to a family that bought and sold horses, Benny earned his keep as a runner for gamblers and bootleggers. He was a horse trader and a tire thief until he moved up the criminal hierarchy ladder.

Benny was an illiterate, but by his late teens, he held an advance degree in ruthless street savvy. Everyone bribed cops, but Benny Binion's willingness to kill competitors made him feared and respected in the Dallas underworld of rednecked racketeers and transplanted Mafiosi.

Binion learned the business under the tutelage of Dallas bootlegger Warren Diamond. By 1930, Diamond was the city's No. 1 rumrunner. "He had the town all buttoned up," a Dallas detective told *Green Felt Jungle* authors Ed Reid and Ovid Demaris. After Diamond's suicide, Binion picked up the bookmaking and gambling slack, and by 1936, he was boss of the Dallas rackets.

True, he felt the occasional need to kill thieves and competitors, real and imagined, but it didn't seem to bother him much. Throughout his life, he alluded to times he'd picked up a gun. Near his death, he quipped to a reporter on Christmas Eve 1989, "I'm still able to do my own killings." Few who knew Benny Binion's history doubted him.

"His M.O. was always the same," a Dallas lawman recalled. "'Kill 'em dead and they won't give you no more trouble.' Binion eliminated four competitors in rapid sequence. The first to go was a gambler named Ben Frieden. Frieden operated three or four policy wheels and was making bundles of money. On September 12, 1936, Binion and his top gun, Buddy Malone, blasted Frieden on Allen Street while he waited for his policy pickups. They emptied their .45 automatics into Frieden, who was unarmed, and then Binion shot himself in the shoulder. Just a superficial wound. Then he turned himself over to the sheriff."

When Binion was indicted, he claimed his shoulder wound had been inflicted by Frieden. Never mind that Frieden was unarmed or that the bullet came from Benny's own pistol. The shooting was ruled self-defense, and the murder charge was dismissed.

"He lost the fix in the '46 elections, so he packed his bag and moved his wife and children to Las Vegas, leaving the whole operation in the hands of Harry Urban," one law-enforcement veteran said.

Benny Binion never officially ran the Horseshoe. When it opened in 1951, he was mired in a licensing dispute. By 1953, he'd been convicted of tax evasion and sentenced to five years in Leavenworth.

Binion maintained a lifelong connection with the underworld. When Russian Louie Strauss, the hit man and freelance extortionist, got greedy with Binion, Benny reached out to Nick Licata, Jack Dragna's go-to man in Los Angeles. He offered a percentage of a future casino deal in exchange for Licata's relieving him of his Russian Louie problem. A few days later, Russian

Louie took a ride with Jimmy Fratianno and Felix Alderisio. It was a ride to oblivion, for he never returned.

Fratianno later admitted that Strauss had been lured to a house under the guise of picking up some money, and while inside, he'd been strangled with a piece of rope. The Strauss murder became such a part of Vegas lore that it gave rise to a popular street expression among lenders and borrowers:

"You'll get your money as soon as Russian Louie comes back to town."

Binion was also suspected, but never convicted, of killing Dallas rackets rival Herb "the Cat" Noble, whose last life ran out when he was blown to pieces. Benny Binion later said, "The Texas Rangers, the FBI, and the whole works knows that I didn't have nothin' to do with the Noble killin'. It would've taken me a half-hour to kill Noble if I'd wanted to kill him. There's no way in the world I'd harm anybody for any amount of money. But if anybody goes to talkin' about doin' me or my family any bodily harm, they become candidates to be takin' care of in a most *artistic* way."

How outsiders perceived Benny Binion was largely dependant upon their perception of gambling itself. He was a felon with a reputation for violence, but he'd became a Vegas legend by creating the world's highest-stakes gambling hall. It was his occupation that set him apart.

Investigative reporters Reid and Demaris, for example, were brutal to Binion. They marginalized his importance in the development of Las Vegas. Perhaps they didn't understand his place as a money man in a valley where cash flow is everything.

"Benny Binion was never a big man in Las Vegas," they wrote. "His operation was always in Glitter Gulch. Rumors have it that he invested money in both the Flamingo and the Desert Inn, and it's probably true that he did; but true or false, he never had juice on the Strip. Even in a den of thieves and murderers, Binion lacked class. He was a barbarian as well as an illiterate. He was loud, coarse, and a pompous bore."

Others were kinder to Binion's legacy. A. D. Hopkins in *The*

*First 100: Portraits of the Men and Women Who Shaped Las Vegas* noted that the downtown statue of Binion on horseback was one of just two historic equestrian statues in Las Vegas. "There's Rafael Rivera, said to be the first white man to find the Las Vegas Valley, and there's Benny Binion, said to be the first to give gamblers a shot at winning big."

Author Deke Castleman observed in *Las Vegas*, "Above all, Benny Binion was a survivor—the Dallas gang wars of the 1930s, the Las Vegas cutthroat competition of the 1940s, the federal confinement of the 1950s. He didn't only survive, he prospered."

His family went to pieces along the way.

At his original licensing hearing, Benny was asked about the two men he admitted killing. Officials only probed into one other of the violent deaths to which he'd been linked.

Binion thought for a moment trying to place the name. Then recognition showed on his face, and he said, "Aw, you're not gonna count that one, too. He was just a nigger I caught stealing my whiskey."

Tax Commission Chairman Robbins Cahill recalled in his oral history, "Binion had this engaging style, and he had the Tax Commission in stitches, just laughing at his killing a man. He said it was self-defense, that the man reached into the glove box, and he thought he had a gun."

Jack Benny he wasn't. Binion was about as down-home country as the plague. Despite all the evidence against him, he was licensed. This display of juice set a standard his offspring attempted to imitate in years to come.

"Meanwhile," Denton and Morris observed in their book, "beneath the public confection, his present was, if anything, more brutal, brazen, and corrupt than his past." Although the state had seen fit to cleanse Binion's reputation, it didn't stop the beatings, occasional homicides—seven in a six-year period by one published account—and the jaw-dropping familiarity Benny kept with judges and politicians, including future Federal Judge Harry E. Claiborne, whose colorful career would be punc-

**207**

tuated by becoming the first sitting federal judge since Reconstruction to be impeached."

In the late 1970s, the Horseshoe's bottom line rivaled that of Caesars Palace and the Desert Inn, which specialized in high-roller services and provided their best customers with private jets and opulent suites. As late as 1987, the Horseshoe won $60 million and netted $19.2 million after taxes and expenses.

"It's better to have a little joint with a big bankroll than a big joint with a little bankroll," Benny once advised Steve Wynn. But Wynn was desperate to nourish his ego. Making a big impression was at least as important to him as the money.

It was sage advice that most of the corporate era's young Turks declined to take, but it served Binion well. Of course, Binion wasn't particular about his customers, and his egalitarian gambling instincts encouraged drug dealer Jamiel "Jimmy" Chagra and marijuana smuggler Rex Caudle to launder their ill-gotten millions at the Horseshoe. Stories of heroin traffickers and Mafia men using the Horseshoe to clean their cash became almost as much a part of the Horseshoe's reputation as its Texas chili and $2 steaks.

◆　　◆　　◆

"I'm very well pleased with my family," Binion said in an oral history made by university students. "They're all good workers. My wife works here, and my daughter [Barbara]. They count the money and look after the office. Jack is the boss. We get along real good."

Those who knew Ted well remember him always wanting to be like his father. The trouble was that Benny had been an outlaw, and in Las Vegas, there wasn't really room for a casino owner who reveled in busting the hands of card cheats and occasionally shooting competitors.

While Ted struggled with his increasing drug problem, running the day-to-day operation fell to big brother Jack. Jack was no pushover. He wasn't shy about taking dealers caught "going south" with chips into the bathroom and forcing them to cough up the tokens and a few teeth as interest. Binion shattered a hand on a men's room stall when a dealer ducked a punch, or so the story goes.

Players caught cheating at the Horseshoe were taken into the security room where they were taught never to make such a mistake again. Stories of hands, ribs, and jaws being broken were common, and Binion's gained a reputation as a place for cheaters to avoid.

However, card counting is legal in Nevada. It's not cheating, but a form of advantage play in which skilled players narrow the house odds. In one case, two card counters at Binion's were taken into the security office and beaten. The incident resulted in charges being filed against three men. What followed was typical Las Vegas justice.

The trial judge and the lawyers were men who regularly dined together with Benny Binion in the Horseshoe coffee shop. They spent their time in court telling funny stories. One couldn't tell the district judge from the defense attorney. The trial included one precious moment in which it was admitted that someone in District Attorney Bob Miller's office had informed Binion counsel Oscar Goodman that a search warrant was about to be served at the Horseshoe for the surveillance tape that would have captured the beatings. Investigators arrived a short time later to find that the tape they sought had suddenly and mysteriously vanished.

In the end, the court treated those responsible for the beatings with the high respect usually given to the friends and family of Benny Binion.

Through the years, Jack Binion took on increasing responsibility for the Horseshoe as his parents aged and some of his siblings proved undependable. "Jack held the whole show together," said a Binion family intimate. "Without Jack, the place would have fallen apart. It's as simple as that."

What was more complex was the role filled by Jack's younger brother, Ted. Jack clearly possessed his mother's focus on the financial bottom line and his father's ability to assemble a loyal team. Ted was different. He wallowed in psychedelic music, drugs, and hedonistic excess. "He liked his black-tar heroin and young whores, that's for sure," said a former Metro lieutenant who'd watched Binion's movements, yet for some reason had never seen fit to arrest him.

Although the police were generally accommodating to the Binions, they made a special place in their hearts for Ted, who in 1976 was a suspect in the murder of Rance Blevins. Blevins was a Horseshoe customer who made the fatal mistake of tearing up the place on his way out the door. The man was "accidentally" shot to death on the street. Ted was at the shooting scene, but ran away. He was found by police hiding in the Horseshoe's casino cage. He wasn't charged in the death although witnesses saw him do the shooting and then pass his gun to a confederate.

Ted Binion was charged in a major heroin-trafficking investigation in 1986. He was able to plead guilty to a misdemeanor. This caused the state Gaming Control Board to investigate his license suitability. Thus began a merry-go-round with regulators that led to his March 1998 banishment from the industry his daddy helped establish.

Friends and family said Ted was the most gifted of all the Binions when it came to understanding the river of numbers and odds that flow through the casino. He understood probability and mathematical theory and could add a foot-long list of figures in his head.

Ted also inherited his father's gift of storytelling. He reveled in recounting stories his father had told him as far back as early childhood when the family was being hunted by Dallas racket rival Herb "the Cat" Noble even after Benny moved his clan to Las Vegas. As a teenager, Ted drove the family Cadillac while Benny talked business in the backseat. He took pride in his father's mob connections and bloody history.

Ted may have been banned from the casino business, but his personal wealth was in excess of $50 million and all the fast-company friends that kind of money could buy. After being pushed out of the casino business for failing state-ordered drug tests and associating with organized-crime figures Herbie Blitzstein and Peter Ribaste, Binion found himself isolated from the Horseshoe and from members of his own family, as well.

Ted and Jack feuded with their younger sister, Becky Binion Behnen, and her husband, Nick Behnen, over control of the Horseshoe. In nasty litigation, the Behnens accused the elder brother of mismanagement and felonious acts. The accusations were floated in the press by a local reporter and haunted Jack Binion for years to come as he sought casino licenses in Illinois, Indiana, Louisiana, and Mississippi.

Ted, meanwhile, was suspected of taking revenge the only way he could—by grabbing hundreds of thousands of dollars worth of casino chips on his way out the door. The chips later turned up, and the Horseshoe's new owners, Nick and Becky Behnen, were forced by authorities to redeem them.

Nick Behnen didn't have a license and getting one would have been difficult due to his checkered history. This included accusations of running an illegal card game and of shooting a man in the face. He was just the sort of character who endeared himself with Benny Binion. Although Ted believed Nick held a Svengalilike spell over his younger sister, the truth was that they acted as a team and initially appeared to have outfoxed the brothers. They also were suspected of being secret informants for state gaming investigators.

◆　◆　◆

Ted Binion was fascinated with the dark side of Las Vegas. He tried to resist its appeal by playing cowboy on the family's 160,000-acre ranch in Montana, but he couldn't stay away.

When he died at age fifty-five, it was from a suspected drug overdose. His body was found on September 17, 1998, at his million-dollar home at 2408 Palomino Lane. Immediately, people close to him believed he died the way he'd lived and that his demons had caught up with him. Family members questioned the accidental overdose theory and suspected foul play.

Ted's estranged sister, Becky, was the first to speak out. She stated her belief that the death wasn't from the obvious cause: a fatal mixture of heroin and the prescription anxiety medication, Xanax.

Police at the scene were skeptical of the skeptics at first for they knew of Binion's fondness for smoking black-tar heroin. Then they saw clear signs that something was amiss. Ambulance and hospital attendants would later testify that Sandra Murphy, Ted's girlfriend who found his body, faked her anguish. She wasn't much of an actress, and her grief appeared staged. Then it became known that Ted's friend, Montana contractor Rick Tabish, had been squiring Sandy Murphy around Las Vegas.

Binion had been dead fewer than forty-eight hours when Nye County Sheriff's Department deputies saw something odd on Binion's ranch property in Pahrump. They found Tabish and several other men using heavy equipment to open an underground vault. The vault contained Binion's 48,000 pounds of silver bars and coins worth millions.

After Tabish was booked on burglary and theft charges, he insisted he was only trying to protect the best interests of Ted's daughter, Bonnie.

Meanwhile, Tom Dillard, a private detective hired by the family, discovered that Murphy and Tabish had shared a room at a Beverly Hills hotel. Although they insisted their relationship was innocent, the army of skeptics was growing.

Dillard's investigative efforts augmented the dogged detective work of Metro Homicide Bureau veterans Jim Buczek, Tom Thowsen, and Sgt. Ken Hefner, and Michael Karstedt of the District Attorney's Office. By early 1999, a grand jury was convened.

Meanwhile, Murphy hired lawyers to obtain her share of Binion's estate, which included the Palomino Lane home and all its contents. Given Binion's propensity for squirreling away cash and gems, there was a strong likelihood the property held many hidden millions.

When Clark County Coroner Ron Flud held the first press

ny Siegel was a most unlikely founding
er.

Meyer Lansky was an early Las Vegas
investor and a major influence on the Strip.

Benny Binion went from Texas horse trader and Dallas racket boss to the
owner of the Horseshoe Club.

Moe Dalitz was the genuine Las Vegas godfather.

Jackie Gaughan: From Omaha betting parlors the king of downtown.

The Las Vegas Club's Mel Exber turned a love of sports into a successful casino.

chael Gaughan expanded father Jackie's
vntown empire.

Caesars Palace and Circus Circus creator Jay
Sarno was the Strips' great idea man.

Howard Hughes bought casinos, but failed to own Las Vegas.

Robert Maheu was known as the man "Next to Hughes," but never saw him while he worked for the eccentric billionaire.

Bingo man Sam Boyd struck it rich in Las Vegas.

Harrah's attention to customer service and bottom line put him ahead of the mob-nmed casino crowd.

Barron Hilton with a portrait of family patriarch, Conrad Hilton.

Bill Boyd took father Sam's carnival style and created an empire.

Ted Binion, center, died of a suspicious drug overdose, and Bob Stupak watched his Stratosphere Tower dream go bankrupt.

Jack Binion is Las Vegas' most unpretentious billionaire.

ndicapping king Frank Rosenthal couldn't
t the odds, or his pals in the Chicago mob.

Casino industry friend Harry Reid went from
baby-faced Gaming Commission Chairman …

… to United States Senate Minority Leader.

FBI boss Joe Yablonsky made plenty of enemies while battling the mob on the Strip.

Former mob lawyer Oscar Goodman reinvented himself as mayor of Las Vegas.

Bill Bennett made Circus Circus a household name before being shoved out of his company.

Controversial cowboy Sheriff Ralph Lamb butted heads with the feds, but was credited with attacking the mob.

Relentless Ralph Engelstad survived the "Hitler birthday party" controversy to amass more than $1 billion in casino and business assets.

Arthur Goldberg reinvented Bally's as Park Place Entertainment.

When Carl Icahn goes bargain shopping, casino men cringe.

Donald Trump, the Vegas Apprentice, has big plans for the Strip.

l Satre turned Harrah's into an international
ning giant.

Gary Loveman: From Harvard to Harrah's
Entertainment.

ms owner George Maloof is on top of the world.

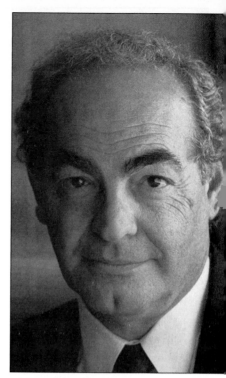

"Golden boys" Tom Breitling (left) and Tim Poster didn't last long as owners of the Golden Nugget, but pocketed millions.

Phil Ruffin is out to prove a hotel man can su ceed in the casino racket.

Japanese slot giant Kaz Okada teamed up with Steve Wynn to create Wynn Las Vegas and pursue casino development in Macau and Singapore.

Convention broker-turned-Venetian impresario Sheldon Adelson made the high-risk transformation into casino industry billionaire.

Terry Lanni has Kirk Kerkorian's trust and the keys to the MGM Mirage kingdom.

Kirk Kerkorian is the Strip's consummate shark, building the largest casinos in the world—and swallowing the competition.

rry Lanni and Kirk Kerkorian have proven an unbeatable team.

modern-day David amid an army of casino Goliaths, Rev. Tom Grey is never at a loss for words.

Peter Morton has taken his Hard Rock theme from T-shirt sales to a billion-dollar casino empire.

conference of his long career on March 15, 1999, the case against Murphy and Tabish took shape in earnest. The coroner ruled Binion's death was a homicide caused by a mixture of heroin and Xanax.

Murphy's attorney, John Momot, observed, "You have a guy who's a heroin addict, a multimillionaire. If he was a porter at the Horseshoe Club instead of a famous guy, I don't think we would be here today. Obviously, there were a lot of enablers who surrounded him, and I'm not talking about Sandy Murphy."

When it was discovered that the forensic analysis of Binion's system was flawed and that he'd not ingested enough drugs to overdose, a new theory of the case emerged. This one was offered by a pathologist named Michael Baden who was hired by family investigator Dillard and testified for the prosecution. Binion, Baden believed, had been suffocated in a method known as "Burkeing" where pressure is applied to the chest as opposed to covering the mouth and nose.

The eleventh-hour second theory, combined with Binion's own long history of drug abuse, appeared to bode well for the prosecution. And the shaky witnesses who fleshed out the prosecution's theory of the killing held together. A jury convicted Tabish and Murphy of murder and lesser charges, sentencing them to the equivalent of life terms.

Their appeals were filed by a trio of prominent lawyers. The team of Alan Dershowitz, William Terry, and Tony Serra persuaded the Nevada Supreme Court in 2003 to throw out the murder convictions and grant each suspect a new trial.

In the second trial, Tabish's ex-wife disputed his alibi for the morning of Binion's death. She said he'd misled people and admitted to her that he was at the millionaire's home early that day. Nevertheless, Murphy and Tabish were acquitted of murder. They were found guilty of burglary, conspiracy, and grand larceny for stealing $7-million worth of Ted Binion's silver and rare coins.

In March 2005, they were each sentenced to serve one to five years in state prison. Murphy was given credit for time served and emerged from prison more defiant than ever. But she rarely mentioned her undying affection for the late Ted Binion.

# Fathers and Sons II

sk Las Vegans to name the most successful Texas gambler to make the grade in Southern Nevada, and they'll invariably answer with the name Benny Binion. It's a good guess given Binion's legendary reputation, but it's incorrect. Although Binion's Horseshoe was once the most-profitable casino in Las Vegas based on profits per square foot, it doesn't approach the success of Beaumont, Texas, native Frank Fertitta Jr.

Fertitta, lesser known perhaps, was vastly more successful than Binion.

Fertitta was identified in a published report as a "cousin" of former Galveston vice lord Sam Maceo. He gravitated to Galveston, which has been described as a "little Chicago" on the Gulf of Mexico. It was a tough place to learn the business.

Maceo ruled the Galveston rackets for several decades. He was a close associate of Benny Binion and Meyer Lansky and was a bootlegging partner of Moe Dalitz. He had political clout in Texas and with powerful United States Sen. Pat McCarran of Nevada.

Unlike Binion, who was convicted of income-tax evasion and forced to put the official title to his club in his family's name, Fertitta was a working man on the ground floor of the casino trade. It was only after he went to work for Argent Corporation at the Fremont casino downtown that he rose in stature and controversy.

Fertitta worked as a casino manager and briefly as general manager for his friend and trusted associate, Carl Wesley Thomas, who for many years was considered one of the brilliant minds in the casino business.

Thomas earned a political-science degree at the University of Nevada, Las Vegas in 1964, but the sort of politics he practiced, they didn't teach in school. He'd knocked around local casinos since 1958 and worked his way up from a break-in 21 dealer to owning his own casinos. Along the way, he developed an eclectic circle of friends. These ranged from the state's top politicians to controversial oil man Jack Urich, Teamsters official Allen Dorfman, Chicago bookmaker-turned-casino-owner Ross Miller, and Outfit killer Anthony Spilotro.

In later years, Thomas also had a fierce defender in gaming attorney Frank Schreck.

Along the way, Thomas developed a bustling slot joint called the Bingo Palace. One of his partners in the Bingo Palace was Frank Fertitta Jr.

Fertitta might have been content to remain offstage and out of the public eye forever, but with Thomas as his partner, anonymity wasn't an option.

Thomas was no ordinary casino man. He was a master at helping casinos run smoothly. He was also a trusted insider when it came to setting up skimming operations for the mob throughout the Argent Corporation, the Tropicana, and all the way back to when the Circus Circus opened in the late 1960s. Charming and glib, well-read and amiable, Thomas had the skeleton key to the city.

Thomas was eventually convicted in a skim operation and placed in the state's Black Book. Fertitta, on the other hand, was never charged with any criminal activity. Still he operated under a cloud of suspicion. By the time the gaming regulatory cavalry arrived, thirteen years had passed since Fertitta was suspected of participating in the Fremont Casino skim.

He testified under oath before a federal trial in Kansas City that he had no knowledge of the skimming at the Fremont where he'd been casino manager. No one could prove otherwise although Thomas, the mastermind of the skim, had mentioned a "Frank" in a wiretapped discussion, which led to the speculation that this was a reference to Fertitta.

Even Fertitta's leading adversarial witness, former Argent Corporation security director Harry McBride, gave mixed signals. In the beginning, McBride said he had no knowledge of the skimming and had never seen Fertitta steal any money. Later, when he was described as "embittered" by Fertitta's allies, McBride did a turnabout. In the Kansas City trial, McBride named Fertitta as part of the skimming crew at the Fremont in 1976.

Several mobsters were convicted of hidden ownership and skimming millions from the Argent casinos. Thomas was convicted of conspiring with Civella family members to steal at least $280,000 from the Tropicana in the late 1970s. He was sentenced to fifteen years. He then cut deals with the government and the Civella family, as well. He agreed to cooperate enough to have his sentence reduced to two years. In exchange for leniency, Thomas said he would testify that at least $80,000 had been skimmed from the Fremont by the mob's insiders.

Even then, Thomas wouldn't name his friend, Fertitta, among the conspirators. In far-reaching cases credited with knocking out a majority of the organized-crime influence in the Las Vegas casino industry, the Fertitta question shrunk to a footnote.

The footnote was, nevertheless, an embarrassment for the Gaming Control Board. The board was criticized for allowing a man believed to be complicit with organized crime to operate a casino.

In 1988, gaming agents Richard Carr and Ronald Hollis produced an investigative report that recommended disciplinary action against Fertitta. Suddenly, it appeared that the lines of communication had gone dead around the office. It was as if someone was screaming and all the other people in the office acted as if they heard nothing.

Las Vegas newspaper columnist Ned Day observed dryly, "He has a lot of important and powerful friends in Las Vegas."

"I never skimmed any money," Fertitta insisted. "I fired Harry McBride shortly after Mr. Thomas left here. McBride was very, very bitter."

Fertitta did not, however, have a convincing answer to the question of why his name and unlisted home phone number were found in papers seized by the FBI in 1979 when it raided the home of Kansas City mob underboss Carl DeLuna.

Also, Fertitta was discussed by mobbed-up Tropicana executive Joe Agosto and DeLuna in a January 1979 conversation captured by an FBI wiretap. Thomas had traveled to Puerto Rico, and DeLuna was attempting to find out who accompanied him.

"He [Thomas] just left Friday," Agosto said. "He took, uh, the other guy with him, uh."

"Fertitta," DeLuna replied.

"Huh? Who?"

"Frank," DeLuna said.

It was later discovered that former Circus Circus operator Jay Sarno and not Fertitta had accompanied Thomas.

In the recorded conversation picked up by a microphone planted in the basement of mob family relative Josephine Marlo, DeLuna, Thomas, and brothers Nick and Carl Civella discussed the Fremont skim. Again Fertitta's name came up.

"At the Fremont, they had people, we had a ball," Thomas said. "We had Frank and [Billy] Caldwell, we had two cashiers, and I got my controller, [Jimmy] Faso plus my security man's fronting it. McBride's outside the door, the cashiers gives Frank the key, they go grab the money, the comptroller's upstairs, he's not actually in, but we take care of him."

Thomas later said, "I had Fertitta and Caldwell at the Fremont."

But those conversations had taken place eleven years earlier. And after a decade, they were just that, a lot of talk.

The Kansas City skim trial was a success for the government. By 1988, only a handful of straight-arrow gaming agents were still obsessed with Fertitta, whom they considered the shark that got away.

Said one Las Vegas casino insider who'd known Fertitta Jr. for decades, "Frank was died-in-the-wool old school. He grew up in the rackets and knew how to keep his mouth shut. And he knew his business inside and out."

Gaming Control agent's internal files gave insight into what lowly working investigators believed, but couldn't prove, about Fertitta: "Subject is currently 100 percent stockholder in the Bingo Palace at 2450 S. Rancho Road, Las Vegas, Nevada, 89102. It is widely accepted that Fertitta is a front man for Carl W. Thomas, his long-time friend and associate from whom he purchased the business.

"Fertitta apparently did not have the financial background or status to make a purchase the size of the Palace. He was assisted by a $4 million loan from Valley National Bank of Nevada. This bank is run by E. Parry Thomas . . . but is directly controlled by Moe Dalitz. Dalitz reports directly to Meyer Lansky in Florida."

In reality, the world of Las Vegas was more complicated than that, and a majority of law-enforcement investigators were ill-prepared for the challenge of seeing beyond the elaborate façade of an industry in dramatic transition from thinly veiled mob joints to sophisticated, if no less treacherous, publicly traded companies. (In the same report, one investigator wondered whether Parry Thomas and Carl Thomas were related. They weren't.)

With few exceptions, local law enforcement had rarely been effective in separating the mob insiders from the casino woodwork. It was only after federal wiretaps collected by the FBI in conjunction with the then-fledgling Organized Crime Strike

Force headed in the West by attorney Richard Crane that the true ownership picture of Las Vegas came into focus.

Although it announced there would be no formal complaint against Fertitta, the Control Board tried to save face by reserving the right to reopen its investigation. Only Control Board member Gerald Cunningham, a former police officer, was outspoken about the lack of interest shown by Chairman Bill Bible and member Dennis Amerine (who'd already resigned to accept a position in the industry) in pursuing the matter. They voted against calling Fertitta for a full hearing, and the majority ruled.

But Cunningham knew that a reopening wasn't going to happen.

"He didn't do anything wrong," lawyer Schreck insisted. "Frank is one of the corporate stalwarts of this community and has always been."

Fertitta's licensing odyssey made a laughingstock of the state's gaming regulatory process. Critics of the process, including former gaming agents, said that Fertitta was protected by his relationships with state officials and his powerhouse attorney Schreck.

In the middle of his licensing woes, the Fertitta family contributed $500,000 in academic scholarships to University of Nevada, Las Vegas and were praised by its president, Robert Maxson, as "wonderful citizens." In August 1989, just weeks after his gaming license and family fortune was saved by providence and perhaps some good old Las Vegas juice, Frank Fertitta Jr. announced that his Palace Station was giving $1 million to build a new tennis complex at UNLV. Local skeptics murmured that it was a community tribute in exchange for the licensing vote.

What of Carl Thomas, the mastermind behind the skimming operations? Fate took a hand in November 1993 when his pickup truck rolled over on a dusty rural road in Oregon. It caught fire, and he burned to death.

With the licensing controversy behind him, the door opened to bigger things for Fertitta and his family. The Palace Station embarked on an ambitious room expansion and not long afterward, broke ground for the $90-million Boulder Station on the Boulder Highway. This move sped the renaming of the formerly seedy corridor "the Boulder Strip." The hotel and casino were an immediate success.

Within five years, the Fertitta family emerged as the unchallenged leaders in the so-called "neighborhood casino" movement in Southern Nevada. They marketed to locals, focused on food quality, gaming value, and popular entertainment, and continued to extend the brand.

In a single decade, Palace Station would go public and become known as Station Casinos. It would expand and acquire other locals casinos, plus two Native American casinos, and even become investors in the influential Greenspun publishing and development companies.

When Frank Fertitta Jr.'s twenty-year-old skimming ghosts briefly reemerged in 1995 as he attempted to develop what would become known as the Texas Station, he left the stage and turned over the reins of his family's publicly traded company to eldest son Frank Fertitta III, who was joined by younger brother Lorenzo Fertitta and trusted insider Glenn Christenson. The Fertittas remained an extremely close-knit family, sharing Sunday dinners and trusting few outsiders.

Station's expertise in the marketplace is beyond controversy.

Station is among the industry's leaders in player marketing. Its Boarding Pass program tracks every nickel of slot and table play and results in an increasingly fine line being drawn when it came to issuing "comps," free rooms, food, beverages and merchandise, to customers.

Station was lauded for donating $50,000 every other month to local charities through its "Caring for the Community" program. Its "Smart Set" program sponsored at-risk public schools near its ever-expanding lineup of spiffy neighborhood casinos. The media rarely juxtaposed the charitable giving with the paychecks of the Station bosses.

Through it all, the company managed to operate without bending to the will of Culinary Local 226. The union wasn't shy about throwing up a picket line on the Strip or downtown, but seemed to have a blind eye where Station Casinos properties were concerned. Union officials offered unconvincing rhetoric when questioned about attempts to organize Station properties. True, the Station group was known for its generous employee-benefits packages and programs, and these included housing services and even day-care options.

The union's more-organized attempt in 2003 to embarrass Station executives by publicizing their generous executive stock-option program was perceived by local media and gaming investment analysts as the first serious attempt to organize.

"It's one thing to align executives' interests with shareholder interests," Culinary research director Courtney Alexander told *Las Vegas Sun* reporter Liz Benston. "It's another thing to take millions of options and grant them to insider shareholders. Then you are simply taking the potential for earnings in the company from the outside shareholders and giving it to the inside shareholders."

Chief Executive Frank Fertitta III's total compensation was $28.2 million, $25 million coming from generous stock options. Chief Financial Officer Glenn Christenson received a $1.1 million salary. His compensation rose to $18.2 million when options were included. And President Lorenzo Fertitta's $2 million salary was augmented by $7 million in stock options

But in the hog-fat casino industry, jaw-dropping salaries and corporate largess were nothing new and in many ways to be expected from companies with double-digit annual net-profit margins. Station Casinos executives could brag that its stock had risen 282 percent in the previous five years. It enjoyed one of the best reputations among all gaming stocks, was considered a *Forbes* "top pick," and lived up to Bank of America predictions by rising above $60 in early 2005.

◆    ◆    ◆

The Fertittas were eminently successful in Las Vegas. When they ventured outside of Southern Nevada, they sometimes ran into trouble. This happened particularly when they let their emotions get the better of them.

When Clark County Commissioner Lance Malone flip-flopped on a vote to approve the zoning for a new casino site, Station Casinos' political affairs coordinator Mark Brown arranged to have an anonymous mailer titled "You Just Can't Trust Lance Malone" to the commissioner's district.

The anonymity was a violation of Nevada law. In the end, the company and Mark Brown and his partner in the ham-handed operation were embarrassed. True, they got the last laugh when Malone was indicted on corruption charges in an unrelated matter.

The Fertittas also took flak for adding City Councilwoman Lynette Boggs McDonald to their board of directors. Although McDonald remained on the board only a short time, she later was named to a county commission post in a district in which Station Casinos had been having difficulty getting zoning and neighborhood support for its planned Red Rock Station casino.

After a rare defeat to develop a neighborhood casino in North Las Vegas, Station's CFO Glenn Christenson admitted, "We've looked at most of the other feasible sites, and we control most of them."

He was not boasting. The Fertitta family placed itself years ahead of their competition in the locals market by locking up choice real estate along the Interstate-215 beltway project that loops the valley. Their land acquisitions were so precise, it made some skeptics wonder whether they knew the location of the beltway ahead of time. With key real estate secured, they were guaranteed to remain competitive in the multibillion-dollar neighborhood casino market for a generation to come. One gaming analyst put it bluntly, "Other folks will have a difficult time finding sites to develop. They're in a very good position."

The Fertittas were willing to pay a premium to ensure their position in the market. In early 2001, the company paid $9 million to buy property near the North Las Vegas Airport that had been owned by Michael Gaughan's Coast Resorts.

If the savvy Gaughan had chosen to build, his casino would have put him in direct competition with the Santa Fe Station, Fiesta, and Texas Station along the "Rancho Road Riviera" at a time when Station Casinos already was being scrutinized for unstable revenues and a substantial debt load. For the Fertittas, it was $9 million well spent and allowed Gaughan to concentrate on his Orleans, Suncoast, and future Southcoast properties.

◆    ◆    ◆

In Missouri, Station nearly lost all credibility. The company's attempt to operate riverboat casinos in Kansas City and St. Charles was a disaster. Their lawyer, Michael Lazaroff, testified that it was his close friendship with Missouri Gaming Commission Chairman Robert Wolfson that helped juice the Fertittas' license.

Lazaroff was monitored by authorities who recorded him making more than two hundred private phone calls to Wolfson during the Station licensing process. Although the company paid unusually large bonuses to Lazaroff, it was never accused of participating in a bribery scheme. Lazaroff, the state's key witness, was also found to have skimmed $380,000 from his law partners at the Thompson Coburn firm. He later attempted suicide.

The company consistently denied wrongdoing, but it paid a $1-million penalty in November 2000 for the Lazaroff incident as well as failing to prevent underage gambling and failing to enforce the state's $500 gambling-loss limit. Perhaps coincidentally, the $1 million was paid to the Missouri School Fund.

Although Missouri officials gave lip service to the importance of maintaining propriety in their fledgling system, they agreed not to comment publicly on the terms of the settlement.

Just weeks earlier, there had been strong gaming industry rumors that Station Casinos, due to its Missouri compromises, was considering selling off to one of the Strip giants. Its stock had dipped into the $12 range and traded at less than half of its high. Ameristar Casinos came to its rescue with a $475 million offer for both Missouri casinos.

The Fertittas jumped at the chance to sell, and Station stock gradually recovered.

Four years later, the ghost of the Lazaroff case haunted the Fertittas when they agreed to pay $38 million to settle a lawsuit that charged them with using improper contacts with Missouri gaming officials to secure their casino license back in 1997.

The Missouri settlement was used as fodder for critics of Station Casinos' plan to secure a gaming agreement for a reservation casino in Allegan County, Michigan, in June 2004 with the Gun Lake tribe of Pottawatomi Indians. A spokesman for the anticasino group "23 is Enough" told *Grand Rapids Press* reporter Ted Roelofs, "Leopards don't change their spots. They engaged in unethical conduct. They are likely to engage in unethical conduct again."

By then the company had broken through outside its Las Vegas stronghold with a hugely successful Indian reservation casino called Thunder Valley near Sacramento. It was so successful that it was having a noticeable impact on the Reno-area gaming market, which traditionally had drawn customers from the Sacramento area.

Lorenzo took time from his executive duties to serve as a member of the Nevada Athletic Commission, and Frank III emerged as a respected and generous contributor to the Republican Party. It was the sort of activity their father might not have dreamed possible a generation earlier.

For a proud son, his father was a man of the people.

"My Dad knew the names of employees and customers, and recognized them when he was walking across the floor," Fertitta III told industry reporter Roger Gros. "Even though we are a much bigger company today, we still try to embody all those cultural things my father put in place that made Station the success it is today."

The Fertittas had mined the seemingly limitless pot of gold and had managed to avoid the pitfalls that had consumed Benny

Binion's clan. The Fertittas had arrived. In many respects, they are the quintessentially successful Las Vegas casino family.

# Fathers and Sons III

No son in Las Vegas ever cultivated his father's legacy more faithfully than Bill Boyd. In a city waist-high with inflated egos, Sam Boyd was an anomaly: He was a gambling man who kept a clean house, watched his bottom line, didn't allow his dreams to become too large, and went home at night to his family.

When Sam died in 1993, his lawyer son Bill made sure that history was kind to his father, whose successful, quiet life seemed destined to be reduced to a Sin City footnote. To make sure this didn't happen, Bill Boyd hired a team of writers to create *The Players: The Men Who Made Las Vegas*, a collection of essays on the gamblers who built the city. There, next to Kirk Kerkorian, Howard Hughes, Benny Siegel, and Moe Dalitz is one of the few profiles ever published about the elder Boyd.

Unlike some of the community's founding fathers, Sam

227

Boyd didn't cut his teeth on big-city dice hustles. He wasn't a mob enforcer or racket boss. He was born in Enid, Oklahoma, in 1910 and learned to be a carnival barker in California at the Long Beach Pike Amusement Park. He ran bingo games from Long Beach to Honolulu and dealt cards on gambling ships off the California coast until he moved his wife, Mary, and son Bill to Las Vegas.

By then, he had more experience dealing to low rollers and average Joes than any of Las Vegas' mobbed-connected money men. He marketed with the coupon books and front-door bally pitches that define downtown gambling halls to this day.

A story Bill Boyd likes to tell is how his father came to Las Vegas on Labor Day 1941 with $80 and through unwavering determination became a wealthy man who "embodied the concepts of integrity, commitment, and excellence."

All true, but there's more to the story.

Sam Boyd carved an early reputation as an honest man in a cutthroat business. He worked at several casinos, many of them tied to organized crime figures, including the Meyer Lansky-backed Thunderbird. In 1952, he was offered the opportunity to purchase 1 percent of the Sahara from Al Winter of Portland, Oregon. Winter had Teamsters connections and gambling convictions, but he was licensable in a Nevada where the friends of Lansky populated nearly every joint.

"If he stayed at the Thunderbird, he would have owed his soul to those guys, and it would have been trouble," Bill Boyd told *The Players* author Jack Sheehan. "I honestly believe this was the pivotal moment of dad's life."

When the Sahara group developed the Mint downtown next to the Horseshoe, Sam Boyd bought 3.5 percent of the deal. He continued to build his bankroll and contacts in the business and banking community. One important contact was Valley Bank's E. Parry Thomas, the man with intimate access to the Teamsters' pension fund loans and the city's deal maker extraordinaire.

At the Mint, Boyd displayed marketing concepts that were

radical for the time and raised the bar by offering live entertainment. He may have been a carny at heart, but no CPA ever had a better grasp of numbers than Boyd. "It was always like a carnival, or a party, with people in hats and balloons everywhere," former Mint employee Rita Taylor told Sheehan. "He'd have a giant birthday party for the Mint each year, and they'd bake this enormous cake, weighing maybe a ton. I thought no one would want to eat it, but people lined up around the block to get a piece of that cake."

In 1971, Boyd bought a 12.5-percent share of the newly constructed Union Plaza downtown and again experimented with live entertainment. He even presented musicals from Broadway such as *Fiddler on the Roof.*

Next, he bought a 26.5-percent stake in the new California Hotel and Casino. Located a block off Fremont Street on Ogden Avenue, the California's location was poor, but Boyd benefited from a Teamsters Central States Pension Fund loan and an uncanny knack for marketing to Hawaiian customers.

Boyd spent part of his formative years as a bingo operator in Hawaii and knew the customs of the Islanders. He not only learned their songs and lifestyle, he knew they would appreciate having rice cookers in their rooms. When Islanders got "rock fever," they were glad to spend a week at Sam's place in Las Vegas and remained loyal to the California long after it became antiquated by Strip standards.

Three decades later, with Bill Boyd at the head of the multibillion-dollar Boyd Gaming, Hawaii remains the California's primary customer market.

Without question, the most-inspired decision of Sam Boyd's life was made in 1979 when he opened Sam's Town. This was a country-western themed hotel and casino on the Boulder Highway. The highway was really just a strip of asphalt running east from Fremont Street and west from the industrial town of Henderson. Sam's Town catered to locals and the RV set and helped create what would become known as the neighborhood casino.

Sam Boyd remained a carnival barker with a love of the game of shouting until a house was full of customers. Although he made smart investment choices in his life, the best move he and wife Mary ever made was sending their son to law school. Bill Boyd graduated from the University of Utah and for a decade practiced law in Southern Nevada.

In 1973, after more than fifteen years as a practicing attorney, Bill made the decision to join his father on a full-time basis. It was a turning point in the lives of both men. Sam was loud, but conservative. Bill was soft spoken, but aggressive. Bill joined Sam in buying the Eldorado Club in Henderson. Although he lacked his father's volatile temper, Bill was determined to raise the stakes.

The younger Boyd would be entrusted with taking the once-mobbed-up Stardust from notoriety to profitability in the post-Frank Rosenthal era. But it was the locals-focused Sam's Town on the Boulder Highway that put the family business into the big money game. Sam's Town was built on just thirteen acres in the drab east end of Las Vegas. By catering to locals with low-priced food and drinks and liberal slot payoffs, he proved that his father's approach was valid even in the new corporate era: Gamblers want value. It is only the definition of value that changes from one player to the next.

When the mob-owned Stardust opened its doors on July 2, 1958, it featured a record-setting 105-foot-long pool, a 16,500-square-foot casino, and the world's largest electric sign that stretched the length of the building.

The casino was controlled by gambling ship operator Tony Cornero, who died of a heart attack while shooting dice at the Desert Inn in 1955. Moe Dalitz and his Cleveland group of investors took over before Cornero's body was cold and finished the Stardust project.

In later years, with backing from the Teamsters, the Stardust was fronted by Allen Glick's Argent Corporation and in the hands of Frank Rosenthal, Anthony Spilotro, and the Chicago Outfit.

In the 1980s, stewardship of the Stardust had echoes all the way to New York, where salty Genovese crime family mob boss "Fat Tony" Salerno discussed the fate of the resort's Teamsters pension fund loan. The era of organized-crime hidden ownership was fading, and college-trained casino men such as Bill Boyd represented the future of the industry.

After operating the Stardust and Fremont for sixteen months after the ouster of Al Sachs and Herb Tobman, the Stardust was hit with a $3.5-million fine for failing to control skimming in the casino. The Boyds moved to buy the properties. "I was somewhat naïve, because it was a war those first three months," Bill Boyd recalled.

At last the Stardust was free of its mobbed-up image. Upon marking the casino's forty-fifth anniversary, Boyd observed, "The Stardust is old Las Vegas, and we have a lot of customers who still enjoy the classic Las Vegas experience."

Sam Boyd died in 1993 at the time the corporation he founded was taking off. His son wished his father had lived to the end of the century so he could have enjoyed the fact that Boyd Gaming then would own a dozen casinos in Indiana, Illinois, Louisiana, Mississippi, and Nevada.

However it was the July 2003 opening of the $1.1 billion, 2,000-room Borgata Hotel Casino & Spa in Atlantic City in cooperation with MGM Mirage that at last put the soft-spoken Boyd on center stage. Boyd might have looked like he was more likely to hop off one of Atlantic City's ubiquitous casino buses than cruise into town in a limo, but he was now a real player in the casino-ownership game.

With its 135,000-square-foot casino and eleven restaurants, Borgata was designed to redefine the Atlantic City casino experience as something worth more than a day trip. Boyd's goal was to attract visitors from across the country and getting them to hang around for several days replacing the hordes of day bus trippers. He told *BusinessWeek*'s Christopher Palmeri, "I've looked at this for a number of years. The timing was right."

The Atlantic City deal came to him in a roundabout manner. The land under the Borgata was originally to have been jointly occupied by Mandalay Resorts and Mirage Industries, but at the last minute, Steve Wynn grabbed the entire parcel. Later Wynn divided the land into thirds and sold a piece to Boyd. After Wynn was pushed out of Mirage Resorts by the MGM takeover, Boyd and the new MGM Mirage agreed to partner. It was the biggest business risk of Bill Boyd's life.

Things hadn't always been that happy for Boyd Gaming. Only four years earlier, it was drowning in debt. But recovery was swift, and by 2003, its stock had risen 18 percent on revenues of $1.3 billion.

The Borgata sent a tsumami through Atlantic City: Its creation forced the competition to improve their properties. Donald Trump looked more than ever like the poseur he is than the competent casino owner he pretends to be.

Atlantic City's older properties had suffered from the opening of the enormously profitable Foxwoods and Mohegan Sun Indian reservation casinos in nearby Connecticut. These were, after all, the same distance from New York City as Atlantic City.

◆　　◆　　◆

Bill Boyd's reputation continued to climb in the industry in February 2004 when he bought Coast Casinos, a locals gaming giant directed by Jackie Gaughan's eldest son, Michael Gaughan. In the $1.3-billion deal, Coast became a wholly owned subsidiary of Boyd Gaming. Gaughan and longtime casino executive Frank Toti held 40 percent of company stock and continued to direct their part of the company.

Suddenly, Boyd found himself at Gaming Inc.'s final table as a Top 10 operator and the largest locals casino company in Nevada.

Boyd's annual revenues increased to $2 billion with seventeen properties and 9,050 hotel rooms—5,300 of those in Las Vegas. Boyd Gaming now boasted 25,500 employees.

It was this elevated cash flow that allowed Boyd to invest in the nearly fifty-year-old Stardust property, which stood to be overshadowed along with north Strip properties by the 2005 completion of Wynn Las Vegas. The Stardust occupied fifty acres and still had untapped potential. This meant Boyd had to reduce its debt ratio and spruce up revenues. The Gaughan merger did just that. Boyd President Don Snyder immediately went public with "much more exciting plans for the Stardust property."

Gaughan's ambition to develop in Southern Nevada did not appear to be hindered by the merger. If anything, he was comfortable partnering up with his old friend, Bill Boyd. Gaughan continued to expand by completing the $350-million Southcoast.

Michael Gaughan came from Omaha and was in many ways the antithesis of the Vegas casino guy. He graduated from Creighton University with a degree in accounting in 1965 and picked up an MBA from USC in 1967. He was downtown legend Jackie Gaughan's most successful son, but beyond his roots, he bore little resemblance to his father. He was a big man prone to stammer, who had been married to the same woman, Paula, for decades, doted on his four children, and for many years raced off-road vehicles. He ran in the famous Mint 400, won High Desert Racing Association events, but quit racing after he survived a 1991 accident outside Reno.

Perhaps the dirty, fast-moving gambling business had prepared Gaughan for racing success. He was handed the keys to the El Cortez downtown at age twenty-two and learned the grind of the trade among the nickel slot players and dollar blackjack bettors.

He teamed up with father Jackie, casino man Frank Toti, and others to open the Royal Inn Casino just off the Strip in 1972. The Royal's location made it a likely loss leader and provided a challenge to the savvy of the young Gaughan.

Michael and Jackie Gaughan began buying up Golden Nugget stock. They became company directors just when a young Steve Wynn was attempting to remake the downtown casino. Although they would make money from their investment in the Nugget, they never forgot that Wynn had forced them out.

Meanwhile, Gaughan and his partners, Tito Tiberti and Jerry Herbst among them, continued their growth first in 1979 with the creation of the Barbary Coast on a sliver of real estate at the corner of Flamingo Road and Las Vegas Boulevard, and later in 1986 with the Gold Coast, a locals-focused hotel-casino that offered a bowling center and movie theater.

Gaughan told a self-deprecating story about how ill suited he was to the hustle of landing a gambling license in jurisdictions outside Nevada. For example, he withdrew his application in Louisiana because officials demanded endless bribes, which he refused to pay.

He made a small-but-profitable killing when he christened St. Louis's *Casino Queen* riverboat in 1993.

Building on the success of the Gold Coast, Gaughan & Company opened the Orleans Hotel and Casino in 1996, followed by the Suncoast four years later. Both locals-oriented casinos had sufficient rooms to cater to value-oriented tourists. Both offered movie theaters, and the Orleans was home to an ice arena and professional hockey franchise.

It was after the September 11, 2001, terrorist attacks that Gaughan's character really began to shine. The Las Vegas economy went into a tailspin as tourists avoided commercial planes. Megaresort operators frightened by the drop in business fired thousands of casino dealers and service workers. Others were given part-time employment at reduced salaries.

In a truly underhanded move, many corporations used the crisis as an excuse to shrink payrolls by dumping senior employees who generally made more money and cost more for their health insurance.

Michael Gaughan cut back on the hours of some employees, but refused to fire any of them. Word spread through town about what a good guy he was. His workers felt a strong sense of loyalty.

One of his most profitable "casinos" didn't require many

employees. It was a grind joint that millions of tourists patronize each year. Gaughan held the slot concession at McCarran International Airport. With 1,308 machines positioned strategically, Gaughan made money whether tourists were coming or going.

In an interview, Gaughan made it clear that he and Toti wanted to take Coast public while the company's older stockholders preferred to cash out. The Boyd merger, he said, gave both parties what they wanted.

Meanwhile, federal law enforcement was investigating former Clark County Commissioner Lance Malone on corruption allegations. Reporters noted the odd relationship between Coast Resorts and Malone, who received a Subway sandwich shop franchise in a prime location at the Orleans casino.

Malone, who was indicted in 2004 for his part in a sweeping political corruption investigation in San Diego and Las Vegas, had never run a sandwich shop before. By this strange good fortune and thanks to Gaughan, he found himself with the second-most valuable Subway franchise in America.

Michael Gaughan admitted feeling sorry for Malone, whom he'd formerly supported, after the commissioner was bounced from office. The sandwich shop deal was unusual, but played no part in Malone's indictment.

In fact, Boyd's offer came not long after other casino giants and their affiliated investment bankers made initial overtures to Gaughan. His profitable and privately held properties regularly attracted suitors from the gaming world. Harrah's Entertainment showed interest, as did fellow locals gaming giant Station Casinos. Ameristar Corporation also appeared intrigued by the profit possibilities.

While it was unclear whether Gaughan intended to downshift into retirement, it was clear that Bill Boyd was one man he trusted implicitly.

For his part, Michael Gaughan had always been the straight arrow of Jackie Gaughan's children while Jackie Jr. fell into the long dark tunnel of drug addiction in much the same manner as

Ted Binion. Jackie Jr. fought heroin addiction and late in his life was a casino manager at Jackie Gaughan's Plaza. He was removed from the premises after he was caught stealing. He later died of a heart attack linked to his drug abuse.

"The family tried everything with Jackie Jr., but they couldn't change him," said one source. "Big Jackie got him I don't know how many jobs. It's a real tragedy, but it just proves money doesn't buy everything in Las Vegas."

But for the most part the Gaughans have avoided becoming just another Vegas statistic.

As a childhood friend of the Gaughan family, former Organized Crime Strike Force attorney Donald Campbell was introduced to the casino culture at Jackie Gaughan's El Cortez. He swam in the hotel pool and laughed when Michael Gaughan threw in live lobsters just to shake things up. One day, Michael set Campbell on a blackjack table, and he watched in wonder as two elderly women fought over the use of a nearby slot machine.

"It had the most incredible impression on me and has stayed with me all my life," Campbell recalled. "Gambling is an intoxicating business, but the Gaughan family has always been down-to-Earth. In all the years I've known them, they haven't changed."

In a town of tip slaves, the Gaughans were known for rewarding loyalty. Longtime employees, even restroom attendants and hotel maids, received fat pensions for staying with the company.

In 2004, Michael Gaughan was named Man of the Year by Temple Beth Sholom and spent much of his free time proudly following the rising prospects of his son, Brendan Gaughan, a professional race driver.

That hard-driving attitude must run in the family.

# 26

# Is There a Caesar in the House?

When *Forbes* produced its annual list of the top corporations in America in March 2004, Caesars Entertainment was ranked as the nation's largest casino company. It was, in fact, the highest-grossing licensed gambling organization in the world. Yet the company, formerly called Park Place Entertainment, was overshadowed on the Strip by leaner, hipper resorts that moved fast and showed a greater grasp of effective marketing.

Like the whale shark, Caesars' size was impressive, but it lacked the teeth of more-aggressive members of the species.

Company observers wondered what Caesars Entertainment might have been like had Arthur Goldberg lived. The intense and dynamic executive died October 19, 2000, at age fifty-nine of bone-marrow failure. He left a legacy as a man who ushered in the era of rapid consolidation to the casino industry.

Goldberg was a practicing attorney with a law degree from Villanova. His casino adventures began one afternoon when he met a friend at Newark Airport. They chatted while waiting for an airline to announce a new departure time for a delayed flight. The talk turned to stocks, and the friend persuaded Goldberg to buy shares of Bally Corporation. The friend assured him it was bargain priced.

Goldberg acted on the tip and bought shares. He was disappointed the stock dropped to half of what he'd paid for it. He looked into the company. Then he spent $12.5 million to buy several million additional shares. In doing so, he became Bally's largest stockholder. At this point, he demanded a seat on the board of directors. He felt that he was a passenger on a huge cruise ship that didn't have a captain or compass.

His was an accurate evaluation for in 1990, Bally was slipping into bankruptcy with $1.86 billion in debts. It had an overall value of about $2.1 billion. At the time, not only was Bally's choking with debt, but it was considered the softest major gaming company in the industry. Its executive compensation packages were notoriously fat, its stock performance dismally thin.

Bally's links to the mob were severed by 1990, but the casino was at the furthest end of the Atlantic City boardwalk and was eclipsed by the competition.

Robert Mullane, as Bally's chief executive officer, had somehow managed to keep the sinking ship afloat. Nevertheless, he was roundly criticized at the 1990 annual meeting for drawing his $1.86-million salary in 1989 when the company was $1.8 billion in debt and its stock tumbled from $24 to $3.

Mullane announced they'd see a new Bally's in the coming year. What he might not have foreseen is that they'd see it without him in the picture.

Goldberg replaced Mullane. He was gracious in praising Mullane's stewardship, saying that some things were beyond his predecessor's control. But he truly impressed stockholders when he announced that he would not take any salary as CEO.

Goldberg once was a New Jersey trucking-company owner.

That toughened him up. As a lawyer, he'd spent part of his legal career fighting off thieves and mobbed-infested unions. He wasn't intimidated by Chicago-based Bally's colorful history.

Within a decade, Goldberg introduced a new style: growth by acquisition. He guided Bally into and out of its bankruptcy and then, with some brilliant moves, shaped it into an almost unrecognizable casino giant called Park Place Entertainment.

Goldberg was following the sage advice of Charles "Toolie" Kandell who told friends, "If you want to get rich, get rich in the dark." Unlike publicity-hungry Donald Trump and Steve Wynn, Goldberg kept under the media radar and out of the *New York Post* gossip columns.

When Bally's casinos in Nevada fell millions behind on bond payments, Goldberg sold off unprofitable pieces of the company. He cut costs, renegotiated debt schedules, and tried not to reveal his state of shock upon learning of the company's real financial crisis.

Within months, the company began to respond.

While Goldberg was busy reshaping Bally Entertainment in Las Vegas and Atlantic City, the company was pounded in Louisiana. Its slot-machine manufacturing subsidiary, Bally Gaming, was entangled in a slot-machine scandal in Louisiana with links to the mob. Despite his distance from the Bally arrangement to provide video-poker machines to distributor Worldwide Gaming of Louisiana, Goldberg was named as an unindicted co-conspirator in the case. Gaming regulators in Nevada and Atlantic City monitored the case closely. However, neither moved against Goldberg because they agreed that Bally was a victim in the investigation.

Fattening the bottom line was one thing, but what Bally really needed was a transfusion. So Goldberg jettisoned the slot-machine and fitness-machine manufacturing divisions. This reduced the company's debt by millions and further increased investor confidence.

Goldberg focused on the thing past executives ought to have been focusing on all along: the gargantuan profit potential in the casinos. After less than six years of restructuring, he sold the new-look Bally's to Hilton Hotels for $3 billion.

He accepted a reduced role in the transaction while he searched for a new conquest. He found one in 1998 in the form of Grand Casinos. This was a company built by high-stakes poker player Lyle Berman, who had secured a management agreement with a Minnesota Indian tribe. The agreement gave Berman entry into the emerging Mississippi casino market. At $1.3 billion, it was just the sort of work-in-progress that intrigued Goldberg. Geographically, it also put him in blossoming markets that didn't directly compete with Las Vegas and Atlantic City.

Then he announced an even-more ambitious plan. He would merge Grand Casinos with the Hilton casinos and spin them into Park Place Entertainment.

Goldberg now headed the largest gaming company in the world, but he was far from finished. With the September 1999 opening of the $785-million Paris Las Vegas, with its fifty-story replica of the Eiffel Tower, he proved he was capable of developing new properties as well as acquiring established ones.

For all his low-key leadership, Goldberg was not without an ego. While analysts clearly respected the job he did in reinventing Bally's in the mid-1990s, they verily gushed over Las Vegas casino titan Steve Wynn, whose success with the Mirage had been credited with reviving Las Vegas. Wynn's Hollywood smile and high profile irked Goldberg, who called the Mirage CEO "a bad Jew." For Goldberg, a man not given to public displays of emotion, this was a supreme insult.

In 1997, when Wynn was considered the public face of corporate gaming, the two clashed over a Republican fund-raiser involving Senate Majority Leader Trent Lott of Mississippi, Bill Frist of Tennessee, and Mitch McConnell of Kentucky at the casino titan's exclusive Shadow Creek golf course.

The event was sponsored by the American Gaming Association, but Wynn used the event as an opportunity to cater to the politicians. As a result, Goldberg, whose Hilton gaming creation was the talk of the industry and eclipsed Mirage Resorts at the bottom line, was incensed. He complained to AGA President Frank Fahrenkopf, and Wynn's leadership role was critically noted in the *Wall Street Journal.*

"There's a perception among some members of the industry that if it's the industry's money being spent, it shouldn't be done where one guy gets the credit for having it at his country club," an industry insider told *Las Vegas Sun* columnist Jeff German. "Let's spread it around and give others some of the credit."

Goldberg believed that gaming should be represented by a trade organization such as the AGA and by men with diverse business backgrounds, not by lifelong casino owners.

◆　◆　◆

Caesars Entertainment came into being through a circuitous route, beginning in 1919 with Conrad Hilton's first hotel in sleepy Cisco, Texas. Hilton's son, Barron, emerged as a player in Las Vegas in 1970 when he acquired the International from Kirk Kerkorian and renamed it the Las Vegas Hilton.

With its off-Strip location on Paradise Road next to the Convention Center and across from a Space Needle-shaped lemon called the Landmark, Barron's Hilton became known as the Las Vegas home of Elvis Presley and quickly established the city as a convention and business destination.

In years to come, with casino insiders such as Jimmy Newman massaging the marketing, the Las Vegas Hilton established itself in the high-roller market that had once been the exclusive territory of Caesars Palace. Hilton's lesser-known acquisition from Kerkorian was the Flamingo, quickly christened the Flamingo Hilton, which gave the hotel company a footing in a prime Strip location and also a lusty cash flow from the midmarket tourists. (The Flamingo Hilton would eventually grow into a 3,626-room behemoth with EBITDA [earnings before interest, taxes, depreciation, and amortization] in 2000 of $116 million, placing it just $3 million behind legendary Caesars Palace and $85 million ahead of the elephantine loss-leader Las Vegas Hilton.)

241

Hilton's gaming pursuits were derailed temporarily when Barron Hilton applied for a casino license in Atlantic City in 1982. The newly legalized gambling town tended to treat Las Vegas people with suspicion. Despite his long years in the hotel business, his relationship with mob-connected lawyer Sidney Korshak returned to haunt him.

Korshak was connected to the Chicago Outfit and other organized-crime operations for decades, according to a variety of law-enforcement sources. And he'd been collecting a $50,000 annual fee from Hilton.

In his 1987 bestseller, *The Art of the Deal*, Donald Trump observed, "The problem was that the Hilton people got a little too smug for themselves. They assumed they were doing Atlantic City a favor by coming to town, when in fact the licensing authorities see it just the opposite way."

Hilton had grown his father's company after he entered the gaming market, but he was never considered one of the Strip's great developers. And he got no respect from such cocky would-be rising stars as Donald Trump.

For his part, Trump had mixed feelings about Hilton. While declaring his affection for him, Trump chided his business acumen and described him as a member of the lucky-sperm club. This was ironic given Trump's own comfortable upbringing by Brooklyn and Queens developer Fred Trump. Donald later described Barron Hilton as a good friend and bragged to talk-show host Larry King that he attended the hotel man's birthday party. In like fashion, although Trump was verbose in expressing his disdain for Steve Wynn, Wynn was an invited guest at Trump's Palm Beach wedding in 2005.

Hilton sold his casino to Trump, only to return to Atlantic City in 1996 after acquiring Bally Entertainment. With the Bally takeover, Hilton became the world's largest casino operator, and Arthur Goldberg emerged as the white knight who would take the Park Place Entertainment giant into the twenty-first century.

If only he had made it that far.

Goldberg's death in October 2000 led to the appointment of Tom Gallagher, a Harvard-trained lawyer characterized in media accounts as "the deliberator." Gallagher, an executive with Merv Griffin's Resorts International in the 1980s, had been corporate counsel for Hilton Hotels. He had startlingly little experience on the casino floor.

The tall, bearded Gallagher was the wrong man to replace the energetic, supremely perceptive Goldberg. The company's stock price fell reflecting that Park Place was now a stumbling, lethargic giant. Insiders said Gallagher blamed the company's downturn on September 11, but it was clear that Park Place wasn't bouncing back as quickly as its competitors.

One reason for its lethargy was its underperforming properties, most notably the venerable Las Vegas Hilton. While the property attracted suitors, selling off Barron Hilton's first casino proved difficult.

Los Angeles real-estate developer Ed Roski Jr. offered to buy the convention-centered hotel and casino. He placed a $20-million check in escrow, but the deal fell apart in January 2001.

Initially, Park Place accused Roski of bad faith and attempted to have a court award it Roski's $20-million deposit and $20 million more in damages. Roski in turned accused Hilton Hotels, which had unsuccessfully tried to buy back the property from Park Place and tried to block the sale to Roski, of attempting to manipulate the Park Place sale following Goldberg's death. Litigation followed, and Park Place ended up cutting a $3.8-million check to settle that dispute. This was but one example of the lack of sound decision making inside the company.

It was just the sort of warfare that wouldn't have been tolerated had Goldberg been alive.

Park Place/Caesars Entertainment executives also were faced with two of the more controversial issues in gaming: questionable credit use and guarding against "advantage play" gamblers.

One case involved gambler Steve Mattes, who obtained an $8-million jury verdict after accusing Park Place executives of causing him to lose millions "due to fraud in the accounting of his markers." The jury awarded $1 million in defamation to Mattes and $1.5 million in punitive damages. On appeal, Park Place was granted a new trial on a legal technicality. The late Arthur Goldberg's reputation took a beating at trial, and Mattes proved, at least to one jury's satisfaction, that the company's allegations that he'd floated bad checks was not merely incorrect, but reckless.

Casino debt collection had long been a delicate dance with customers, who traditionally could not be forced to make good on the credit they'd received. But Clark County District Attorney Stewart Bell, with the full endorsement of the Strip casino titans, in the 1990s began preferring charges against slow-paying high rollers, causing no small amount of embarrassment to the players while generating millions of dollars from outstanding markers.

Highly skilled advantage players, professional gamblers who counted cards and played in teams, suffered from another problem in the highly monitored world of Las Vegas casinos. Some casino corporations not only kept a keen eye out for their presence in the house, but they sometimes detained the players in constitutionally questionable behavior.

Longtime gambling observers, however, would be quick to remind those players that at least their hands hadn't been broken, a common method of treating the problem in the old Las Vegas.

Meanwhile, Tom Gallagher, part of the team that helped Goldberg spin off Park Place from Hilton, left the company in November 2002. His lack of success at the helm of the world's largest casino company didn't discourage him from mounting a respectable campaign for Congress in Nevada in 2004.

Park Place not only needed a new skipper, it needed a new course. Observers generally agreed that Wally Barr, who'd been loyal to Goldberg and didn't become embittered when he was passed over as CEO, was the right man for the job.

Goldberg admired Barr from the start. One of the late chairman's best friends, Clive Cummis, told the (Newark) *Star-Ledger* reporter Judy DeHaven, "He saw that Wally was a real talent."

Barr was schooled in the mechanics of the company from the operations end of the business. He'd been a casino auditor and worked successfully within the Nevada and New Jersey gaming markets. He maintained an affinity for Caesars Palace.

When he took over in September 2002, the understated Barr had to overcome the perception that Park Place was a stagnant, twenty-nine-casino behemoth with $4.7 billion in annual revenues that was wallowing in nearly $5 billion in long-term debt. He had to show that the company had focus and direction. These were the things major investors look for almost as much as quarterly profits.

The best way to do that was to recapture a little of the Goldberg magic. Barr did so by changing the company's name to Caesars Entertainment, which immediately turned the corporate perception away from Atlantic City to Las Vegas.

"The new name will strengthen our position as a global leader in the gaming industry and drive increased name recognition of the company, our corporate objectives and our strategy," Barr announced. For all Goldberg's wisdom, choosing the Boardwalk-centric Park Place as the company's name in 1998 had been an image blunder.

In Las Vegas, the original Caesars Palace underwent a much-needed $250 million redesign. This included the creation of a $95-million Coliseum theater for pop diva Celine Dion. Add to that a $380-million hotel tower and convention facility, and Caesars was poised to freshen its laurels. Caesars now advertised itself as the resort where guests could "Live famously."

A record number of guests would have to do that and more to offset the bloated $3-billion purchase price Park Place had made to acquire it and similarly branded properties after a bidding war against an apparently bluffing Steve Wynn. The appointment of the dynamic Mark Juliano to run the newly directed Caesars gave observers hope that the Strip's venerable high-roller paradise's best days were yet to come.

Dion's platinum-record popularity aside, Caesars also carved out a relationship with her husband-manager, casino whale

Rene Angelil. Angelil was known to gamble millions at his favored casino, and the pact with his wife ensured he'd be spending a large piece of his vast fortune at Caesars, where he was rumored to hold a percentage of the theater designed to his spouse's exacting specifications.

There was another side to Angelil that surfaced when a South Korean woman, Yun K. Sung, accused him of rape. With his wife's career about to be reignited in Las Vegas, Angelil paid $2 million to Sung to keep what he characterized as her false allegation out of the press.

After Angelil cut the hush-money check, it was Sung's turn to feel the heat. She was suspected of failing to redeem $950,000 in casino markers and faced the possibility of felony charges from the district attorney's office. She also was believed to have returned to Angelil for another payoff, this time $20 million.

It was only after she'd been paid once that she filed a police report, a move that backfired when police charged Sung and her husband, Ae Kwon, with extortion.

Meanwhile, the sex-assault allegations and extortion charges associated with the Angelil-Sung case had no affect on Dion's popularity with fans. Next, Caesars added to its entertainment coup by signing piano-rocker Elton John to a long-term, multi-million-dollar contract to alternate with Dion.

By March 2004, Caesars Entertainment was being touted as one of the last bargain stocks in the Gaming Inc. portfolio: Not because it was performing up to its potential, but at least in part because Barr had acknowledged that serious problems existed and was correcting them. With the Caesars Entertainment name change had come a renewed energy in the once-complacent company.

Caesars Entertainment had survived, but remained a weakened company. And in Las Vegas that meant it was a natural for a takeover.

# Carl Icahn Goes Shopping

## 27

The Carl Icahn legend includes the story about how the brilliant young philosophy graduate from Princeton launched his business career with a bankroll won at a small-stakes poker game. It's a colorful tale sprinkled with green-felt romance, but no matter the smattering of truth it contains, only a rube would take it seriously.

It's understandable that a man considered the ultimate stock-market gambler might want people to believe player's luck led to his status as a billionaire and placed him among the most-dangerous casino sharks in Las Vegas. It's a striking image and dovetails nicely into Las Vegas's hyperbolic history. But it's a bit like saying crazy Bobby Fischer became a chessmaster after playing a game of cracker barrel checkers. It doesn't account for the quirkiness of the character and the genius of his work.

Understanding the real Icahn isn't easy because the man

remains an enigma even to those in the business press who follow his career closely. In March 2005, *Fortune* magazine called him "Icahn the Spoiler."

He has almost single-handedly rewritten the meaning of aggressiveness in American business. What this means for the future of Las Vegas is simple: If Carl Icahn wants to, he can feed on any of the gambling world's corporate giants. In a corporate casino culture defined by the wealth and maturity of Kirk Kerkorian, Icahn is younger, almost as wealthy, and far more aggressive than the old MGM business lion.

True to form, Icahn has made his billions by picking off the weakest companies first, although he doesn't close every deal he starts. His runs on Tappan, Marshall Field's, American Can, Phillips Petroleum, TWA, Texaco, USX (formerly U. S. Steel), and, more recently, Reliant Energy, Kodak, and Global Crossing have made him a fearful presence.

The mere mention of his name is enough to send shivers through corporate bosses.

One summer morning while shaving, a news report on NBC caught his attention. It concerned a proposed merger between two pharmaceutical companies. Mylan, the company planning to take over King Pharmaceuticals, was watching its stock price fall rapidly. Icahn made a few phone calls. By sunset, he owned one million shares in Mylan. Within two months, he was that company's largest shareholder. His 9.8-percent stake was worth more than $450 million.

It was probably that kind of whim that inspired him to acquire his first casinos. He became the owner of the Stratosphere Tower and two Arizona Charlie's casinos in Las Vegas. He also bought the Sands in Atlantic City. These holdings only suggest what he could do if he put his mind and money to it.

In late 2003, Icahn's name was floated in connection with the possible $150-million to $200-million acquisition of the Las Vegas Hilton, a 3,500-room convention and business hotel and casino.

While dilettantes such as Donald Trump were dabbling with verbalizing about acquiring the Riviera or perhaps building time-share high-rise condominiums on the Strip, Icahn was circling larger prey. He understood to establish a real presence in Las Vegas one had to fill hotel rooms. It was obvious that with a critical mass of in-house casino patrons, the corporate casinos could prosper even in the face of high-interest bond payments and cutthroat competition.

Here, again, Icahn's deep pockets and his Wall Street connections gave him an edge. His place in the casino forum was an improvement on the breed of casino men defined by the excesses of Steve Wynn, the creative expansionism of the Mandalay Resorts group, and the corporate stiffness of Harrah's Entertainment. Icahn, if he wished, could carve pieces of many corporations and, with a focused management plan, amass a competitive operation with little personal risk and large returns.

The Stratosphere was a dream situation for him. It had underperformed since its 1995 opening, was mired in management shake-ups, and suffered from its poor location.

He bought it for a fraction of its original $550-million construction cost.

When the Becker family ran into licensing trouble, Icahn strolled in to pick up the little locals gold mine, Arizona Charlie's on Decatur. A second neighborhood casino was later added.

Icahn was born on February 16, 1936, in Brooklyn and raised in Queens by strait-laced, middle-class Jewish parents, Michael and Bella Icahn, who wanted their son to be a doctor. They couldn't foresee that he would become a Wall Street speculator whose very name would strike terror in the hearts of those who were vulnerable to a takeover.

Icahn's most notable achievement at Princeton came in his senior year when his research thesis, "The Problem of Formulating an Adequate Explication of the Empiricist Criterion of Meaning," won first prize. His unauthorized biographer Mark Stevens says this gave him "a philosophical frame-

249

work for applying his considerable intellect to real-life challenges."

Icahn remarked, "Empiricism says knowledge is based on observation and experience, not feelings. In a funny way, studying twentieth-century philosophy trains your mind for takeovers. . . . Thinking this way taught me to compete in many things, not only in takeovers, but in chess and arbitrage."

The empiricist ethic was hard-wired into Icahn's thinking when he stepped through the door of his first brokerage firm, Dreyfus & Co. He had quit medical school because he saw wealth in his future without a stethoscope. He fancied himself a Wall Street outsider brilliant enough to beat insiders at their own game.

Icahn came of age among other corporate raiders in the 1980s. Actually, he'd made bold moves on Wall Street for more than a decade before his name made headlines. It was just that, by 1989, his deals were large enough to attract the attention of the national business press.

Icahn succeeded without one component common to many of his contemporaries, who thrived on endless image making. He didn't court the press. He once showed up late for an important interview with a reporter from a major business publication. Instead of impressing the writer with tales of his achievement and self-importance, he fell asleep during the questioning.

One story tells of his meeting with a major Drexel Burnham Lambert official and excusing himself to change his socks. It was an apparently compulsive ritual he repeated on other occasions. With Icahn, it's impossible to say the man changes his mind as often as he changes his socks.

In the late 1970s, Icahn added real-estate investment trusts to his acquisition targets list. He ran roughshod over such organizations as Chicago's Baird & Warner Mortgage & Realty Investors. He bought up their stock, jacking up the price, then sold it for millions in profits to finance his takeover.

In 1979, Baird & Warner was renamed Bayswater Realty & Capital Corporation. Bayswater was the section of Queens, New York, where Icahn had grown up after his family moved from Brooklyn. By the time the ink was dry on the corporate papers, Icahn was selling off its assets and turning his attention to the struggling Tappan appliance corporation. He ran that one to the ground with his stock buy-and-sell activity.

Insiders quoted in Mark Steven's *King Icahn* point out that Icahn knew nothing about kitchen ranges and had no interest in owning the company for the long term. He was like a bored lion who stalks and hunts down an antelope not because he's hungry, but merely because the animal is slow afoot.

Icahn was so immersed in wheeling and dealing that he wouldn't take time out for a honeymoon. His wife, Liba, accepted reality. She told an interviewer, "Sometimes I feel there's no reason for him to work anymore, but then where is he going to go from here? In regular families, the husband works, and there is always something financially to look forward to. Husband and wife are building toward security. With Carl, accumulating more money is not going to make any difference. He doesn't need any more money. He just loves the game."

She stopped accepting things as they seemed when she discovered that busy Carl was having an intimate relationship with his secretary. She tried to have her prenup thrown out, saying that she'd signed it because she was pregnant and Carl said he would marry her only if she would sign a prenuptial.

Icahn has been described by some as a bully who takes advantage of the weak and ailing. He has a bit of the pugilist in him. He's at times a relentless school-yard scrapper, at others a punishing brute, and at others a skilled strategist with a desire to outbox an opponent and then knock him out. He's a heavyweight bruiser disguised as a Princeton-schooled philosopher. It's no surprise, then, that throughout his life, Icahn has viewed his work more in terms of a heavyweight fight or a military campaign than a series of business transactions and corporate negotiations.

"I'm like a gunfighter you hire to save the town," he once said. "That gunfighter is there to do good. However, he'll do what he does only if he knows he'll get paid for it."

Icahn's instincts are impeccable. He picked his way through the turbulent 1980s junk-bond era. He fended off skeptics who believed his ruthlessness, like that of the Drexel crew, would immerse him in legal problems. While competitors headed to federal prison camps, he emerged on the other side of the decade still running, still raiding, still intimidating, but, at last, settling into his one-man acquisition phase.

Icahn's reputation as a high-rolling sports bettor raised a few embarrassing questions during his Gaming Control Board license hearing. In the end, he appeared more like a Las Vegas guy than he was. The fact is, he had far less in common with a Benny Binion than with the legendary Bernard Baruch. And for Icahn, a man worth billions, what was a mere $500,000 wager on a Super Bowl game? Nothing more than a diversion from the far-greater gambles in Las Vegas that were made for his voracious appetite.

One development threatened the image of the Stratosphere. In 2003, law-enforcement sources cited the presence of a prostitution ring in the hotel. It included penthouse strippers and porn stars who performed for and serviced high rollers. With rates as high as $2,500 per hour, these working girls were bound to be noticed.

Icahn did not appear to be aware of this activity. If anyone in upper management could be tied to it, Icahn's gaming license would be at risk.

The Stratosphere was not alone in providing sanctuary for high-class hookers. After Howard Hughes bought the Sands and barred "women selling sexual favors," the lobby and casino floor of the Sands became like a perennial hookers' convention.

Not all Icahn acquisitions were successful. Seizing a corporation is one thing, running it quite another.

"Icahn has been a great critic of the management of American industry," labor negotiator Theodore Kheel told Mark

Stevens in *King Icahn*. "When he took over TWA he said, 'I'll show you how to do it.' But he fell flat on his face. He did a miserable job of running the airline."

Operations were not Icahn's strong suit. Neither was this his philosophical goal. As it is said about some military campaigns, Icahn was keenly concerned with winning the war. He paid little attention to the peace that followed. He was a conqueror, not a workaday drone.

Congress fretted over Icahn's maneuver to shirk liability for $1 billion in unfounded TWA pension-fund obligations by insulating the company from his other assets. By wide margins, Congress passed legislation aimed directly at Icahn's personal protection plan. The fund was an estimated $1.2 billion in the hole, and Icahn was presumed to be on the hook. But he wore down Pension Benefit Guaranty Corporation officials and in the end wound up making a $200-million loan to the foundering airline company to effectively freeze its pension plan.

Employees might recover the money they'd put in, but not a penny more. Icahn thus saved himself an estimated $1 billion in liability by doing what he'd done so well for so long: battering the opposition into stalemate or submission.

Nearly a decade after he sold TWA, Icahn still had it on his mind. When American Airlines attempted a takeover of TWA, which had entered yet another bankruptcy, Icahn reappeared. He'd managed to carve out a lucrative buyout when he departed TWA—an option to purchase hundreds of millions in discount tickets in exchange for a $190-million loan to the desperate airline.

While TWA treaded water in the mid-1990s, Icahn took advantage of the Internet revolution in the travel industry. He created Lowestfare.com, a travel booking Web site that offered low prices for airline tickets, especially on TWA. Icahn might have left the airline's front office, but his influence was a passenger on every flight.

Icahn's vampire act drew lawsuits by TWA management, but he prevailed in court because the deal had been cut with everyone's knowledge. He could not be blamed if his foresight was superior to that of his opponents. "It took hundreds of millions of dollars from TWA's revenue base," an airline official told *BusinessWeek*'s Ronald Grover.

Carl Icahn was a veteran of several Wall Street wars. He'd fought and survived every attempt by Congress to make him an outlaw. Still, little in his experience prepared him for the strange science at work at City Hall in Las Vegas when his Stratosphere went before the City Council and Mayor Oscar Goodman to get approval for a thrill ride.

For theme-park fanatics, the proposal was a dream come true. Riders would travel from up the side of the Stratosphere tower, across Las Vegas Boulevard, and back in something akin to a NASA-approved luge run. The company has assured critics that its ride would travel on superquiet polyurethane wheels and passengers would travel in an enclosed environment.

However, residents complained that Stratosphere's super ride would make too much noise and detract from the renewal going on in an area riddled with cheap motels and adult bookstores.

The mayor had made much of the neighborhood's resurgence and promised to support the residents. His immense popularity was enough to turn a majority of the council against Icahn's proposed ride despite heavy lobbying by veteran attorney John Moran Jr.

Icahn spent big dollars to surround himself with experts, but they failed him on the Stratosphere.

"This would never happen in New York," Icahn told Mayor Goodman.

"This isn't New York, Mr. Icahn," Goodman replied.

Icahn's position only worsened when it was reported that Stratosphere officials had threatened area Councilman Gary Reese with political repercussions. Reese was a Goodman favorite. The charge was denied by Stratosphere's president and chief executive officer, Richard Brown.

Icahn might have intimidated investment bankers and corporate CEOs, but Goodman, a one-time mob lawyer, had clients who were killers and underworld bosses. He wasn't impressed. By the time word of the meeting circulated at City Hall, Icahn had also lost the vote of City Councilman Larry Brown, a Harvard graduate. Council members Gary Reese and Lawrence Weekly also shunned the billionaire.

With less than twenty-four hours to go before the fateful City Council meeting, Icahn discarded his expert entourage and took the elevator to the tenth floor of City Hall for another meeting with the mayor.

He returned with a smaller attraction for the Stratosphere, whose rooftop already sported a roller coaster and "Big Shot" rocket ride. His $20-million super-thrill ride was doomed.

Except for the Stratosphere thrill-ride controversy, Icahn maintained a low profile in Las Vegas. He was widely known in casino-marketing offices as a man who was capable of betting any amount on a sporting event. But beyond the handy proximity of legalized sports betting and all-night action in the casino, Las Vegas seemed an ill-fitting place for the iconoclastic Ivy Leaguer. His name appeared in neither Las Vegas newspapers' gossip columns, and even some Stratosphere executives admitted they rarely saw their boss.

Restaurant owners, meanwhile, confirmed that they'd served meals to Icahn, and to them, he came across as more shy than aloof.

Stratosphere's Richard Brown kept saying publicly that Icahn was interested in expanding his casino holdings in Las Vegas. There were lots of deals, but few piqued Icahn's interest.

One property, the Las Vegas Hilton, appeared ideal. Park Place Entertainment had struggled to keep it competitive in the wake of Chairman Arthur Goldberg's death, but managers began to see it as a white elephant despite its 3,000 rooms.

It could be a gold mine in the right hands, but whoever operated the hotel had to understand the market and not be distracted by what was happening at the Strip's brighter, newer megaresorts.

*Barron's* first reported the Securities and Exchange Commission disclosure of the interest of Icahn's American Real Estate Partners in purchasing a 3,000-room Las Vegas hotel. The underperforming, three-decade-old Hilton was worth approximately $200 million, a price Icahn would pay as long as he knew he was getting the best of it. As if to underscore the psychological machinations at work, not long after the SEC filing was made, Icahn told a reporter that negotiations weren't active. Not until his price was met if his past history was prologue.

In the end, Icahn turned his back on the Hilton.

But he clearly wasn't willing to maintain an absentee-landlord status at his casinos. In late 2003, Icahn rattled the Sands in Atlantic City by firing General Counsel Frederick Kraus and Chief Financial Officer Timothy Ebling. The pair had been with the company for two decades and were considered to be stabilizing forces within a tumultuous operation. They'd guided the Sands through bankruptcy reorganization in 1998 and had separated the Sands from its parent company, Great Bay Casino Corporation.

The firings may have been beneficial, even necessary, but it was also pure Icahn, a man for whom the bottom line remained the only line with his time. Twenty years of loyalty didn't equate to profit.

The Sands was like an old ship taking on water. Its cash balance was down for two consecutive years, and its earnings before interest, taxes, depreciation, and amortization were off 36 percent. Losses had risen sharply, and its long-term debt topped $110 million.

Not even Icahn, with his icy reputation, could resist the rise in popularity of poker in America. Television programs featuring a "world tour" of top professionals as well as celebrity card games dotted the airwaves.

Whereas Binion's World Series of Poker had long held a slice of interest each year in the late spring, with the final table often being featured on ESPN, the poker fever now sweeping the nation sent the game into prime time. By early 2005,

*Barron's* reported that some 200 poker Web sites were making an estimated profit of $2 billion a year.

Icahn saw an opportunity and added a twist for his "Million Dollar Deal: Showdown at the Sands." For a $10,700 buy-in, players not only got a crack at a million dollars, but were also offered dinner with Icahn himself.

Of the event and its creator, one publicity writer enthused, "Legend has it that Icahn, who owns the Stratosphere and two Arizona Charlie's properties in Las Vegas, began his investment career with $4,000 in poker winnings in the early 1960s."

"I thought, why not take a shot?" Icahn told a reporter with uncharacteristic nonchalance. "The worse I could lose is a million bucks."

His enemies would never admit it, and he didn't dwell on the sentimental, but there is a human side to the driven Icahn. For example, he makes substantial contributions to children's rights advocacy groups, sponsors homes for single mothers and the poor, and contributes many millions to create scholarships.

Icahn has the potential to be the most dangerous, most successful operator in Las Vegas, although he has yet to show that he's willing to spend the time and effort it would take to compete against the likes of Terry Lanni, Steve Wynn, Glenn Schaeffer, Sheldon Adelson, and Michael Gaughan.

The Arizona Charlie's casinos are neighborhood properties that focus on local quarter slot players than national marketing. The Stratosphere literally straddles the divide between a Strip property and a downtown grind joint. And the Sands in 2005 continued to underperform in an Atlantic City market that in 2003 added the sparkling Boyd Group resort called Borgata.

The most-successful operators have been those who devote themselves to the day-to-day casino activity. The gaming product is virtually the same everywhere. A slot machine is a slot machine although microchip payoff percentages may differ, and a blackjack table is a blackjack table even with more generous rules. It's the personal service and image marketing that make the differences in Las Vegas.

Icahn, whose other business interests have always been hands-on affairs, has acted more like an absentee owner than one of the Strip's commanders.

When a longtime Icahn observer was asked the billionaire's ultimate goal in the gambling business, he responded with a short answer to the question "What does Carl Icahn want?"

The simple reply: "Carl wants more!"

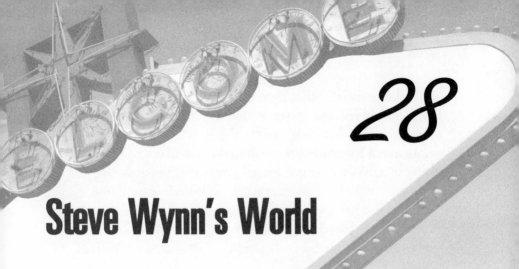

# Steve Wynn's World

T he smile says it all.

With his capped teeth, handsome surgically enhanced physical presence, and reputation as a charismatic public speaker, gaming mogul Steve Wynn has been dubbed "the Great Casino Salesman."

Until he was unceremoniously bought out of Mirage Resorts in March 2000, Wynn was the most dynamic, visible, and volatile figure in the gaming industry. Perhaps the only thing he sold more effectively than casino culture and his gaming properties was the Wynn legend itself.

He was the son of an East Coast bingo-parlor operator and gambler and was immersed in gambling even as a child. Nevertheless, Wynn was educated in the Ivy League. In interviews, he has spoken with nostalgia of the time when, as a ten-year-old boy, he was taken by his father, Michael Wynn, to Las Vegas.

Wynn recalled, "I remember thinking, 'What a place to live! What an incredible, outrageous environment! What a glamorous, colorful, totally bizarre environment this is! The fellows who control this town must be having a ball.'"

Michael Wynn was there to gamble and because he wanted to open a bingo concession at the mob-dominated Silver Slipper. His license application was rejected by the Nevada Tax Commission. Steve recalled that his father lost all his money and returned to his bingo hall at Waysons Corner, Maryland, a defeated man.

A decade later, Michael Wynn died during heart surgery. Steve, then a student at the University of Pennsylvania, was thrust into the family business. But he wasn't comfortable with the grind life of a bingo caller, even though he admitted years later that he owed everything he had to his bingo-parlor experience.

He used his father's contacts to buy a working percentage of the Frontier in a deal put together by Maurice Friedman. The Frontier was controlled behind the scenes by members of the Detroit mob and Meyer Lansky.

Wynn's Frontier experience deserves close examination.

His first foray into Las Vegas as an adult was disastrous. Following his father's death, the twenty-five-year-old Wynn paid $45,000 to buy a 3-percent stake in the Frontier. Of that, $30,000 was borrowed from a family friend named Frank Goldman. As part of the deal, Wynn was put in charge of the slot and keno departments. In October 1967, Wynn bought two more points in the project. While others toiled in obscurity, young Steve Wynn made contacts at the highest levels of Las Vegas banking society.

What was intriguing was that the Las Vegas neophyte was able to parlay his contacts and obtain his $30,000 loan from Valley Bank through E. Parry Thomas, the powerful Vegas figure.

Meanwhile, the Frontier's management facade was cracking.

Friedman and his cohorts had been exposed for their Detroit mob connections. Names that surfaced included those of mobsters Anthony Zerilli and Michael Polizzi. Then there was point owner Bernard Sindler, an associate of Meyer Lansky.

How Wynn found himself in such company has long intrigued Las Vegas historians. When the Frontier was finally busted in a federal hidden-ownership case, Wynn was called to testify, but was not implicated in any of the criminal activity. He managed to come through the investigation unscathed.

He'd swum among the sharks and survived. More importantly, he emerged from the dangerous waters with a companion and lifelong friend in E. Parry Thomas. Thomas, as detailed earlier, was the most important casino financier in the first fifty years of the Las Vegas story.

When a grand jury was convened to weigh evidence of hidden ownership in the Frontier, Friedman and his friends quickly decided to sell out. They found an eager buyer in Howard Hughes, the billionaire who inexplicably paid $24 million for a property worth perhaps half that. Although he had to divide his profits with his behind-the-scenes partners, Friedman had made his score.

Four years later, several members of the Frontier group were convicted in Los Angeles federal court in the hidden ownership case. By then Friedman had turned cooperating witness.

By then, too, thanks to banker Thomas, Wynn was several rungs up the ladder to bigger things. Thomas is credited with introducing Wynn to Best Brands, a Las Vegas liquor distributorship. Best Brands, a subsidiary of Schenley Industries, was known for its Dewar's Scotch and its historical ties to Prohibition bootleggers Lewis Solon Rosenstiel, Samuel Bronfman, and Lansky.

Despite the dream advantage of selling liquor in Las Vegas, Wynn ran up debt. His markers to Best Brands were eventually forgiven by Schenley.

Wynn sold Best Brands and with the $121,000 he collected from the sale, and the help of J&B Scotch executive Abe Rosenberg, he bought a 1.1-acre piece of real estate for $1.1 million from Howard Hughes. It just happened to be located next to Caesars Palace.

As the legend goes, Hughes never sold property. He made a rare exception for Wynn after a meeting with Parry Thomas, who gave Wynn a $1.2-million loan from Valley Bank.

Wynn announced that he'd build a slender casino between Caesars and Flamingo Road on one of the "Four Corners" of the Strip. This threat enabled Wynn and Abe Rosenberg to sell the land for $2.25 million on October 27, 1982. Wynn's share of the profit was $687,000.

He was going places fast, and Thomas was guiding him. Next, Wynn bought blocks of stock in the troubled Golden Nugget casino downtown. Thomas once attempted a takeover of the casino through Continental Connector Corporation, but was hamstrung by the Securities and Exchange Commission.

Wynn would have no such problem, and, for the first time, he found himself in a position to do something for Thomas. He bought 92,000 shares from casino man Jerry Zarowitz, whose associations ranged from Genovese crime family boss Anthony Salerno to New England mob boss Raymond Patriarca.

Wynn moved into the Golden Nugget's front office. He unceremoniously ousted President Buck Blaine and embarked on an ambitious remodeling plan.

Once Wynn assumed control over the cash flow, the Golden Nugget's profitability began to grow. The hotel and casino gained a reputation for service and sparkle that reminded visitors more of a Strip place than of the increasingly ragged Fremont Street. When Wynn added a tower to his hotel and copious amounts of brass and marble, upscale restaurants, and special events featuring Frank Sinatra, the Golden Nugget became dominant in the downtown market. It was Wynn's laboratory and playground.

While at the Golden Nugget, he began flexing political muscle. When he decided to expand the hotel across Carson Street, he didn't build above it. Instead he persuaded elected officials to approve a plan to close the street. To this day, the Carson Street Café unofficially commemorates Wynn's first major political victory. There would be many more to come as he learned how to manipulate judges and politicians with contributions and publicity.

However, early attempts to expand his casino empire beyond Las Vegas created problems and led to several defeats.

In Atlantic City, Wynn's license application was stalled because several women accused him of using cocaine. This coincided with his being mentioned in a Drug Enforcement Administration investigation. He produced affidavits refuting the claims of some of his accusers, who were casino workers and admitted drug users themselves.

Others recanted their stories, and Wynn was licensed. He immediately embarked on turning Golden Nugget Atlantic City into a record-setting casino. It became known for its brilliant commercials that featured Frank Sinatra and a self-deprecating Steve Wynn.

If the New Jersey license was difficult to obtain, approval to operate in Great Britain would prove impossible. The British Gaming Board relied on intelligence gleaned from New Jersey and Nevada authorities, as well as a confidential report from the New Scotland Yard.

After being advised he wouldn't be licensed in Great Britain, Wynn withdrew his application.

While the failed British casino foray was quickly forgotten in Las Vegas, it surfaced years later when I wrote *Running Scared: The Life and Treacherous Times of Las Vegas Casino King Steve Wynn*. Wynn attempted to block the biography's publication, then sued for libel in Kentucky. The suit was later dismissed with prejudice.

Not accustomed to being criticized on his home turf, Wynn also sued for libel over the publication of a Barricade Books catalog advertising *Running Scared*. I was dropped as a defendant in that lawsuit, which targeted publisher Lyle Stuart.

During the six-day trial, jurors were asked to scrutinize a fragment of a single sentence in the catalog that Wynn's attorneys claimed had defamed the public-figure plaintiff who enjoys a celebrity status in Las Vegas that rivals that of Wayne Newton.

The jury ruled in Wynn's favor at the trial, awarding him $3.1 million in damages. The Nevada Supreme Court overturned the decision, and the case was later settled with Stuart unbowed and no money changing hands.

Wynn hadn't won—in fact, his obsession with the case contributed to issues that eventually forced him to sell Mirage Resorts—but he'd sent a message to the world that he would fight to maintain his image in Las Vegas.

Reflecting back two decades, the Golden Nugget became one of the best-known small companies in gaming. Then Wynn became mired in a licensing dispute in Atlantic City. The problem was the Golden Nugget's casino marketing executive Charlie Meyerson. As an illegal bookmaker, Meyerson had booked Michael Wynn's wagers.

"Uncle Charlie" played host to dozens of members and associates of organized crime from New York to Florida. They were good customers. Testifying in the above libel trial, he was asked about ninety names in his black book of customers. All had Italian names and by a strange coincidence, most were members of or associates of the Genovese crime family.

Did Meyerson know that? Asked that question while under oath, he shrugged. "I didn't ask because I don't know or care what my customers do for a living."

The mid-1980s hearings were highlighted by the revelation that Mel Harris, a friend of the Wynn family, was hired as a vice president for the Atlantic City casino despite his total lack of experience. As if that weren't strange enough, Harris had twice been seen entering the Palma Boys Social Club in East Harlem to visit with Genovese crime family underboss Anthony "Fat Tony" Salerno.

When the FBI reported that information to Wynn and showed him the photographs, he immediately asked for and received Harris's resignation.

There were other oddities, such as the hiring of mob-connected marketers Irving "Ash" Resnick and "Big Julie" Weintraub.

Wynn explained it all and kept his license. But the flavor of the investigation angered him, and a short time later, he sold the Atlantic City Golden Nugget and announced that he would never return to such an inhospitable locale.

Atlantic City survived without him.

♦  ♦  ♦

If Parry Thomas helped create Steve Wynn's business life, then Wall Street junk-bond king Michael Milken brought him to maturity by showing him how to finance the $700-million Mirage with junk bonds.

Nothing like the Mirage had been seen before. A huge aquarium was the backdrop to the check-in counter. A faux volcano in front of the hotel attracted hordes of gaping tourists as it spewed flames and perfumed the air every fifteen minutes. A dolphin pool in the rear allowed visitors to enjoy the mammals. Siegfried & Roy presented a show in a special theater built for them at a cost of millions that gave new meaning to magic and illusion.

The Mirage became the place to be for high rollers.

With high-interest financing arranged by Milken, Wynn proved an army of skeptics wrong when the Mirage opened in 1989 and almost immediately generated the more than the $1-million-a-day drop necessary to break even.

The Mirage also provided a stage for Wynn to practice his various passions, one of which included surrounding himself with celebrities. He seriously considered creating a "Jackson attraction" theme park with Michael Jackson, only to have the plan fizzle when the pop singer was accused of child abuse the first time. Ten years later, Wynn was surprised to learn that Jackson had listed him as a character witness in his March 2005 trial for child abuse. Almost totally blind now because of his retinitis pigmentosa, he had no intention of appearing in a courtroom.

For years, one of the most-luxurious suites for high rollers at the Mirage was called the Michael Jackson Suite. It was decorated in ways designed to please Jackson.

Wynn also created an upscale submarine sandwich shop called Dive! in partnership with friends Steven Spielberg and Jeffrey Katzenberg.

Perhaps the greatest illustration of Wynn's freewheeling corporate lifestyle was his creation of the $48-million Shadow Creek golf course. This heavily secured facility located in North Las Vegas was not far from a waste-disposal transfer station. It was characterized by some observers as the single greatest perquisite in America's corporate benefits game.

Wynn built a spacious home for himself and his wife and two daughters on the property. It was surrounded by thousands of imported pine trees, streams, and ponds. He held tight to the keys to the kingdom: Only personal friends and select high rollers were permitted to play the course.

That philosophy stoked the curiosity of the nation's celebrity golfers and also of the Internal Revenue Service. Still, in Las Vegas in the early 1990s, to have a locker at Shadow Creek was to be a member of a very elite club.

High-rolling Japanese billionaire Ken Mizuno's locker was next to Wynn's. Basketball star Michael Jordan also had a locker there. But it was Mizuno's presence that intrigued federal investigators. They wondered whether the millions he'd been losing at the tables at the Mirage was simply the act of a gambling sucker or an investment from a man connected to Asian organized crime. Mizuno eventually took a fall in Tokyo on fraud and tax charges.

By then, Wynn had built the Treasure Island resort next to the Mirage. It was distinguished by a free attraction on the Strip in front of the hotel. This was the popular pirate-ship battle in Buccaneer Bay, an echo of the famous attraction at Disney's amusement parks. It was an instant hit with a segment of the travel demographic that, with the exception of Circus Circus, had never been marketed to: families with children.

Wynn wasn't alone in his pursuit. The Excalibur pushed a playful Arthurian-legend theme and contained an enormous arcade. The Luxor offered an entire floor of high-tech games and rides. The MGM Grand Hotel and Casino created a theme park based on *The Wizard of Oz*. But Wynn was the only casino mogul to add his own made-for-television infomercial starring a small boy and called "Treasure Island: The Adventure Begins."

The family marketing push fizzled, and critics chastised Las Vegas casino owners for their tacky pursuit of families in a tourist town built for adults.

Wynn quickly distanced himself. "This is a place for big kids," he said.

◆　　◆　　◆

Only for big kids? So was Wall Street.

With Thomas in retirement and Milken in prison for twenty-two months, Wynn had to rely on himself. He embarked on a financial road show to raise money for his proposed $1.6-billion Bellagio.

The Bellagio was considered the most-ambitious casino resort idea in history. The Bellagio would be a tribute to Italy's Lake Como region and would include a lake with a dancing-waters show set to classical music. Millions of dollars in fine art would hang on the walls of its pay-to-enter art gallery and its gourmet restaurants, one of which was named the Picasso.

Wynn announced that there would be a massive glass ceiling in the lobby created by artist Dale Chihuly. This would be an enormous glass flower arbor to give guests a sense of tranquility in the midst of the Las Vegas bedlam. It would cap the entrance to the most-luxurious Las Vegas resort ever.

The ceiling cost $2 million to design and construct.

"Bellagio will become the alternative to Paris as a weekend getaway," Wynn announced.

But the unspoken question was would it earn back its investment and actually turn a profit for bondholders who'd bought into Wynn's vision?

The Bellagio was indeed spectacular. It lived up to its promises. Its problem was that it drew much of its best players from the customer base of its sister casino, the Mirage.

Wynn had outdone himself and in the process undone himself by doubling the debt load of the company to $2 billion and raising eyebrows throughout the investment community. Then it was reported that he was using his own millions and millions more in stockholder funds to buy, mostly at auctions, the creations of Picasso, Renoir, Monet, and Modigliani. Wynn sweetened his purchases by ramming an art tax-relief law through the Nevada legislature.

Mirage stock began to lose its strength. As its price fell, stockholders became more aware of Wynn's personal lavish lifestyle. He once used the company plane to fly from Las Vegas to Idaho just to bring him some Chinese food.

He promised a Broadway-worthy musical in his showroom and the latest offering from Cirque du Soleil, but managed to alienate some stockbrokers and analysts during a road show by lip-syncing the words to songs from *Miss Spectacular*, a Jerry Herman musical he proposed for Bellagio.

"They couldn't get out of that room fast enough to phone in their sell orders," an eyewitness told the *New York Post*.

While Mirage Resorts stock was falling in price, Wynn was locked in a nasty battle with Donald Trump. The tactics used by both sides distracted Wynn and made his company more vulnerable. When stockholders thought he should watch his stock price and improve his bottom line, he was flying to Europe with singer Paul Anka on a private plane to buy more art. He could afford it: The company picked up the tab for his use of an MD-80 jet, and he arranged for it to pay him $5.2 million a year for the privilege of leasing his personal art collection.

In 2002, Donald Trump's attorney Donald Campbell said that federal law enforcement had opened an investigation of Wynn under the code name "Operation Snake Eyes." Campbell was poised to embarrass Wynn and his security henchmen for their alleged corporate espionage efforts, but the carpet was pulled from under him and the case settled.

Trump and Wynn had said things about each other that an

average person would never forgive. These two were quintessential opportunists and saw a lot of themselves in the other. They became friendly enough for Wynn and his wife to be invited to Donald Trump's wedding in 2005. It was Trump's third marriage. Wynn had been married twice, but to the same woman.

Now Wynn had a larger issue on his agenda: Out of the blue, a takeover offer was presented to his board of directors by Kirk Kerkorian, the crafty fox who owned MGM Grand. The initial offer was rejected by the board whose members included Wynn's wife, Elaine, and several close friends. When Kerkorian raised his bid and stockholders simultaneously filed class-action suits against Wynn and the Mirage, the board had little choice but to accept the buyout offer. Negotiations ended twelve days after the initial bid with MGM acquiring Mirage Resorts for $21 a share, or $6.7 billion.

Wynn didn't need welfare assistance. His share of the buyout was an estimated $500 million. But the sale shook him up for it cost him what was even-more important than the money: his power base.

"The game he'll miss is perks galore, and few know how to play the angles better than Steve Wynn," business writer Ronald Grover observed.

Nor had anyone received more credit for redefining the new Las Vegas. Steve Wynn was down, but not out.

# The Comeback Kid

Steve Wynn quickly showed he was a comeback kid.

After selling the company that had been his personal kingdom, he was quoted as saying that he would never again deal with Wall Street or the media.

A month or so later, he purchased the venerable Desert Inn hotel-casino and golf course. Calling it a birthday gift for his wife, Elaine, he said he would demolish the building and build a resort to top all other Las Vegas resorts.

Wynn gathered the veteran staff of the Desert Inn and assured them he would keep the hotel and casino open "for at least another year." Two weeks later, he closed everything and fired the entire staff.

If he were to make his comeback, he'd need a grand plan. More important, he'd require the kind of capital that institutional investors weren't likely to advance without a long list of assurances. In their eyes, he had to prove himself all over again.

More than anything, Steve Wynn needed a partner.

♦　　♦　　♦

271

Shortly after the twentieth century became history, Steve Wynn, the person most credited with sparking the new Las Vegas, was a man without a casino.

With nearly half-a-billion dollars from the MGM buyout and the tax man's clock ticking, Wynn bought the Desert Inn and its adjacent undeveloped acreage for $270 million. Shortly thereafter, his Valvino Lamore limited-liability company scooped up lots in and around the Desert Inn Golf Course for $47.8 million.

Wynn was on his way to amassing what appeared to be the last best collection of real estate on the Strip. He promised to build a hotel and casino that would make Bellagio obsolete. With his usual flare, he christened it "Le Reve," or "The Dream," after a Picasso painting of that name that he owned. This portrait of a young woman, Picasso's lover, was rife with phallic imagery.

In the wake of his unceremonious dumping by Mirage Resorts, his announcement was received skeptically by those familiar with his expensive tastes and flamboyant history as a developer. Most of the cash he'd walked away with from the MGM buyout was invested in the new property.

In 1950, the Desert Inn had been the fifth hotel-casino to open on the newly named Strip. It set a new standard for Vegas opulence and service and eventually expanded to 715 rooms with a 30,000-square-foot casino and championship golf course. But as new modern palaces sprung up, it fell from the ranks of the contenders on the boulevard.

With Wall Street still snickering over his well-documented excesses as Mirage chairman and all but his most loyal institutional investors taking a wait-and-see attitude, he sought capital elsewhere. He found his mark in Japanese pachinko king Kazuo Okada. The deal appeared simple enough: Wynn sold a 50-percent stake in Le Reve's development company to Okada for $260 million. Wynn had found a billionaire partner.

While his attorneys and frontmen pursued the purchase of the remaining homes lining the Desert Inn's award-winning golf course, Wynn worked twelve hours a day on his dream project. Simultaneously, he did some fence mending with Wall Street investment houses.

Okada remained in the background as the Gaming Control Board began the arduous process of investigating a foreign gaming giant. Although some Control Board insiders had long looked upon Okada with suspicion—some of Japan's original pachinko operators had been associated with the infamous Yakuza organized-crime syndicate—the fact was that Okada had been doing business in Nevada for a quarter-century through his Universal and Aruze slot companies.

Although Universal had become dormant in recent years, there was a time when it was the most-aggressive slot company in Las Vegas. By the late 1980s, Universal was a dominant player in the Nevada market with more than 10,000 sales and had sold thousands of machines to Europe, Asia, Australia, and South America. Okada took profits from his slot-machine sales and bought two dozen hotels and office buildings, as well as a chain of pizza restaurants. He also met Steve Wynn through attorney Frank Schreck, whose career profited handsomely from his relationship with both men.

"Universal virtually transformed casino gambling in the 1980s," wrote Jeff Burbank in *License to Steal: Nevada's Gaming Control System in the Megaresort Age*. "Its innovative computerized slot machines became the most popular among players who thought Universal's were more fun and paid out more often. The higher volume of play translated into higher casino profits."

When the Mirage opened in 1989, it featured more than seven hundred Universal slot machines with their jackpot outcomes determined not by the traditional mechanical slot infrastructure, but by what was then an innovation. It was the computerized "random number generator."

When Universal attempted to expand the "near-miss" function of its machines, wherein the slots are programmed to exploit players by showing jackpots just above or below the pay line in a Pavlovian strategy, Gaming Control regulators were called upon to investigate the company.

The near-miss function raised the issue of whether Nevada casino regulators were doing enough to protect customers from being tricked by technology. The state had always prided itself on guaranteeing the gambler an honest game, and the near-miss functions were programmed to hold the sucker at the machine until his or her pockets were empty.

"Everyone has done it, and they have always done it," Schreck lectured the Gaming Control Board in a hearing. "We should not be penalized."

The head of the Control Board's gaming lab, Ed Allen, argued against approving the near-miss. In the end, after two hearings, the Nevada Gaming Commission voted against allowing the near-miss function, and Universal fell from the ranks of the state's slot giants.

Nevertheless, Okada was expanding his empire. He continued to dominate the slot and pachinko business in Japan. (Pachinko is a pinball-like gambling game popular in that country.) By the time he entered into his partnership with Wynn, Okada appeared ready to emerge as a major player on the Strip.

Okada's background check was complicated by a series of miscommunications. Despite his lack of cooperation, he seemed to be on the verge of being approved when it was learned that he was under investigation in Japan for tax irregularities.

There was media speculation that Okada's tax problems would end his partnership with Wynn and scuttle the project. Okada was accused of concealing $35 million in income from 1996 to 1998. According to Kyodo News Service, Aruze was assessed $14.9 million in fines. Although Aruze USA technically was a subsidiary of the controversial parent corporation, the Okada clan had been in charge since founding the company in 1969, and even Wynn's glib personal spokesman, Billy Vassiliadis, couldn't come up with a defense.

Gaming Control Board Chairman Steve DuCharme, a former police officer, had no difficulty capturing the essence of the investigation. "Sometimes individuals or companies use aggressive methods to reduce taxes that turn out not to be in accordance with tax law," he told a reporter. "On the other hand, sometimes they make an outright attempt to evade paying taxes."

Okada appeared to have been playing a game in which he'd controlled both ends. He had arranged for Aruze to purchase the near-dormant Universal, a company he also owned, at what some regulators believed was an inflated price. It was a move DuCharme likened to insider trading and might have come complete with "phantom transfers" of money in an effort to make Universal look more financially attractive than it was.

Control Board Chairman Dennis Neilander asked, "When it comes to taxes, I ask if there was a willful attempt to evade taxation."

Wynn remained steadfast in his support for his indispensable partner.

Lesser players with inferior political and legal contacts might have tossed in their hand, but Okada was Wynn's partner, and Wynn was one of the best manipulators of the Nevada legal system in the history of gaming. With Schreck's assistance, Okada waded through a morass of questions by the Control Board. In the end, he was victorious.

Okada was licensed on June 4, 2004. His gaming-regulatory process had been slowed by the tax investigation in Japan. It became a foregone conclusion once Nevada authorities were assured that the Japanese investigation had not centered on his actions as chairman of the $1-billion Aruze Corporation. Although regulators and journalists were quick to point out that Okada had been licensed by Nevada for more than twenty years for his Universal Distributing, these stories failed to mention that his earlier licensing also had been difficult because of personal tax problems.

He was found guilty of tax evasion in 1984 in Japan according to a Gaming Control report. That fact didn't keep him from selling his popular slot machines in Nevada and elsewhere.

The realities of the new Las Vegas marketplace made

Wynn's fantasy of private ownership a pipe dream. If he wanted to top Bellagio, he would need not just a moneyed partner, but large long-term financing. This was the sort found on the Wall Street which with he claimed to have been so disenchanted.

Now Wynn had only to address issues of his own profligacy and make assurances that his new project would stay within its estimated construction cost. Bellagio had gone from a $1.3 billion to $1.6 billion project, shaving potential profits before the front door opened to the public. Between overruns and Wynn's lavish spending, analysts looked askance at Wynn's leadership.

But the Desert Inn site indeed was special. Its 220 acres featured enormous water rights, a precious commodity in parched Southern Nevada. With 2,000 feet of Strip frontage and another 2,500 feet lining Paradise Road, it held the potential to become a veritable casino continent near the heart of the biggest gambling/tourism enterprise the world had ever known. Wynn was right about the land: It was an imprint a casino developer might only dream about.

When the time came to generate the working capital necessary for the $1.85-billion plan, an initial public offering was brokered at $23 a share. However, in October 2002, Wynn's investment bankers found a chilly reception in the marketplace. Some looked at Wynn's dismal bottom line showing at Mirage Resorts. Others were influenced by post-September 11 skittishness.

The $23-share price was out of the question. The offering price dropped to $21, then $20, then $18. It fell to $13. Now the investment bankers were forced to increase the offering from twenty million shares to thirty-two million in order to generate the $400-million target.

Wynn and Okada bought shares of their own stock, but by late October, "WYNN" began trading on the NASDAQ stock market despite the fact the company would only take on debt in its first thirty months in operation. That fact was reflected in its flat trading price, which dipped into single digits before creeping upward. But creep upward it did with Wynn's publicity

276

machine operating on all cylinders. By March 2005, the price had risen to $74.

In local gossip columns, Wynn wasn't above floating coy comments and planting zingers in the form of his latest raid on rival gaming company executives. The avid art collector let it be known that he had been among those present when an anonymous $104-million bid was made for a Picasso at a New York auction in May 2004. The man who'd vowed he was finished with the press became easily accessible as his new resort project grew closer to completion.

Wynn's plan called for $374 million to flow into Le Reve. He renamed it Wynn Las Vegas.

The Las Vegas construction-financing plan included a $340-million, high-interest second mortgage of the sort Wynn used to build the Mirage more than a decade earlier. The company also arranged for a $1-billion bank credit line, assuring that it could purchase restaurant equipment and furniture. Total cost: $2.7 billion.

Although the original deal called for Wynn and Okada to own even more of the company, the compromise still left them in an ownership position that exceeded Kirk Kerkorian's share of MGM Mirage.

In its corporate filing, Wynn was careful to report that the jet and art gallery operation would be "included in the Company financial statements." To some, Wynn was sending a message to skeptics who wondered whether he'd learned from past mistakes.

"The Company previously leased the Wynn Collection from Mr. and Mrs. Wynn at a monthly rate equal to the gross revenue received by the gallery each month, less direct expenses, subject to a monthly cap," the pro-forma states. ". . .Under the new terms, one-half of the net income, if any, of the gallery is retained by the Company."

Wynn's reputation as a bully resurfaced only weeks after he became owner of the Desert Inn. He attempted to evict residents of the Desert Inn Country Club Estates, whose homes lined the golf course. Initially, Wynn's plan was to acquire enough residences and lots to control the homeowners' association. Those who held out for a higher sale price or just plain refused to move faced formidable legal gamesmanship.

When control of the homeowners' association failed to garner the required result, which was to rapidly clear the area, a concrete-batch plant was built near the homeowners. Wynn bought more than fifty lots and homes in an effort to redevelop the property. A dozen homeowners with residences that lined the golf course refused to sell. Sharon Greenbaum, of the homeowners' association board, challenged the casino man, whose longstanding influence with the Nevada judiciary and politicians was legendary.

Wynn's attorney, Marc Rubinstein, said the casino mogul was "prepared, if necessary, to build around the existing homeowners." If so, it wouldn't have been the first time Wynn had isolated a reluctant seller. A decade earlier, he isolated an apartment-complex owner during the development of Treasure Island.

Greenbaum, however, was no pushover. She mounted a counterattack on the man she called a bully, saying he'd acquired homes and let them go to ruin in part to alienate the remaining residences. "There are rats and homeless people living in these houses," she told reporter John G. Edwards. It was a claim Wynn's attorneys refuted.

In the end, District Judge Mark Denton listened to arguments from both sides and ruled, rather courageously, given Wynn's volatile and vindictive reputation, that the residents had a right to remain on their property without harassment.

The golf-course border could not be used to drive them out. They not only had property rights, but their residency meant they also had an interest in the golf course. Whether they would want to continue living in homes located so close to such an enormous casino resort remained to be seen.

Wynn later benefited from the passage by the Nevada legislature of Assembly Bill 139, that specifically protected the water on his project from the oversight of the Public Utilities Commission. Residents of the Desert Inn Golf Course worried that their historical ties to the water use would be affected by the law, but were assured their interests would be respected. The course's original fifty-three homes were hooked into the Desert Inn's well.

In the end, Wynn Las Vegas became a forty-five-story resort with 2,700 luxurious suites. Its elegant casino occupied 111,000 square feet. It boasted an expansive water feature and lush setting. It offered fine dining, unprecedented shopping including a Ferrari dealership on site, and enough convention space to challenge MGM and Venetian for a place at the top of the market.

And it had all become possible because of the relationship he'd carved out with slot pachinko king Kazuo Okada.

"I just love him to death," Okada said of his partner at the resort's groundbreaking.

The two men from different cultures shared more than a common investment. They also knew the complications of being the leaders in their families and having brothers who were, to say the least, complicated characters.

At sixty years old, Kazuo's brother, Tomoo, wasn't a kid anymore. He'd lived in Las Vegas and had been expected to shepherd his family's vast slot-manufacturing and business interests. But Tomoo was too easily seduced by Las Vegas' hedonistic nightlife.

When Japanese law-enforcement authorities investigated what must have appeared to them a scheme to transfer untaxed funds out of the country, Tomoo was considered the weakest link. He embarrassed his brother, shamed his family, and endangered its massive investment through his profligate spending, notorious carousing, and questionable business moves. No matter how the tax investigation turned out, he would no longer be trusted within the company.

Instead of being put out to pasture, on March 1, 2003, he decided to take his own life in a traditionally Japanese way: death by ricin. Tomoo had ample understanding of chemistry. He mixed up a fatal dose of ricin from a handful of castor beans. After brewing the poisonous residue, he injected it and gradually began to fail. When a family member discovered him in the throes of a slow suicide, he was transported to a local hospital where he refused treatment and died.

Kenny Wynn's career as director of Wynn Development and Design also came to an abrupt end in early 2004 when information surfaced that tied him to a federal child-pornography investigation called Operation Predator. The fifty-year-old reportedly used his credit card to acquire access to online kiddie porno images.

In all, more than 100,000 names worldwide were captured during the investigation, which resulted in a series of indictments. A search warrant was served at Kenny Wynn's residence in February 2004, but he was not indicted. He was fortunate that his career made him a lower priority as law enforcement pursued users with jobs linked to children.

United States Customs officials were more concerned with school-bus drivers and day-care center employees than the brothers of casino titans.

Steve Wynn was overheard lamenting his brother's abhorrent behavior, adding that he was relieved that his mother hadn't been alive to see the headlines linking her youngest son to child pornography.

As the story faded from the local press, space was filled with updates from the Wynn Las Vegas construction site.

One month before Wynn Las Vegas was scheduled to make its debut, Andrew Bary, writing in *Barron's*, estimated the cost to complete construction at $2.7 billion. He described it as "yet another pile of glamorous bricks and mortar."

Wynn Las Vegas opened its doors in April 2005, and "the Great Casino Salesman" was poised to make a dramatic comeback.

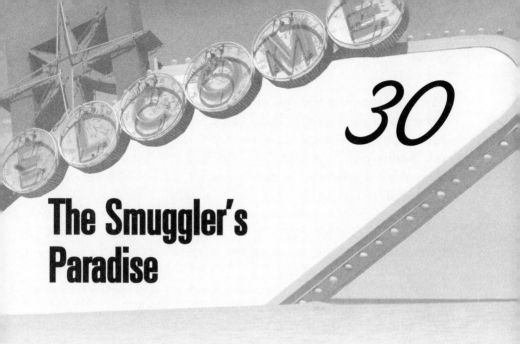

# The Smuggler's Paradise

W hen it came to controlling a major gambling hub, the Las Vegas guys had nothing on the ubiquitous Ho Hungsun in Macau.

Known as Stanley Ho, he accomplished his goals without shooting up the island. Instead, Macau's notorious Triad thugs handled the gunplay, and Ho maintained his image as a respectable businessman.

As director of Sociedade de Turismo e Diversoes de Macau (STDM) for forty years, Ho was the undisputed casino king of the Portuguese island. Located across Pearl River from Hong Kong, Macau was known throughout the world as a crossroads of Asian vice. It was a paradise for mobsters, smugglers, and prostitutes of many nationalities. It was also known as the exclusive turf of Stanley Ho.

That changed on midnight of December 20, 1999. It was then that the People's Republic of China took over control of

Macau, ending the Portuguese colonization that had existed for more than four hundred years. The Chinese assured Ho that it had no plans to change the island for at least fifty years, but the new ruler opened the door to competition in the casino business. With a gambling market exceeding $2.5 billion annually and unlimited growth potential from nearby China, opportunity was seductive to casino moguls everywhere.

Macau has a long history of Triad mob violence and the tight control by organized crime of the money-lending and prostitution rackets. If the streets teemed with tattooed Triad members and sallow, square-shouldered Russian Mafiya men and if more than five hundred of the approximately seven hundred inmates in the territorial prison were Triad members, the outside casino men appeared unconcerned. Neither did they give a second thought to the fact that Triad members outnumbered Macau's police by a 2-to-1 ratio, nor that the infamous 14K Triad boss Wan Kuok-koi, alias "Broken Tooth Koi," had a reputation at least as bloody as Al Capone's.

No matter. There was gold in that there island, and Las Vegas casino owners were determined to mine as much of it as possible.

Yes, they knew that the VIP gambling salons at several casinos, though officially under the supervision of Stanley Ho, were really run by mob insiders who marketed junkets and provided various "services" to their customers. In that world, Ng "Market" Wai was an example of a force to be reckoned with.

Would the Chinese takeover change all this?

People who knew the score found the thought of a Macau suddenly transformed into a model of propriety difficult to believe.

For generations, Macau was a center for trafficking in humans for prostitution and slave and indentured labor. Legal gambling halls were introduced to the island in the 1850s, which ironically made Macau a progressive place by the Las Vegas moral and business models. It also was a hub for trading in opium and gold.

Treaties with other nations had little effect on business in Macau. If the world frowned upon opium trading and whore running, it was of little moment to the island's pirates and pimps. And as long as the Portuguese government exacted its share of the profits, it turned a blind eye to irregularities, making sure only that Macau remained open and running.

All of which, one might think, would have changed with the rise of Communist China. But Portugal was not a country with clean hands. It had aided the Nazis in World War II by providing them with supplies in exchange for pillaged gold. Macau became known as a black-market capital.

Portugal eventually settled its debts for a small fraction of the tons of gold it received. Macau stood at the center of the world gold trade for decades, and much of the Nazi gold found its way into the coffers of the Chinese government. Trade sanctions by the United States were softened by the supply of illicit gold.

"If this theory is true, then an extraordinary scenario emerges: capitalist Macau, ruled by then fascist Portugal and equipped with Nazi gold, helped communist China survive throughout its first difficult years of existence," writes Bertil Lintner in *Blood Brothers: The Criminal Underworld of Asia*.

But all that was history, wasn't it?

Now there were billions to be made, the strongest kind of bait to attract such faraway sharks as Las Vegas tycoons Sheldon Adelson and Steve Wynn.

Whatever the dangers, the risk was justified by potential casino profits. Adelson and Wynn hurried to stake their claims. Nor were they discouraged by the fact that casinos are taxed at a whopping 35 percent of their gross revenue or that casinos accounted for 59 percent of the island's total tax receipts.

Ironically, these were the very same men who went wild when any heretic in the Nevada state legislature dared to suggest that the gaming tax be raised to 9 percent.

Macau was not one of those inviting islands in the sun, and yet in 2005, gross gaming revenues will exceed $5 billion. Profit promises were immense. Macau is the closest gambling city to more than one billion Chinese customers. These were a people with an appetite for gambling who were barred from legally gambling in their home provinces.

By 2020, the Chinese government was expected to issue as many as 100-million worldwide travel visas, which was good news for Macau and other gambling and travel destinations, as well.

Sands Venetian president Bill Weidner told *Las Vegas Review-Journal* reporter Rod Smith, "We believe we can help bring a major portion of those to Las Vegas."

In March 2002, the Galaxy gaming consortium headed by Sheldon Adelson and Hong Kong business tycoon Lui Chi Wo made history in Macau when it became the first casino not controlled by island billionaire Stanley Ho Hung-sun.

Those who have studied Adelson's business history may have wondered when the mercurial mogul would file his first lawsuit in Macau. They didn't wait long, for Adelson squared off against one-time business associate Moshe Hananel, the former president of Adelson's Israel-based Interface Partners International. Hananel claimed he'd used his influence on the island to connect Adelson to officials who sped the licensing process and gave him a tremendous advantage over the competition.

Hananel was fired and argued that Adelson had reneged on his promise to give Hananel a 12-percent share of the gaming operation in exchange for helping him get licensed by the notoriously dicey government.

Adelson, through his attorney, David Friedman, called Hananel's claims false and the actions of a "disgruntled former employee." If Hananel hoped for a settlement from the pugnacious Adelson, his hope was in vain. Instead of retreating as his Macau casino grew close to its spring 2004 opening, Adelson went on the attack. He filed a lawsuit that accused Hananel of misappropriating funds.

After granting Adelson a gaming license, Macau officials indicated an interest in entering the emerging Asian convention and trade-show business. This was new territory for Macau, but right up Adelson's alley.

"Macau is going to surpass Las Vegas," Adelson predicted to a group of exhibit managers, while being careful to add that Las Vegas's future was also bright. If he was concerned about the Macau market vulturing the Las Vegas market, it didn't show.

Adelson's casino opened on May 18, 2004. It contained 360 betting tables, almost three times as were in the Venetian. A table at the Sands Macau earns an average of $6,000 a day—or twice that earned by tables in the Venetian. The typical gambler in Las Vegas makes an average wager of $25. In Macau, the average is $85. Chinese gamblers also are eager to play more hands per hour, and at their request, cards are brought to the table already mixed so no time is lost in shuffling.

On the day it opened, more than 50,000 people pushed through its doors to try their luck. Adelson had beaten his hated rival Steve Wynn by at least two years. Although analysts noted that Adelson's dealers were slower than the competition, and as a result early income statements showed the Sands Macau hold (profits after all bets and expenses have been paid off) was less than its competition, it was an instant winner and a big addition to the Venetian owner's portfolio.

In fact, the Macau operation, dollar for dollar, generated the sort of income that could fuel Adelson's many expansion plans in Macau and back in Las Vegas, as well. Who needed Wall Street, Initial Public Offerings, and meetings of angry stockholders when he owned his own Asian money machine?

Adelson did things differently. As with the Venetian, the Sands Macau didn't make high rollers its priority. This protected him against a substantial short-term hit if some whale happened to get lucky. Vegans still recalled when Kerry Packer, an Australian billionaire, hit the MGM Grand for more than $20 million in forty-five minutes playing blackjack and baccarat with minimum $250,000-a-hand wagers.

On Adelson's opening day, it was reported that the fifteen casinos still controlled by Stanley Ho managed to generate $8.7 million. It was low for Ho, but still impressive. It was a not-well-kept secret the wise old bird Ho had known for years: With

285

so much of the market covered, and so many players streaming into his casinos, all he had to do to continue his huge success was to practice patience.

In addition to the 360 table games, Adelson's casino opened with 850 slot machines in a million-square-foot facility that left ample room for growth. With nearly two dozen restaurants and lounges, Sands Macau didn't neglect the creature comforts so familiar in Las Vegas posh resorts.

*Forbes* observed, "The deal with the Macau government obligates Adelson's group to spend $1.1 billion within 10 years. But although Adelson's refinancing of Sands Inc. . . . includes an allowance of up to $40 million for Macau, he also quietly revealed in an earlier 10K filing that his Las Vegas Sands Inc., which is privately held but issues public bonds, isn't 'obligated to pay' anything on the project. His only commitment is an option for a 30 percent stake. Who was staking Adelson? His less visible partners, who consist of prominent local (Macau) families."

And by breaking ground on the $240-million, million-square-foot Galaxy only days after receiving the government's go-ahead, he put himself at least a year ahead of Wynn's more-polished but less-certain venture. Adelson immediately talked about adding a second resort complex on Macau's flashy Cotai Strip. Estimated price tag of his Macau dream project: an incredible $10 billion.

If Stanley Ho was sweating the entry of the Las Vegas sharks into the Macau waters, he did a good job of disguising it. He remarked, "I won't be afraid of ten Sands casinos."

Although Ho might never admit it, Adelson's entry threatened to do to the Macau king what the Strip did to downtown Las Vegas. Ho's Casino Lisboa billowed cigarette smoke and was a second home for whores and loan sharks. When it was the only game in town, none of its thousands of customers—most of whom would never get to Las Vegas—knew what they were missing. That's what made Adelson's challenge formidable.

"We are the only casino with roots in Macau," Ho's spokes-women Nancy Wong said. "We have more than forty years of experience and a good network of hotels, retail, and property businesses."

Ho designed a forty-story hotel tower expansion at Lisboa. He took a page from the MGM Grand, a company with whom he was rumored to be negotiating. He announced that, like MGM Grand, he would build an amusement park and cultural village.

Ho had more business than he could handle. Adelson's inva-sion wasn't so much a threat as a chance to challenge the Macau master. While high rollers everywhere are given the best accom-modations, midlevel players at Lisboa complained of the crowd-ed casino and their near-anonymity. It was this group who stood to benefit most from the casino competition and distinctly "Las Vegas" atmosphere that Adelson offered.

Ho could no longer take players for granted because his monopoly position was gone. He took a lesson from an old dead associate, Triad godfather Yip Hon. Yip Hon was the visionary who saw the water-taxi service to the island as an essential com-ponent to the success of his own properties, but focused on his Hong Kong-to-Macau ferry operation, Shun Tak Holdings, to grow the market by delivering more players to his doors.

The company also entered into negotiations with Adelson's Sands/Galaxy Casino to purchase blocks of ferry tickets. This caused observers to wonder whether the Ho family understood what it was in for.

◆　◆　◆

Steve Wynn finally drew his pistol ready for action after the Macau legislative assembly passed more-relaxed lending rules. Wynn's hesitation might have been wise given Macau's crime culture and his own historic licensing difficulties.

Now Wynn would have to compete with the formidable Ho and the tenacious Adelson. The upside for Wynn was his choice of a site. He clearly took on Ho when he bought 6.5 hectares directly across from Lisboa that had been used for overflow parking.

His lack of a major investment in the island—under $25 million as of mid-2004—gave some skeptics pause, but on Wall Street, Wynn had regained footing in the fund-raising market. Despite offering nothing except the promises of profits to come, he managed to fund Wynn Las Vegas from those very Wall Street people whom he had publicly vowed never to deal with again.

At least in the short term, the Las Vegas sharks' daring swim in waters rife with decades of corruption and Triad influence appeared to be paying off.

But were these gamblers actually gambling themselves? The danger to the operation came not from the mysterious Triad, but from the Chinese government, which could at any moment decide to take control of the Macau gaming market.

## 31

# Sheldon's is Bigger

If Steve Wynn didn't have Sheldon Adelson in his life, he would have to invent him. Seldom in the turbulent history of the Las Vegas casino business have two casino-owning titans been more intense about wrecking each other's careers. *Forbes* in March 2005 quoted Adelson calling Wynn "a liar" and "an egomaniac" and described the two as detesting each other and knocking heads for a decade.

On the surface, they couldn't be more different.

Wynn is the quintessence of Vegas polish. Tall, well groomed, stylish, a charismatic speaker. To many, he defines the new Las Vegas casino owner. Wynn plays down his Jewish ancestry (the family's name was changed from Weinberg) and revels in being schooled by his father, a professional gambler.

Adelson is a squat, croaking micromanager with a wisp of vanishing gray hair and the ability to make even a welcome speech sound like a direct order. He is proud of his Jewish Ukrainian ancestry and is a dedicated supporter of Israel. He maintains business ties with that country.

The seventy-one year old Adelson likes to remind interviewers that he wasn't born with money or "swaddled in green felt" like others among the Strip's wealthiest casino owners. His father was a Boston taxi driver, and his mother ran a knitting shop. As an infant, Sheldon was so tiny, and the family's home so small, that his first bed was a dresser drawer.

But Sheldon Adelson has made a name for himself in business by not doing things in small ways. For example, he developed the Computer Dealers Association (COMDEX) convention into one of the world's largest trade shows. And he is planning to make the Venetian the world's largest hotel complex.

Owning the COMDEX show without having a hotel and casino to complement it made for an incomplete business model. In April 1989, Adelson, through his Interface Group, bought the Sands from Kirk Kerkorian for $110 million. Only one year earlier, Kerkorian had purchased the Sands and Desert Inn from Howard Hughes's Summa Corporation for $161 million.

While Adelson may have gotten more ghosts than gamblers for his money, the legendary Sands stood in a prime location. When it originally opened in December 1952, it was the only game in town for high rollers. Baccarat was introduced in its halls when Frank "Tommy" Renzoni brought the game to America from Havana. Renzoni's behind-the-scene "auspices" were the notorious Cellini brothers.

What helped the Sands stand out was its entertainment policy. This was directed by former Copacabana nightclub impresario Jack Entratter, a pal of mob boss Frank Costello. The Sands set a new Las Vegas standard when it featured a rotating ensemble that included Frank Sinatra, Dean Martin, Sammy Davis Jr., Joey Bishop, and Carol Burnett.

The Sands was home to Sinatra and his Rat Pack.

That warm relationship with Sinatra ended after several years on a warm spring evening. Sinatra was furious because he'd tapped out his credit line and the baccarat-table supervisor wouldn't authorize more chips. Sinatra charged into the Garden Room followed by two of his gofers and confronted Carl Cohen, a Sands owner.

Cohen had once been a boxer. Sinatra, having drunk too much, made a racist remark. It was not at all in keeping with his norm. The 300-pound Cohen stood up slowly from his table and punched Sinatra in the mouth. One punch was all it took to floor America's legendary crooner. He lay on the floor and shouted to his two gofers, "Do something!"

Cohen turned to them, fists ready. In a gentle voice, he asked, "What would you like to do?" The two men hurriedly backed several feet away. Meanwhile, Sinatra retrieved the two front teeth caps that had been knocked out of his mouth.

Finally able to stand up, he promised, to whomever was in hearing range, that he would take down the Sands by having his fellow Rat Pack members work elsewhere in Vegas. But Dean Martin, Sammy Davis Jr., and Joey Bishop were fond of the Sands and continued to appear there.

This happened shortly after Israel had scored a triumph in the Six Day War with Egypt. The Sinatra-Cohen encounter gave birth to the line "Never fuck with a Jew in the desert."

◆ ◆ ◆

The IRS intensified its inquiry into phantom ownership, counting-room skimming, and other potentially dangerous situations. One owner, Charley Kandell, was so worried about the situation that he suffered a mild nervous breakdown. The other owners weren't too complacent, either. Enter a solution. Howard Hughes bought the Sands for $14.6 million.

Years later, when Adelson's Interface Group acquired the property, the Sands was a kitschy shadow of its former self.

Adelson bought and sold dozens of businesses. He'd owned a small airline and a large tour-and-travel agency, American International Travel Service. News articles on Adelson called him "dictatorial" and noted that he had "a penchant for suing."

But the Sands deal would prove to be the happy turning point in his career.

Adelson's business beginnings provided an education that no university could match. On a lengthy list of holdings were Boston-area vending machines and bars of the sort that were favorite targets of the Patriarca crime family and the Winter Hill Gang. He had to be vigilant.

In *Black Mass*, Dick Lehr and Gerard O'Neill tell the story of two Boston vending-machine operators from a company called National Melotone, which ran into trouble from local organized-crime figures James "Whitey" Bulger and "Stevie the Rifleman" Flemmi.

The gangsters had their own vending interests and used intimidation to secure the most-profitable bar locations. When Melotone complained about these tactics to the Boston office of the FBI, its owners were startled when, instead of coming to their rescue, the agents advised them to mind their own business.

Years later, it was revealed that veteran Boston FBI agent John Connolly was allowing Bulger and Flemmi to run rampant in exchange for providing information on La Cosa Nostra characters. "If they wanted to prosecute, he was willing to, you know, to prosecute us," Flemmi recalled in an account in *Black Mass*. "But he said that they'd have to go into the witness protection program because of who we were."

"Back then, everybody paid," former Boston Mafia figure Anthony Fiato said. "One way or another, you found yourself in partnership with those people. They missed nothing, and they demanded respect. You don't show J. R. Russo or Larry Zannino or Whitey Bulger or Howie Winters the proper respect, and you don't have to worry about having a business anymore."

On arriving in Las Vegas, Adelson sailed through his gaming-licensing hearing. He had to answer some sticky questions about loans he'd forgiven to underworld characters. He also had to explain his friendship with controversial Boston gay-bar owner Henry Vara. (Among his many holdings, Vara owns the Great Barrington Fairgrounds racetrack in Massachusetts.)

Among Vara's many questionable holdings was Jacque's Cabaret, a Bay Village transgender bar notorious for its open prostitution. It also featured regular sightings of gangster "Whitey" Bulger. One of Jacque's neighbors said he grew weary of encountering "estrogenized men having sex on my front steps."

Adelson's Interface partner Irwin Chafetz, however, had a more difficult time. While he did his reputation no favors in Nevada, Chafetz was a philanthropist in the Boston area. Ridiculed in Nevada, he later received honorary doctorate degrees from Boston and Suffolk universities.

Longtime hotelman Henri Lewin, whom Adelson chose to operate the Sands, fared little better before the Control Board. Although Lewin had been a successful casino executive in Las Vegas for many years, he had ties to labor fixer Rudy Tham and Hawaiian debt-collector Johnny Yakoobian.

Although the Control Board unanimously recommended denial for Chafetz, the acrobatically limber Nevada Gaming Commission voted to reverse the recommendation.

The Sands' original cylindrical architecture had been eye popping. By the 1990s, it was a hopelessly outdated. Adelson was intrigued by the Strip, but was battling money problems. He aspired to rank among the top Boulevard developers. To do that, he'd need more working capital. He found it when he sold COMDEX and lesser trade shows to Japanese software manufacturer Softbank for $862 million in 1995.

Adelson moved on to the Venetian, but he did so without Chafetz and some of his other controversial partners from Interface. He combined his newfound wealth with a complex junk-bond financing deal and so was able to bankroll the Venetian, his grandiose dream project.

Adelson wasn't satisfied with just being a high-flying business-man. He yearned to spread his conservative, antiunion philoso-phy. He spent $2 million to support local candidates, and his battle against the Culinary Union made him such a polarizing figure that his support for anyone was like the kiss of a black-widow spider. He was hated by a large segment of the voters.

In 1998, with the Venetian under construction, Adelson financed a $2-million advertising blitz. Its purpose was to oust two incumbent commissioners and prevent a new one from gaining a seat. It fizzled like wet fireworks.

He joined forces with his sometime nemesis, Steve Wynn, and the two men spent freely to defeat a bid for Congress by Shelley Berkley. Despite their efforts, Democratic candidate Berkley was elected to Congress and subsequently was reelected.

While Republican Kenny Guinn was on his way to defeating Jan Jones in the governor's race, Guinn's strategists acknowledged that one of the turning points in the campaign was the rejection of Paycheck Protection, which would have prohibited using union dues for political action without written consent from individual members, and the wide dislike for Adelson.

"Paycheck Protection was a critical issue, but our decision had a lot to do with Sheldon Adelson," one top Guinn insider said.

Adelson was constantly battered by criticism because of his resistance to the Culinary Union's organizing efforts. He offered wages and benefits to hotel and casino service workers that were in some ways superior to the union's Strip contract.

By going to war with the Culinary Union and throwing cash around, Adelson, a staunch Republican, allowed himself to become the Democrat's best friend.

"The easiest way to beat Sheldon's candidates is to remind voters they're Sheldon's candidates," said Democratic political strategist Dan Hart. "He's his own worst enemy."

Adelson had one success. He got former police officer Lance Malone elected to the County Commission. Malone was defeated after one term in office following an ethics scandal and was later indicted in a federal corruption case.

Adelson once claimed a swastika written in soap had been found at his home. Rumors of death threats surrounded him when he was battling the Culinary Union. Soon the outspoken casino boss was traveling with armed, ex-Mossad bodyguards who made little secret that they carried guns even when they accompanied Adelson to an editorial board meeting at the *Las Vegas Review-Journal.*

Adelson's obsessive concern was evident in his attention to detail. Even notorious micromanager Steve Wynn raised his eyebrows at Adelson's relentless focus not only on the material that went into the Venetian, but the cost to the penny of each bolt of cloth, slab of marble, and roll of carpet. Adelson took pride in discussing the quality of the Berber carpet and the way he negotiated its purchase at the best possible price.

During the construction of the Venetian and Bellagio, the *Wall Street Journal* reported that Adelson sparred with Wynn over whose suites were larger and more opulent. It was evident that size mattered to both men.

Within a few months, it was clear the Venetian was progressing too slowly. Rumors swirled around the job site where Adelson's assistants delivered work-change orders to dozens of subcontractors who toiled under the umbrella of general-contracting giant Lehrer McGovern Bovis.

In the spring of 1999, as the Venetian's opening day approached, Adelson invited a contingent of local press people to review the progress on the project. He was clearly admitting that the job wasn't being completed on time.

The 3,036-suite Venetian opened May 4, 1999, to invited guests in black tie and formal gowns. Not even the razzle-dazzle could keep hidden the fact that many of his best suites weren't ready. Celebrity guest Sophia Loren was among a number of invitees forced to stay at other hotels.

Journalist Jeff Burbank, author of *License to Steal,* called it "the most inauspicious debut of any Las Vegas megaresort."

The resort's construction had been riddled with costly change orders. The biggest losers in the battle were the subcontractors. They had performed thousands of hours of work and couldn't collect their money. Many went bankrupt.

Bovis sued Venetian for $97.2 million for work completed. Adelson fumed. He countersued for $201.4 million, claiming construction defects and the building giant's inability to finish the job on time had cost the Venetian a fortune in lost revenue.

The Bovis case was heard by District Judge James Brennan. Evidence files contained more than 10,000 documents. The trial lasted ten months, making a new Nevada record for a civil case.

In the end, a Las Vegas jury determined that the Venetian owed Bovis $44 million. Bovis, in turn, was required to pay Venetian $2.3 million for construction defects.

At the Venetian's opening, Adelson was heard to remark, "Either I'm the stupidest guy around or the biggest crapshooter in town."

He was neither, but he was at the high-stakes table. The Venetian, with its superior rooms, upscale restaurants and spa, splendid marble interior and gondoliers paddling through a glass-covered faux canal, was the latest competition for the town's three other top-class hotels.

Questions persisted about the Venetian's viability as a high-roller casino. What made the resort viable was its million-square-foot Sands Expo convention center. With the facility packing in tens of thousands of conference-goers each year, and convention space leased at a premium, Adelson had a built-in customer base that promised to overcome weaknesses in the fledgling casino's marketing program. With all those laptop-toting businessmen in the house, Adelson believed he could overcome the project's high-interest financing and show a healthy profit. In which case, he was prepared to finance his next tower and build his palace in Macau.

The conservative Adelson remained an enigma in the hedonistic casino subculture in part because of his devotion to Israel.

Authors Sally Denton and Roger Morris observed, "Adelson, the billionaire promoter and right-wing Zionist with business and political ties to Israel, had the same tough mentality as the Strip's former overseers."

And he was even tougher on those who tried to embarrass him.

♦  ♦  ♦

Adelson and Wynn continued their rivalry in 2005 as they expanded their footprints on the sand. Wynn accused Adelson of not providing enough parking space for customers and employees. Adelson responded by building a seven-story underground parking garage at his Palazzo new addition.

The Venetian announced its Palazzo project next to the Venetian would have fifty-five floors instead of forty-two floors. This meant the new building would be 718 feet high instead of the previously announced 460 feet.

The reason was clear.

Wynn's new project would be only fifty stories and 613 feet high.

It appeared Sheldon's would remain bigger.

In 2004, he opened a $1-billion credit line in August and in September, he filed a $350-million IPO. After enduring snickering ridicule by analysts when he shopped the original financing for the Venetian project, Adelson now was warmly received. His initial public offering was an opening-day sellout. In less than five years, Adelson had gone from being a suspect to a prospect with the success of his Venetian and Sands Macau casinos.

Married and with five children, his driving personality doesn't let him take time out to enjoy what he has achieved. The son of the Boston cabby had arrived and was now worth upward of $17 billion according to an estimate in *Forbes* magazine.

If he could manage to keep his ego in check and not waste energy sparring with his neighbors on the Strip, there was no stopping Sheldon Adelson.

# Young Lion

## 32

Ahron and Lily Kerkorian came to America from Armenia with a strong work ethic and ambition. Like many of their countrymen, they migrated to the California farming community of Fresno. That's where Ahron's determination to get ahead would be realized. That's where, on June 6, 1917, the Kerkorians' youngest child, Kerkor, was born. The family spoke Armenian around the house, and it became young Kirk's first language.

Kirk Kerkorian rose from those humble beginnings to become one of America's wealthiest men and one of the most-important figures in Las Vegas history. His early business education came not from Harvard or Wharton, but from the streets.

The writer William Saroyan would emerge as Fresno's most celebrated son of Armenian heritage, but the Roaring Twenties would bring an end to the security of the Kerkorian family's eth-

299

nic community. A recession sent Ahron and his family to Los Angeles in search of work, and that is where young Kirk learned English and his older brother, Nishon, developed his boxing career.

After sitting still through the school hours at Fifth Avenue Grammar School, Kirk sprinted to the corner of Arlington and Jefferson avenues to peddle the *Los Angeles Evening Express* to men coming home from work. Later, he labored at a car wash steam-cleaning engines, bought, spiffed up, and sold used cars, caddied at a local golf course, and even joined the Depression-era Civilian Conservation Corps to earn extra money to augment the family's income while his father labored at his vegetable market only a few blocks from where the Forum would be built in Inglewood.

An anecdote in Dial Torgerson's biography, *Kerkorian: An American Success Story*, gives insight into the father's talent for business, a trait he passed down to his son. An unseasonably cold spring in the Imperial Valley had produced a scrawny watermelon crop, and farmers felt defeated. Ahron and his boys traveled to El Centro from Los Angeles in the family Buick. There the father made the farmers an irresistible offer. He'd give them $50 up-front for their crop and also water and travel expenses to deliver the crop to Los Angeles. The farmers took him up on his offer, and Ahron found a market for the melons. By summer's end, Ahron had an $18,000 profit.

Although Ahron Kerkorian wouldn't always be so successful—he gained and lost the family grubstake several times—Kirk Kerkorian would carry the lesson of the watermelons with him for the rest of his life.

Meanwhile, big brother Nish dreamed of stardom and developed the boxing skills he'd honed in Fresno from trainer Kinky Chevreshian. "I remember as a kid having to fight for everything I wanted," Nish once said.

Los Angeles in the twenties was Mecca for fight fans. If he wanted to make a name for himself, Nish had come to the right town. He emerged as a punishing mauler nicknamed "the

Armenian Assassin" and made headlines by knocking out a journeyman named Joe Arcenigo in sixteen seconds at the Legion Stadium in Hollywood.

Nish, with his prominent nose and heavy Armenian eyes made all the more prominent by his punishing career, rang up 108 victories as a professional. Years later, when his little brother was gathering headlines as one of America's most-successful businessmen, the former fighter would sip cocktails and recount his days in the ring at his Nishon's restaurant in Las Vegas.

By then, young Kirk Kerkorian had set aside his fleeting career as "Rifle Right Kerkorian" after challenging a Pacific Boxing Federation amateur welterweight title and winning acclaim for his tenacity in the ring. But his opponents in business would agree that Kerkorian's pugilist's heart hadn't changed merely because he'd turned in his boxing trunks for a tailored sports coat.

"When you're a self-made man, you start very early in life," Kerkorian said. "In my case it was at nine years old when I started bringing income into the family. You get a drive that's a little different, maybe a little stronger, than somebody who inherited."

Kerkorian dropped out of school in the eighth grade and continued to box and work menial jobs. In 1939, he was assisting Ted O'Flaherty with the installation of wall furnaces in what held all the promise of another dead-end pursuit.

O'Flaherty had a dream of his own. He was a licensed Piper Cub pilot flying out of the Alhambra Airport. He persuaded Kerkorian to join him for a test flight, and Kirk was hooked. He received his advanced pilot training from Florence "Pancho" Barnes at the legendary Happy Bottom Ranch and for a short time worked as a flight instructor.

In World War II, Kerkorian joined the Royal Air Force and flew Mosquito transport planes for the Air Transport Command from Montreal to Scotland. Many pilots lost their lives on this dangerous flight, but Kerkorian was unscathed. He banked the $1,000 per flight and was a frequent flyer, making thirty-three flights in thirty months.

After the war, Kerkorian used his savings to buy a $5,000
twin-engine Cessna. He flew charters for anyone who could
afford the fare. One of the more-notorious men who could
afford the fare was Benjamin Siegel, who was struggling to
complete the Flamingo.

In July 1945, Kerkorian's Cessna was observed bouncing
among the superheated desert currents. He was flying scrap-
iron dealer Jerry Williams from Los Angeles to Las Vegas, and
as he descended onto the small airstrip, he couldn't have imagined becoming a legend in what was then a sea of sand and
greasewood.

For a man of passionate pursuits who was not yet thirty, the
El Rancho Vegas and Hotel Last Frontier were places where
fantasy and reality blended and easy money was just a dice roll
away. Kerkorian recalled years later, "I was overwhelmed at the
level of excitement in this little town. The best times of my life
were in Las Vegas."

Kerkorian gambled heavily for a while. One of the turning
points of his career came in 1970 when a New York state legislative hearing on crime revealed that he had been taped in a
1961 conversation with Genovese crime family capo Charles
"Charlie the Blade" Tourine. The discussion concerned the
transfer of $21,300 from Kerkorian to Tourine through the
Blade's frontman and friend, Hollywood gangster-actor George
Raft. His was quite probably a gambling debt.

Kerkorian warned Tourine not to deposit the check immediately because "the heat is on," no specific explanation was
given for the conversation during the hearing, Tourine was a
percentage holder of mob casino interests as well as a well-connected bookmaker.

By the time the conversation surfaced in 1970, Kerkorian
had long since been licensed by Nevada casino regulators. The
authorities scoffed at the notion of a mob connection to the
high-flying financier, who, by then, owned the Flamingo and
International hotels.

After several losing sessions at the tables, Kerkorian realized he had no future as a player. Although he would gain the moniker the "Perry Como of the craps table" for his cool whether up or down a few thousand, Kerkorian realized that the only way to beat a casino was to own one.

That took lots of money. And this was a time when banks weren't interested in having their good names sullied by being associated with the gambling business.

Kerkorian made his first fortune in the airplane charter and transport business, buying and selling World War II planes and building up his inventory with help from an understated and immensely loyal man named Fred Benninger. He bought a dilapidated charter operation, Los Angeles Air Service, and in 1965 christened it Trans International Airlines. He grew it into a handsome business that leased private jets to those who could afford them.

TIA not only made him millions and groomed innumerable contacts, it provided Kerkorian with a laboratory in which he could test his business acumen. Taking TIA public was an ideal proving ground for future stock forays with International Leisure, MGM, Columbia, and Chrysler.

His business success made him a celebrity in the Armenian-American community. It demonstrated its respect for this favorite son by buying stock in his company. TIA stock rose above $30, and by the time he sold the company to Transamerica in 1968 for stock eventually worth $104 million, Kerkorian emerged as an Armenian-American success story.

He parlayed his new wealth into a 30-percent interest in Los Angeles-based Western Airlines, which for many years promoted itself as "the Only Way to Fly." He showed a clear understanding of the corporate concept.

Kerkorian's first big Las Vegas deal came in 1962 when he bought eighty barren acres across from the Flamingo and next to the Dunes. The $960,000 purchase price didn't include the coveted corner piece. Two years later, however, when Vegas visionary Jay Sarno went looking for a site for his Teamsters-backed Caesars Palace idea, he came to Kerkorian and cut a deal to become a tenant for what was to become the most-famous new Las Vegas casino. Including rent and $5-million sale price in 1968, Kerkorian made $9 million on the deal.

Between the Caesars score and the sale of his TIA ownership, Kerkorian was in position to make his first major foray into casino ownership. He couldn't have chosen a more opportune moment, for by 1967, the hidden owners of the Sands, Frontier, Landmark, and Flamingo were in the process of being exposed and exiled from their paradise. Kerkorian bought the house that Benny Siegel built, the fabulous Flamingo.

At the time, the Flamingo's majority owners were a couple of characters named Morris Lansburgh and Samuel Cohen. Kerkorian flew to Miami with *Las Vegas Sun* columnist Paul Price and health-club owner Lem Banker, playing gin rummy with the former and being entertained by the street stories of the latter. Although the connection between Lansburgh and Cohen and Lansky was obvious to those who knew how Las Vegas really operated, Kerkorian kept his distance from the notorious organized crime financier and the characters the press of the day referred to as "Miami hotelmen."

When an FBI investigation and wiretaps uncovered Lansky's presence around the Flamingo and his receipt of a $200,000 fee with the sale of the casino, Kerkorian faced more scrutiny, but came away unscathed. The Flamingo was suspected of being the site of an enormous skimming operation linked to Lansky. Lansburgh and Cohen eventually were convicted of tax charges. Lansky caught a Vegas break when federal Judge Roger Foley declared him too ill to stand trial.

If the Flamingo represented Kerkorian's toe in the water, his creation of International Leisure and the construction of the International Hotel and Casino off the Strip next to the Convention Center was his big splash. A 17-percent public stock offering raised $26.5 million and sent him on his way.

By October 1968, the International took shape despite those who questioned its behemoth size, thirty stories high and a whopping 1,512 rooms, and off-Strip location covering eighty acres on Paradise Road next to the saucer-shaped Convention Center. Critics believed all these things would doom it to failure similar to that experienced by the Space Needle-clone Landmark.

At $5 million, the land had been a bargain. Howard Hughes was on his obsessive casino-shopping spree, overpaying for his acquisitions. Kerkorian was often compared to the heralded, reclusive Hughes. Kerkorian's detractors liked to call him "a ham sandwich Howard Hughes."

Although the two warred over property deals, were super-competitive, and butted heads behind the scenes, Kerkorian just smiled when the Hughes name was mentioned.

"He's a mountain, and I'm a molehill," Kerkorian said in typical self-deprecation.

The Las Vegas press was cordial when it came to coddling its new casino titan, Hughes, still he was a landlord who built nothing. As former aide Robert Maheu observed, "Hughes didn't make the new Las Vegas, but he got it ready by buying up the mob joints and cleaning up the town's reputation as a haven of hidden ownership."

Kerkorian wasn't content with owning one casino. He wanted to build the largest hotel in the world. It would be named the International. Meanwhile, the Flamingo, served as a training center for the larger property, and Kerkorian summoned his detail-driven friend Benninger. As Kerkorian would later recall, and Benninger would deflect, it was Benninger's idea to buy the Flamingo and use it as a training ground for future International employees.

Benninger was responsible for bringing aboard the tough Sahara vice president, Alex Shoofey, who plucked nearly three dozen of the north-Strip resort's executives to fill the Flamingo. Among the gems was a young casino manager named Jimmy Newman, who would go on to be recognized as one of the most-powerful gambling operations men in the business.

In its first full year under Kerkorian's team, the Flamingo netted nearly $3 million—almost ten times more than its previous owners had reported. Federal agents and Justice Department officials did the math: If the previous years' gross was more or less consistent with Kerkorian's bottom line, that meant previous owners had skimmed millions. The revelation helped Kerkorian gain Securities and Exchange Commission approval for a first public offering.

But even with the success of the Flamingo, the public offering, and his other assets, Kerkorian was compelled to borrow at high interest from foreign banks. These foreign loans sapped his bankroll. After he was rebuffed by the SEC when he attempted a second public offering—the Justice Department was frustrated with what it perceived as Kerkorian's lack of cooperation in the Flamingo skimming investigation—he sold off blocks of International Leisure stock to Barron Hilton at fire-sale prices. For $180 million of his stake in the company, Kerkorian managed to generate just $16.5 million at the sale window. He no longer controlled the giant hotel-casino he'd envisioned, built, and filled with innovations that included a youth hostel and featured Broadway musicals.

He brought in Barbra Streisand to open the main showroom, and Elvis Presley made his comeback there, but after the new boss took over, the name of his remarkable carpet joint was changed to the Las Vegas Hilton.

Even after selling the Flamingo and International, Kerkorian had only good things to say about Las Vegas.

"I don't think there is a sky here," he said. "You see the sun 95 percent of the time. You see the most beautiful hills, which look like they are only down the road yet they really are fifty miles away. It's like living in Palm Springs if you forget the Strip.

"It's a way of life, and I don't speak of it that way because of the gambling. Here one can come and relax and afford to play and eat the best food and see top entertainment and swim and enjoy more of everything."

◆　　◆　　◆

Kerkorian wasn't supposed to get his hands on MGM Studios. The fat-laden, undervalued entertainment icon was an intended feast for Howard Hughes. But Hughes was distracted. Beverly Hills attorney Greg Bautzer interested Kerkorian in the prospect of owning the famous movie company.

Kerkorian and Bautzer calculated MGM stock was worth $400 million, or $69 a share. At the time, MGM stock was trading at $25, and the studio was losing money with a Harvard Business School graduate at its helm.

Eighth-grade dropout Kerkorian decided to try his luck and began to take control of the company, eventually reworking the board of directors and handpicking a new president, James Aubrey. MGM immediately responded to the resuscitation.

"He's a quick study," Bautzer said of Kerkorian. "In the end, he was to become more knowledgeable about MGM than I was."

Although he'd buy and sell MGM stock through the years, he would maintain a keen interest in the company.

In 1969, he acquired a 40-percent stake in MGM and immediately exercised his clout to make the foundering studio more efficient. Minor stockholders, some of whom had held their shares for decades, were frightened by Kerkorian. When he persuaded board members, his critics called him boorish and sneaky. When he declined to attend stockholder meetings, they called him arrogant and aloof. What they failed to appreciate was Kerkorian's style was understated. He disdained dressing up, loathed public speaking. It was arguably the one area of his life that was affected by his lack of education.

Kerkorian took a financial bath on his sale of the Flamingo and International, but he vowed to fight another day. Still a wealthy man, his reputation in Las Vegas was poor. He still had something to prove.

Less than one year later, he started proving himself by pushing MGM into the casino business—much to the chagrin of many of its longtime stockholders.

Kerkorian paid a group of Las Vegas men for the land across from the Dunes and catty-corner from Caesars Palace that had been home to the Bonanza Club. Moe Dalitz, who was among the sellers, made $1.8 million on the sale. Kerkorian wanted once again to create the largest casino hotel in the world.

To accumulate the working capital necessary to complete such a project, he sold some of his large stake in MGM. He carved a deal to relinquish the studio company's theaters and other real estate in foreign markets and found a buyer in Cinema International Corporation, an MCA and Gulf & Western/Paramount creation that, according to *Dark Victory* author Dan E. Moldea, was created to avoid violating American antitrust laws.

Interestingly, the deal that bankrolled the MGM Grand Hotel was negotiated by Kerkorian and MCA boss Lew Wasserman with legal guidance from powerhouse attorney Sidney Korshak.

"Mr. Korshak was very close to Wasserman and Kerkorian and played a key role as a go-between," then-Gulf & Western Chairman Charles G. Bluhdorn recalled in Moldea's book, *Dark Victory: Ronald Reagan, MCA, and the Mob.* "It was a very, very tough negotiation that would have broken down without him."

If ever there was a deal that was close to Kerkorian's fighter's heart, this was it. While the International had been big and innovative for its time, the MGM project reflected Kerkorian's passion: It combined his love of classic Hollywood with the sorts of touches that were unprecedented in their day in Las Vegas. The 2,100-room hotel would feature a jai-alai fronton, a 1,200-seat showroom, a lounge featuring showroom-caliber entertainment, a hall of fame walk of movie memorabilia, and a casino floor with a high ceiling that made the room look large enough to land commercial flights. (Years later, in his study of casino design, gaming executive Bill Friedman noted that the high ceiling was a crippling design flaw that went entirely against the intimate-play psychology of most casino customers, who preferred lower ceilings even inside megaresorts.)

While the casino was criticized for being too wide open for players who liked to gamble in a secluded setting, the highlight of the MGM might have been its custom theater, which was lined with luxurious couches and offered cocktail service while showing classic movies.

Kerkorian stood on the sidelines during the MGM's 1972 groundbreaking ceremony. Although most of the $107-million construction cost was his responsibility, he wasn't interested in the spotlight. Instead, in an interview many years later, he gave credit for the completion of his Las Vegas projects to his loyal pal, Fred Benninger. "He built the International," Kerkorian said. "He built the old MGM, and he built this MGM. It was all Fred Benninger."

The MGM was an instant hit when it opened July 5, 1973. This expanded the horizons of Las Vegas casino developers. It scoffed at naysayers who said it was too large to turn a profit and over the next seven years presented some of the biggest names in show business.

And then came the day the MGM Grand burned.

# The Lion Never Sleeps

*33*

In a career adorned with many successes, eighty-seven-year-old Kirk Kerkorian's defining moment in Las Vegas casino history rose not from great triumph, but from the ashes of tragedy.

The man best known for ushering in the megaresort era and constructing the world's largest hotels three times cemented his reputation as a stand-up guy in the wake of the November 21, 1980, high-rise fire at the original MGM Grand Hotel.

The blaze killed eighty-seven people and brought the wrong kind of international attention to Las Vegas. For the first time in the city's history, there was considerable consternation and debate about the true safety of the hotels.

Kerkorian was then the largest holder of MGM stock. At the time of the fire, he was in New York in negotiations with Columbia Pictures executives.

The catastrophic fire was due to a faulty electrical system on the first floor. Although the blaze was intense, many of the guests who perished did so from smoke inhalation. Hundreds of guests and service personnel were injured.

The fire gave rise to tales of thievery on the chaotic casino floor by customers, dealers, and even rescue workers. Also reported were feats of great heroism by firefighters and some of the guests. At least two people died because they refused to leave the slot machines, and their bodies were literally melted to the machine metal.

On learning of the tragedy, Kerkorian immediately flew back to Las Vegas. He met with Fred Benninger and hotel president Al Benedict and asked, "Where do we begin?"

In an interview with the *Las Vegas Review-Journal*'s Dave Palermo, Kerkorian spoke publicly about the fire for one of the few times in his life. Although Benedict admitted that the idea of cutting their losses was "in the back of everybody's mind," it wasn't Kerkorian's first concern. He knew there was more at stake than a building and a bankroll. His reputation was at stake.

He told reporter K. J. Evans, "How could I walk away while that whole team was out there, taking the brunt from everybody? I had to be a part of it, I couldn't walk away, I just couldn't."

Time is a healer, and the MGM reopened eight months later with a new guest tower and what would be advertised as a $5-million, state-of-the-art fire-safety system. Statements that the hotel was now the safest building in the world was not lost upon the public. Room reservations were being booked at a record rate, and the hotel was fully occupied night after night.

It was as if one of the worst fires in Nevada history had never happened.

Deirdre Coakley and Hank Greenspun noted in *The Day the MGM Grand Hotel Burned*, "On the night of July 30 [1981], the curtain went up on Jubilee in the Ziegfeld Theater, Dean Martin alternated with Mac Davis and Lonnie Schorr in the Celebrity Room, and in the movie theater, naturally, was the old Garbo film *Grand Hotel*."

The MGM Grand was back, and Kerkorian could breathe again.

Although the fire resulted in protracted litigation, Kerkorian would always be able to say he hadn't ducked his responsibility or hidden from the criticism.

Still his career was not without its roller-coaster ups and downs. In his battle with Columbia Pictures, a lawyer for that studio complained that Kerkorian controlled both of the MGM companies and manipulated them for his own purpose.

"They declare dividends when he needs cash," the attorney charged.

Kerkorian suffered when Denver oil man Marvin Davis beat him out for control of 20th Century Fox a decade later. Although he structured a deal to combine MGM with United Artists, he decided against the suggestion that he buy up all the outstanding shares in 1983. In 1986, he made a deal with Ted Turner to sell him MGM/UA while he reacquired United Artists.

Las Vegas historians seem to have forgotten that Kerkorian once lost a chance to buy the Dunes because he bid $150 million and Japanese billionaire Masao Nangaku bid $5 million more.

By mid-decade, MGM Grand stock stayed in the $10 range. The casino was in full operation, but neither it nor its sister casino in Reno seemed to enhance MGM's prospects. Rarely one for sentimentality, Kerkorian solved his wilted stock problem by selling the two casinos to Bally for $596 million in 1986. He relieved himself of the hotels with a sizable profit. Still something was missing. Kerkorian's legacy, if he cared about such things, was incomplete.

A year later, with Benninger still working loyally behind the scenes, Kerkorian signed an agreement to buy the Sands and Desert Inn from the late Howard Hughes's Summa Corporation for $167 million. With these purchases came acres of valuable land and the Desert Inn Golf Course and Country Club.

Where Hughes took pride in almost never selling off his acquisitions, for Kerkorian, a business was a chess piece to be moved on a board.

Kerkorian was poised to become the dominant force in the movie industry. Instead of holding to that course, he sold his stake in United Artists for $1 billion. In doing so, he generated the bankroll for future projects without giving up control of MGM's television and movie businesses.

Six months later, he was betting again on Las Vegas.

In October, Kerkorian's MGM Grand Incorporated paid $123 million for 117 acres at Tropicana Avenue and Las Vegas Boulevard. The site was large enough for a 5,000-room hotel, a large convention area, a 15,000-seat Grand Garden arena, and a 40-acre theme park that would feature a *Wizard of Oz* theme and contain a roller coaster and a log ride.

In July 1991, Kerkorian sold the Desert Inn Casino for $130 million to help finance his new MGM project. As usual, he made money on the deal. A few years later while he sipped a cocktail at Nicky Blair's, he reminisced about his life in Las Vegas. The Desert Inn, he said, was the only property he ever regretted selling.

Kerkorian had a new place to hang his hat. For the third time in his career, he'd built the largest hotel in the world. The new MGM opened in 1993 and put Kerkorian back among the industry's leaders.

What began as an 85,000-square-foot casino stretched to more than 100,000 square feet by the time MGM opened its doors. Other additions followed, including high-roller salons and high-limit slot areas.

The plan to capture a piece of the family travel market would prove a major miscalculation. Las Vegas finally wised up and dropped its hypocritical "family friendly" advertising.

Creation of the new MGM Grand had been overseen by Benninger. At his side was former Golden Nugget President Bob Maxey, a bulldog-tough operations man who was in charge of getting the place up and running. Maxey's blunt style was suited to the chaos prior to the opening. However, it was no secret that he had persuaded Kerkorian to open without Culinary workers in the kitchen, bars, and in housekeeping.

"One man who seems intent on both spending, and making, more money than anyone else in Vegas in the years ahead is Kirk Kerkorian," author David Spanier observed in his book, *All Right, Okay, You Win.* "I got that impression from the way men were digging up trees from the rolling green sward of his new property. 'We've got $4 million worth of trees out there. We're moving them all, at a cost of $1.8 million,' said Bob Maxey, in a tone which implied that if you look after the pennies, the millions will take care of themselves. 'Then we'll move them all back in.'"

What Spanier, an astute visiting poker writer from England, failed to note was the fact Maxey's stated fiscal responsibility ran counter to MGM rival Steve Wynn's well-known extravagance. Wynn had purchased thousands of mature pine trees and hundreds of pounds of needles for his exclusive Shadow Creek golf club in an effort to make the new course appear seasoned. It was a little dig at Maxey's former employer and Kerkorian's rival. If Wynn had chided the MGM's product and management as grand but unspectacular, Kerkorian's boys were always available to remind others that Wynn's properties looked better than they performed at the bottom line.

In public, Wynn and Kerkorian's men were complimentary of each other, but Maxey made little secret of his dislike for his former boss' fast-lane lifestyle. And Wynn was known to sniff at what he considered only so-so attention to detail at the lion's place.

Both men, each in his own way, engendered staff loyalty. Even though he would be eased out of the executive position and into retirement, and afterward the MGM would warm up to the Culinary Union, Maxey remained fond of Kerkorian.

"Kerkorian doesn't think of himself as old," Maxey said. "He plays tennis every day. He's energetic, he's interested, he doesn't look seventy. You'd think he was my brother. He believes he can do it."

That was sixteen years ago.

In 2005 at age eighty-seven, Kerkorian won the "85 and over" division of a tennis competition at California's Newport

Beach. He does most of his tennis playing at the Beverly Hills Country Club.

One of the great misreads of Kerkorian is the long-held media perception he is a "billionaire recluse." A billionaire, to be sure. In March, 2005, *Forbes* estimated his personal fortune at $9 billion and growing. He was listed as the forty-first wealthiest person in America.

Kerkorian is anything but a shut-in standing in the shadow of Howard Hughes. Granted, he rarely grants press interviews and has shown little need for or interest in personal publicity. However, a hermit he is not. He is often seen dining with friends he's known half his life. These include retired police chiefs, sheriffs, and others who were loyal to him as he rose in wealth and power.

There's usually a chauffeur with him who doubles as a bodyguard. Kerkorian enjoys himself whether having drinks with retired Las Vegas Sheriff Ralph Lamb or dining at Piero's Italian Cuisine with Barron Hilton. Often he eats alone and unnoticed.

In a rare interview, he told a reporter, "I'm far from being reclusive. I have thirty- or forty-year friendships that I prefer to meeting new people. I go to an occasional party, but just because I'm not out in public all the time doesn't mean I'm antisocial or a recluse. I'm at a restaurant three or four nights a week."

A more personal view came from MGM Mirage chairman Terry Lanni, the former Caesars Palace executive who emerged as the corporate gaming era's preeminent leader following the takeover. For years, Lanni, who spent most of his time in Beverly Hills and not on the MGM's enormous casino floor, had watched Kerkorian drink only an occasional cup of green tea at annual board meetings, sit in the second row of the casino's popular prizefights, reimburse the company for expenses that include air travel, and even stand in line at some of its restaurants. Although many reporters describe the MGM Mirage as "Kerkorian's casino company," he's managed to maintain his perspective and hasn't forgotten he isn't the only stockholder.

Kerkorian avoids many of the diversions of his youth, including gambling.

He played a competitive game of tennis well into his eighties. He maintained a lengthy relationship with tennis professional Lisa Bonder. That relationship produced a child and a question of paternity that led to heated litigation. According to press reports, Hollywood executive and Democratic Party supporter Stephen Bing was rumored to be the father of Bonder's child.

Perhaps Kerkorian was hard to pin down as a larger-than-life casino industry character for another reason: It represented only a slice of his business empire. Where Las Vegas legends Benny Binion, Bill Bennett, and Steve Wynn were full-time casino men, Kerkorian was something of a three-sport letterman. Had he remained in the airline business, he would have ranked among the industry's most-important influences. Had he stayed with the movie business, he surely would be known as one of its titans.

True to his understated, but no less relentless drive, Kerkorian not only endorsed MGM's expansion into new gaming markets, including the casinos at Primm Valley on the Nevada-California state line, Detroit, and on the island of Macau, but he made substantive runs on major corporations outside the casino industry.

He made national headlines when he sought to gain a controlling stake in Chrysler Corporation. His foray was rebuffed. According to Bloomberg News, Kerkorian lost the 1995 Chrysler takeover bid because he couldn't raise the $13 billion he needed. Chrysler officials called him a "terrorist," but his criticism of their lack of quality control and fiscal sobriety proved accurate. Three years later, he watched his prediction that Chrysler, the No. 3 car manufacturer in America, was a sleeping giant.

Those who understood Kerkorian's style never doubted that he would profit from the merger of Daimler-Chrysler scenario. In 1998, he saw his personal fortune increase on paper by more than $1 billion in two days after merger talks between Chrysler and German luxury car giant Daimler-Benz.

Kirk Kerkorian was the lion who never stopped feeding.

It was a lesson Steve Wynn learned when Kerkorian's team scooped up flashy, but financially troubled Mirage Resorts for $6.7 billion, including its debt. While Lanni barely contained his glee at besting Wynn, Kerkorian never gloated publicly even though he'd heard tales of Wynn's caustic criticism of him. Actually Kerkorian tried to soothe Wynn's wounds by complimenting Wynn's creative talent.

He could afford to be generous. He was undisputed king of the Strip. MGM Mirage emerged as the most dangerous player in the rapidly consolidating casino industry.

True to his nature, it wasn't long after he captured Mirage that Kirk Kerkorian was ready to hunt again.

Throughout his early career, Kirk Kerkorian was sniped at as a cut-rate Howard Hughes. Then, just when he looked to become the king of Las Vegas, his first MGM Grand burned.

The second MGM Grand completed his Strip comeback, but it wasn't until 2000, when MGM swallowed Mirage Resorts, that Kerkorian emerged as the undisputed leader in Las Vegas.

When MGM Mirage stepped forward in 2003 and announced its intention to acquire flashy Mandalay Resort Group, local historians might have begun to wonder whether Kerkorian's hunger for Las Vegas dominance would ever be satiated. One thing was certain: No one would remember him as a "ham sandwich Howard Hughes."

Unlike the Hughes era, when Nevada was the only state with legalized casino gambling and the billionaire's attempt to purchase the Stardust was held up by federal regulators for fear of creating a hotel room monopoly on Las Vegas Boulevard, Kerkorian's career had lasted into the age of gaming proliferation. Even with his billions, it would be impossible to dominate an industry that had spread to a majority of states and had grown into a multibillion-dollar business on Indian reservations across the nation.

Given MGM Mirage's clean status with regulators, it was hardly surprising that its $7.9-billion acquisition of Mandalay, which operated Circus Circus, Excalibur, Luxor, the hip Mandalay Bay, and other casinos, would be approved without so much as an arched eyebrow by the Federal Trade Commission.

That made approval at the state level a foregone conclusion, and regulators who voiced concerns about the anticompetitive components of creating monolithic gaming corporations in a state so dependent on the industry for tax revenue, they did so with the understanding that they were basically hopeless to do much about it.

A major corporation, save for those busted by federal investigators, hadn't lost a casino license in the history of Nevada gaming. The state's legislature wasn't going to touch the monopolistic aspects of casino consolidation, and Nevada governors hadn't put pressure on the industry in a generation.

Gaming Control Board member Bobby Siller, one of the more outspoken men to hold such a position, raised the issue of good corporate citizenship in a hearing, but added, "MGM chose to expand in Nevada. Nevada is home."

Gaming Commission Chairman Peter Bernhard liked to think Nevada had done its regulatory best after a four-hour meeting that resulted in a unanimous vote for approval. He said, "Even if it met federal antitrust standards, we still had to make the independent judgment that it was in the best interest of the state based on the criteria of our regulations."

Added Commissioner John Moran Jr., "We had to go further and not just be a rubber stamp of the FTC."

Just how far was the commission willing to go?

Given the state's historical embrace of gaming from the days of Benny Siegel to the time of Kerkorian, it's hard to imagine a set of circumstances that would have compelled the Control Board and Commission to halt a level of consolidation that sent shivers through lowly casino employees and union members, who knew well the unwritten tradition of blackballing workers by Strip resorts.

In July 2004, with the FTC scrutinizing MGM Mirage for anything that it might act in an anticompetitive way, the casino company let it leak that it had eliminated the "no rehire" box on its applications. A corporate spokesman said it was meant to ensure fairness in hiring and rehiring between the company's megaresorts. It also was an acknowledgment of the voiced concerns of casino employees, who traditionally had served at the whim of capricious floor supervisors, shift managers, and bosses.

The fear was that if an employee was sacked from one casino job or had a personality clash with a manager, he or she might not be hired at another casino owned by the same company. It also was no secret that in the past some casino companies had allowed midlevel managers to leverage sex and cash from prospective dealer applicants in exchange for favored shifts.

"It's clearly an important issue for us," MGM Mirage spokesman Alan Feldman said. "The no-rehire policy, such as it was, had been substantially watered down in recent years. There clearly was a point in time in years past where it was a pretty stern policy.

"I think it's the sign of an industry that's evolving that this practice has morphed into something which is less and less relied upon.... The one thing that has always been unique about Las Vegas is that when casino employees get terminated, they've always been able to walk right across the street and get another job. When one entity controls a third of the jobs on the Strip, obviously, that has the potential to change the equation. But MGM and Mandalay are two of the most progressive companies in the industry."

MGM Mirage executive Jim Murren observed, "The Treasure Island competes with New York-New York. And they're compensated on the results of their individual properties. We compete against ourselves."

As a longtime casino dealer advocate and president of the tiny International Union of Gaming Employees, Tony Badillo is one of few consistent critics of big gaming's policies and practices. Badillo was suspicious and outspoken about MGM Mirage's minor policy changes.

"The fact is that the casino powers have demanded that Nevada statutes include the 'at-will' provision in its employment law, and the legislature has dutifully complied," he said. "The implications are that gaming managers can fire, or threaten to fire, any employee without a reason or cause, i.e. at will. Were they required to give a reason, it would provide the employee the means to contest the action. This, the casinos do not want.

"They say they need this absolute and uncontestable power over their workers. Why? Other industries manage just fine without it. One must ask: Why does the gaming industry need this power?"

The answer appeared simple: It came with the clout that accompanied owning nearly half the casinos on the Strip.

"Other questions we need to ask before we allow these megamergers to take place is: Who will be looking out for the rights of the casino workers?" Badillo asked.

After being vilified by African-American political activists for failing to recruit and promote minority employees, a charge that might have been leveled at any Las Vegas casino company, MGM Mirage embarked on a sweeping program to enhance its workplace diversity. The result was one part progressive business practice, one part public-relations campaign.

Chairman Terry Lanni, who'd endured stinging slights hurled from activists from Las Vegas, Detroit, and New York in recent years, was proud of his company's No. 31 ranking on *Fortune* magazine's top 50 businesses sensitive to minority hiring. He also said MGM Mirage had worked hard to do more business with minority-owned businesses. And the American Gaming Association, the industry's unified front organization, created an online diversity guide meant to help minority businesses and gaming companies improve communication.

Although the gaming industry could boast few women and minorities in high management positions, MGM Mirage's sensitivity was a sign it and other companies were sensitive to the largely accurate public perception that the nation's gambling bosses remained mostly white males. But in a racket that had been reluctant to integrate, slow to get wise to civil rights and immigration, and had once been led by a billionaire recluse who was frightened of Black people, big gaming had come a long way and finally appeared to be growing up.

The true front-line racial questions would be asked nightly in the Strip's hottest dance clubs, where hip-hop music blared, but stories were still told of black customers being forced to wait in line long after others were allowed inside.

◆    ◆    ◆

But what of the Mandalay Resort Group's corporate hierarchy? In keeping with most corporate takeovers, the "vanquished" received a royal send-off with more than $76.3 million in realized stock options divided among its top executives.

Mandalay's Chairman and Chief Executive Officer Michael Ensign, received $28.7 million in options while his longtime casino partner, Vice Chairman William Richardson, received $21.3 million.

The savvy players sold 6.4 million shares of company stock for a combined $209 million in 2003 just weeks before the news broke that MGM Mirage was circling. In June, MGM Mirage made a play for Mandalay at $68 a share. The offer was rejected, more out of pride than a lack of interest, and a $71 follow-up offer was accepted.

Ensign and Richardson had been content to remain in the background throughout their careers. They had benefited from the creative leadership of Mandalay President Glenn Schaeffer, who had joined the company in its previous incarnation as Circus Circus, had gained and lost the trust of Bill Bennett, and had outshined Steve Wynn and his Bellagio by turning Mandalay Bay into the most exciting high-end casino experience on the Strip. Schaeffer was a 1977 graduate of the Iowa Writers' Workshop. He founded and financed the International Insitute of Modern Letters, lobbied hard to land the City of Asylum writers retreat in Southern Nevada, and brought a stylish and intelligent aesthetic to Mandalay Bay.

Schaeffer would receive $13.7 million in stock compensation and later became involved with the new Fontainebleau hotel and casino project on the Strip.

Other Mandalay directors received lesser amounts, but it was enough to buy salve for the deepest wounds.

MGM Mirage emerged with twenty-eight casinos in five states and more than 75,000 employees. MGM Mirage also controlled more than half the hotel rooms and an even-higher percentage of the high-roller suites, a market it was sure to dominate despite the approaching opening of Steve Wynn's sparkling Wynn Las Vegas.

Consolidation was the way of capitalism, and the gaming industry practiced that philosophy at hyperspeed. But it was also true that Mandalay, with the eclectic Glenn Schaeffer at the helm, was considered one of the most dynamic and forward-thinking companies on the Boulevard. Its Mandalay Bay attracted a broad range of customers and offered tailored experiences for players of all sizes. The property included a Four Seasons Hotel and a new suite-centric high-rise called The Hotel.

Although industry observers said the Mandalay purchase made MGM Mirage "extraordinarily dependent upon visitors to Las Vegas," that's where nearly forty million players were.

In all, Kerkorian's company would create a supersized casino company that would generate annual revenues of $6.9 billion and a whopping $2.1-billion cash flow.

And there were plans to develop the $4.7-billion Project CityCenter on sixty-six acres south of Bellagio. Its features: another 4,000-room resort with high-rise condominiums and businesses. In addition, MGM also had another ninety-seven acres on or near the Strip that could be developed when the company saw fit.

MGM Mirage was also looking outward, signing a casino-development deal in the United Kingdom with Peel Holdings PLC of Manchester. The partnership called for $1.1 billion to be spent to build casinos in Glasgow, Liverpool, Manchester, and Salford. One casino would feature a 20,000-seat sports stadium. Additionally, the company was attempting to acquire interest in greyhound tracks throughout England, no doubt with an eye on the expected liberalization of legalized gambling in the country.

Although Terry Lanni and Jim Murren had taken over many of the day-to-day operations, and Bobby Baldwin and John Redmond held positions of trust and responsibility, in the end MGM Mirage remained a Kirk Kerkorian creation. It reflected his understated philosophy and relentless competitiveness.

Kerkorian's personal wealth fluctuated from one business deal to the next, and depending on the source, the difference can be sizable. But whether he was worth $7 billion or only $5 billion, he still ranked among the richest business tycoons in America. As he pressed on toward ninety, rising early and playing a daily game of tennis, it's easy to wonder why he continued to push so hard to maintain a dominant position in business.

Was he that greedy? That driven? That bored with other elements of his life? Did he consume the competition out of necessity or because it was simply in his nature?

He had his special projects, charities, and diversions, to be sure. He'd given many millions toward Armenian disaster relief and has made donations on a smaller scale to charities in Las Vegas.

What's most telling about his character is the fact he still managed to project the image of the understated, self-deprecating son of Armenian immigrants who is pleased with his success, but neither dazzled by the bright lights nor quite secure that it all is real. While other casino titans were busy using the contacts by networking with presidents and Oscar winners, Kerkorian seemed content to dine with friends of thirty years.

What's easy to forget is the fact that, after a half century of association on Las Vegas Boulevard, Kerkorian had outlived most of his earlier celebrity pals, men like Cary Grant, who once observed, "In his business he has always conducted himself well, honestly, and equitably. He is a very easygoing person, and I agree with his approach. I don't think any business can be conducted with pressure. It escalates into war, and then no business gets done. He delegates responsibility to his key employees ... and he places full reliance on their opinions.... He is the most honest, straightforward, and considerate person I know."

Grant's opinion of Kerkorian was charming and probably as accurate as any view of the man, but it was made to author Dial Torgerson in the days before junk bonds and rapid corporate takeovers changed forever the competition in Las Vegas. It failed to account for Kerkorian's ability to wield the razor in dealings with Columbia and MGM studios. At times in his career, Kerkorian has been a bruising businessman.

Bruising, restless, and always hungry.

That restless hunger, as much as the era of consolidation in the casino industry, explains why Kerkorian's MGM Mirage felt compelled to buy up one of the most-sparkling corporations in all gaming, Mandalay Resort Group.

"In the last four-and-one-half years, Nevada has grown rapidly, and there has been more interest worldwide," Kerkorian told the Nevada Gaming Commission. "I have to believe the same thing will happen again."

With his record of success and dominant position in the marketplace, who dared doubt him?

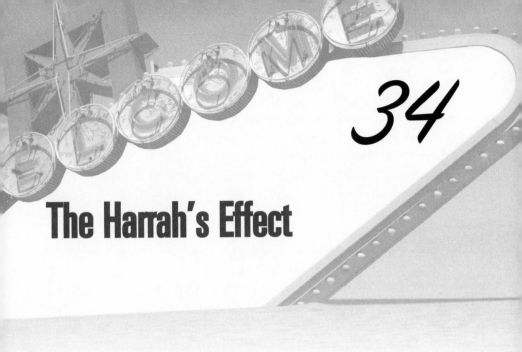

# The Harrah's Effect

**34**

**B**ill Harrah was known as his own man, and it showed.

His lack of underworld connections made him a gambler of distinction when he opened Harrah's Club on June 20, 1946.

The son of a Venice, California, attorney who also owned a bingo parlor, Harrah started in the gambling business at an early age. He quit college after one year to work with his father. Then he opened his first hole-in-the-wall bingo parlor on October 31, 1937, in Reno, America's divorce capital.

As with other gamblers of his generation, the move from California to Nevada was motivated by the desire to avoid police problems. Harrah, a slim, understated fellow, probably would have been chewed up in the mobbed-up Las Vegas of that era, but being situated in Reno gave him a buffer of immunity.

327

By the time he opened Harrah's Tahoe in 1973, his profits were the envy of Nevada gaming and a benchmark for investigators wanting to know what an honest casino that kept only one set of books actually generated in profits. By contrast, some of the mob-controlled gambling castles in Las Vegas kept three sets of books: one for the IRS, one for the stockholders, and one for the behind-the-scenes owners.

Bill Harrah's casino was immaculate and carpeted at a time most others in town were grimy sawdust joints. He collected antique automobiles, but he wasn't flashy and didn't court the press. He cut an independent swath from the beginning, and his seven marriages were as close as he ever came to being owned by others.

He believed in investing lavishly in entertainment and gave red-carpet treatment to his performers. These included such top headliners as Sammy Davis Jr., Bob Hope, and Frank Sinatra.

"Just as Bugsy Siegel recognized back in the 1940s that his Hollywood celebrity friends would attract the masses to his Flamingo casino, Bill Harrah understood that his casinos could draw large crowds by offering world-class entertainment at affordable prices," Robert L. Shook wrote in *Jackpot! Harrah's Winning Secrets for Customer Loyalty.*

Harrah was so successful and "on the square" that caustic gaming-industry critic Wallace Turner devoted a chapter in *Gamblers' Money* titled "If They Were All Like Harrah . . ."

Turner, a *New York Times* reporter, wrote in 1965, "The people with foresight in Nevada, those who sit and think about the future of the state's gambling business, look upon Bill Harrah as a shining example. If more gambling houses were in the hands of men like him, one is told over and over, then the future of Nevada gambling would be completely safe."

Harrah was impressive in Turner's eyes because he had "not brought scandal to the gambling business, and because he has supported attempts by the state to control the gamblers." Turner added, "He is the absolute owner of all his gambling places, and this in itself is a rarity."

Harrah flew to Rome once a year to have his suits and shirts custom made at Brioni. He was so concerned with his appearance that he pinned notes to his suits to remind him who had seen him in the clothes, so as not to repeat himself.

That mania was expressed in many ways at Harrah's. For example, he was among the first owner to develop a list of corporate rules including one that required daily department reports. Let psychologists scratch their heads, Harrah's quirks translated into greater efficiency and profit.

Overweight workers were told to shape up or risk being fired. At a time when a majority of dealers and pit personnel at other casinos had learned their skills in illegal joints, Harrah showed a preference for clean-faced young people to brighten up his casino floor.

Even though he gave few interviews, Harrah was not unaware of the impact of the press on his casino profits. He hired Jackie Cannon, brother of New York columnist Jimmy Cannon, to wine and dine media people. Over time, Cannon was able to plant hundreds of blurbs and anecdotes in the national gossip columns of Walter Winchell, Earl Wilson, and others.

Harrah understood the soul of casino men and the need to keep greed reined in by regulation. To do otherwise, he believed, would be ruinous.

"The gambling operator has no rights to his license, and it can be taken away from him anytime he gets out of line," Harrah said. "That's the way it ought to be."

Even the insightful Bill Harrah didn't envision the dramatic expansion of legalized gambling in an America where greed would make a transition from mortal sin to business model.

The irony of Harrah's warning is that he was at the forefront of those who sped the transition from private ownership to corporate control. His image as a clean operator did much to erase the stigma of mob influence from a pariah industry.

Harrah feared corporate ownership, but he took his company public in October 1971. He did this to finance the construction of a hotel tower at his Lake Tahoe casino. Also because his many divorces had drained his personal wealth.

In his lifetime Harrah's casino interests remained confined to northern Nevada. Although he was said to have an interest in opening an Atlantic City casino, he didn't live long enough to make it happen.

When he died on June 30, 1978, Bill Harrah's reputation was in better shape than his finances. Between his investment in properties and his string of costly divorces, his estate was in shambles. His primary asset was his six million shares in Harrah's.

Within weeks of his death, the company that bore his name began its dramatic transformation. Harrah's longtime attorney, Mead Dixon, negotiated the sale of Harrah's Corporation to Holiday Inns Corporation. By 1980, the Harrah's brand would grace a casino on the marina in Atlantic City. While in Las Vegas, the company opened doors to what would first be called the Holiday Casino, a slot-oriented riverboat knockoff on the heart of the Strip.

Mike Rose was a Harvard-educated lawyer who had melded into the hierarchy of Holiday Inns through his association with company franchisee Roy Winegardner. Rose climbed to the top of the Holiday corporation hierarchy and saw the potential in adding casinos to its portfolio. This move caused some longtime board members to resign from the company.

Rose's father had been the slot manager of Moe Dalitz's Desert Inn, and Rose himself had worked as a desk clerk at the Castaways. More than anyone at Holiday, Rose understood casino-business profits,

Holiday paid $300 million for Harrah's and entered the gaming business at a high level. Rose had made the jump from desk clerk to chief executive officer in a few short years. His father would have been proud of him, but the late Harrah might have been shocked when Rose sold half of the company's famous automobile collection for $100 million and gave the other half to the city of Reno for the tax write-off. So much for sentimentality.

Rose spun off its Holiday Inns brand in 1990. The leaner company was called Promus and included Harrah's, Embassy Suites, Hampton Inn, and Homewood Suites.

A year later, Phil Satre was named president of Promus. If the Harrah's brand had a leader who could fill its namesake's shoes, it was Satre, a straight-shooting lawyer and former Stanford football player who joined Mead Dixon's law firm in 1975.

Satre worked with Rose, the company's future chairman, to open Harrah's Marina in Atlantic City. But a deal gone sour with Donald Trump sent Harrah's into a tailspin. After spending millions of dollars, and losing millions more, it was discovered Trump had paid himself exorbitant bonuses for bringing the project in under budget. The war was on.

Trump was, as always, obsessed with promoting himself. He courted the media. Satre and Rose fought to get him to pay his share for a much-needed parking garage. "To Trump, business is too much about ego," Rose told Robert L. Shook. "He was not always successful at many of his businesses, because he appears to run them to satisfy his incredible ego."

The Trump-Harrah's war ended with Dixon, Satre, and Rose taking a beating while learning an invaluable lesson.

Although not every one of Harrah's new casinos on dockside, riverboats, and Indian reservations was problem free, each broadened the company's reach in an industry mostly known for its megaresorts on the Las Vegas Strip.

In some ways, Satre the attorney never left the football field. He was still a linebacker at heart and admitted building his value system from his time spent in a helmet and shoulder pads. This included the season when underdog Stanford defeated Ohio State in the Rose Bowl. Satre told Shook, "That season influenced my business career because it made me realize that a team, or for that matter any organization, can set a goal and with the right planning process, achieve success."

He practiced that team rule every day at Harrah's. He also retained his sense of humor. At a company meeting in 1998, Satre roared onto the stage on the back of a Harley-Davidson

331

and proceeded to lecture his staffers on the importance of brand identification and loyalty. Until his retirement, Satre was known for his open-door policy with employees. He had taken what Bill Harrah had created and improved on it by adopting many of the same rules the founder had followed.

Under Satre's leadership, Harrah's created a massive customer database that was the envy of competitors. Linking a series of casino-customer bases was controversial for it raised the question of whether individual casino managers would steal players from each other instead of seeking new ones.

Harrrah's opened its first riverboat casino in Joliet, Illinois, in 1993. This was followed in close succession by casinos in Vicksburg and Tunica. Shreveport, North Kansas City. Phoenix came in 1994, being the company's first Indian reservation casino.

Following another spin-off in 1996, which further focused the heart of the company on its winning casino product, Promus faded, and the Harrah's Entertainment name emerged with Rose still chairman and Satre as president.

The Harrah's imprint was expanding, but its stock was faltering. The expensive marketing program was intriguing, but the real question was whether it was effective. Satre, whose own life became tumultuous after his wife was diagnosed with leukemia, had come to a crossroads personally and professionally.

Satre said, "To get the level of execution I wanted, I had to get rid of the naysayers—the people who were stuck in the past and refused to move forward. This meant bringing in new talent."

That meant no more Mike Rose, whose retirement in 1997 failed to slow Harrah's expansion model. Over the next five years, the company opened casinos from the Great Smoky Mountains of North Carolina, to New Orleans, to just outside San Diego.

In addition to building its own places, Harrah's acquired casinos in bunches.

Its purchase of Showboat in 1998 meant that it owned properties from Atlantic City to Sydney, Australia. Its 1999 acquisition of the flashy Rio All-Suite Hotel & Casino in Las Vegas gave it the sexy new image it had been lacking. This was followed by the opening of Harrah's New Orleans where the company had an exclusive on land in the Big Easy. That year, *Computerworld* magazine ranked Harrah's No. 2 among its Top 100 Best Places to Work in Information Technology.

Harrah's fast-running machine was noticed by *Forbes*, which in 2000 listed it among the 400 top-performing companies in the United States. As if to celebrate, Harrah's acquired Players International and another half-dozen gambling operations, mostly in the South. A year later, it added Harvey's Casino Resorts to its list and later acquired Horseshoe Gaming Holdings Company for $1.45 billion.

Just sixty-five years after Bill Harrah opened his doors in Reno, Harrah's Entertainment boasted thirty-six casinos, 1.5-million square feet of casino space, 14,200 rooms, and 42,000 employees.

Harrah's had accomplished what authors Wallace Turner and David Johnston feared: the spread of the legalized gambling brand from coast to coast. Gambling hadn't been packaged as a sin, and it wasn't fronting for some ancient mob family. Satre's company was as close to all-American as a casino concern would ever be, and company-connected scandal was almost nonexistent.

Satre announced his retirement effective January 1, 2005. His handpicked replacement was Gary Loveman, a Harvard-trained lawyer and former associate professor at the university's Graduate School of Business Administration. Observers could ponder about how the gambling business had changed since the days of Moe Dalitz.

Satre had been impressed with Loveman after hearing him give a marketing seminar. Loveman's association with Harrah's started as a marketing and branding consultant, subjects close to Satre's heart. For several years, Loveman was one of the best-kept secrets in the industry. Eventually, he was named chief operating officer at a $1.5-million salary and the perquisites that go with such a position.

Loveman was a dynamic public speaker. His sharp mind was matched by his sharper tongue. He hadn't grown up in the business, and those who watched him talk down to members of the Nevada Gaming Control Board wondered if he appreciated his place in the arc of gambling history.

Loveman in many ways may be the quintessential new Las Vegas corporate boss: educated, intelligent, and arrogant. Like MGM Mirage's Kirk Kerkorian and Terry Lanni, Loveman didn't make his home in Las Vegas. Nor did he live in Memphis, headquarters for Harrah's.

Privately, veteran gaming regulators made little secret of their dislike for Loveman's cocky style. But if "gaming entertainment" has truly gone so mainstream as to be inseparable from kiddie-theme parks and movie metroplexes, then Loveman might be the perfect man for the job.

Gambling history had plenty of men who, by innate instinct, understood the mind of the gambler. Loveman took this skill to the next level by applying a meticulous brand-loyalty philosophy, retail-marketing concepts, and intensive customer service and quality control. Loveman's team is credited with breakthrough marketing technology and customer tracking.

Lest any player naively believe his gambling was anonymous when he stepped inside a Harrah's casino, Loveman prided himself on being able to breakdown each visitor's stay. One goal was to get them to the tables as quickly as possible without making them feel rushed.

"For gamers, precisely because they live their lives for that sense of anticipation, that's a huge deal," Loveman told *International Gaming Business* magazine. "When I got into this business I was amazed. Here's a business that makes money when people gamble and yet we find one hundred ways to keep you from gambling. We keep you on line to check in, and we keep you on line to get your car. Then we keep you on line at the credit window, and we keep you on line to get a jackpot paid or when a machine breaks down . . . it's just nuts."

Loveman wasn't shy about striking back at anyone who

spoke of legalized gambling's downside. "We still have people with absolutely no credibility who are quoted in important newspapers such as the *Chicago Tribune* and the *Wall Street Journal* saying that gambling leads to the destruction of the family, that it decays the city centers, that it is connected to organized crime, or creates higher levels of criminal activities," he said. "These statements are demonstrably false."

In some ways, Loveman was cut from the cloth of Bill Harrah, a master of marketing whose bottom-line-driven efficiency helped open the door to corporate ownership.

In the new century, Harrah's big idea had blossomed into a gaming-industry giant. It had crafted its marketing concepts into ever-expanding profits, and its hunger for expansion was not sated.

So it was only natural that when the once-mighty Caesars Entertainment stumbled, Harrah's was waiting to gobble it up.

Las Vegas has often been touted as a place of grand thematic experimentation, but in truth most first-generation casino bosses thought a lot alike when it came to the decoration of their gambling joints.

Benny Siegel has received undue accolades for his Flamingo project, which in reality was lifted from a string of mob-run art-deco motels in Miami Beach. The Desert Inn, Sands, Dunes, and Sahara were promoted as posh, but held fast to a desert theme as obvious as Southern Nevada's summer sun. Even the Landmark was a knockoff of the Seattle Space Needle.

Jay Sarno changed all that in 1966 when he and his partners created Caesars Palace. With its hedonistic Roman theme, toga-clad cocktail waitresses, and bacchanalian atmosphere, Caesars redefined casino design and raised the gambling experience to unprecedented heights.

Sarno would go on to see Circus Circus built in 1968, a big-top themed casino with live circus acts including trapeze artists sailing high above the gambling floor, but he died in 1982 before his 6,000-room Grandissimo project left the drawing board.

Thanks to a warm relationship with Teamsters boss Jimmy

Hoffa, beginning in 1958, Sarno and business partner Stanley Mallin had access to funds to finance their increasingly sophisticated motel ideas. After building cabana-themed motels in Georgia, Texas, and California, Sarno found himself in Las Vegas, where he spent much of his free time and most of his money.

Although Sarno was a degenerate gambler who as a young man wasn't above pawning his clothes to generate table stakes, a terrible businessman who lost a fortune despite owning pieces of huge cash-generating casinos, and patsy for mob intimidation who once welcomed mob hit man Anthony Spilotro as a tenant and vendor at Circus Circus, his creation was an immediate hit and almost overnight became the standard by which all other casinos were measured. Caesars became the greatest brand in gaming history.

"Sarno's legacy is found in virtually every casino that styles itself as a fantasy world that is one step removed from reality," University of Nevada, Las Vegas gaming research historian David Schwartz observed. "It took the rest of the industry about two decades to catch up to Sarno's vision, but that vision is firmly entrenched today."

It was that magical brand, perhaps more than anything else, that Harrah's Entertainment lacked despite its three dozen properties, formidable profits, and powerful name in the casino industry.

With MGM Mirage's successful $7.9-billion bid to buy out Mandalay Resort Group, effectively creating a Strip casino colossus with eleven resorts and more than 78,000 rooms on a single street, Harrah's had a quick decision to make: continue to cast an ever-wider net for players, or increase its stake in the center of the action on the Strip.

In the end, the decision became obvious. And Caesars Entertainment made it easier by underperforming after September 11. Only weeks after the MGM Mirage announcement, Harrah's stepped up and made a $9.4-billion offer for Caesars Entertainment, a move that if approved would give it five formidable Strip resorts, more than two of every ten hotel rooms on the Boulevard, and, more importantly, a chance to grab the highest high-roller action by owning the legendary Caesars. The deal would again make Harrah's the largest casino company in the world with fifty-one operations from California to Uruguay.

The lack of acrimony associated with the buyout fueled Caesars stock price. The nearly $10-billion deal was almost too easy.

In October, Phil Satre announced his impending retirement and Gary Loveman was poised to take control. Satre could not have left the company in healthier shape. Its $118.8-million third-quarter net profit set a company record. Satre had spent a stellar career growing Harrah's into a rock-solid Fortune 500 company.

In fact, some observers would say Harrah's was in such great shape because Satre had been wise enough to explore new markets and not attempt to challenge for supremacy on the Strip. He never let his ego get in the way of sound business sense as he built the company from four casinos to nearly thirty. He could claim many major victories, but it had been the small ones that made Harrah's a powerhouse.

Ironically, the buyout proposal came at a time Caesars Entertainment finally appeared to be rising from its knees in the marketplace. Its fourth-quarter 2004 profits were up substantially, and even its Atlantic City property was running on all cylinders again. "Caesars' positive announcement does not come as a complete surprise," Deutsche Bank analyst Marc Falcone told *Las Vegas Review-Journal* reporter Howard Stutz. "Based on our New Year's observations, room rate surveys, and meetings with property and company management, we had anticipated that both Las Vegas and Atlantic City experienced a particularly strong New Year's Eve holiday celebration. We believe this announcement bodes well for other gaming operators."

To ease federal trade commission monopoly concerns, Harrah's sold its two Tunica, Mississippi, properties and also a gambling operation in East Chicago. Sales agreements were reached with Columbia Sussex and Colony Capital for a range of casinos, which also included the Atlantic City Hilton, Bally's Casino New Orleans, and Caesars Tahoe.

That would still leave Harrah's Entertainment with fifty casinos, easily the largest, with MGM Mirage a distant second in numbers, but enjoying a far-greater presence on the Strip.

The Harrah's-Caesars combination would annually generate $9.4 billion in revenue with an industry-best cash flow of $2.3 billion—enough to fuel Loveman's plans for continued expansion.

In addition to the federal go-ahead required for such a monopoly-threatening transaction, theoretically the sale would also hinge on the approval of multistate gaming regulatory agencies. Here is where the lack of control of licensed gaming properties showed. Neither Mississippi nor Nevada was expected to raise more than a perfunctory issue with a deal that was sure to make Harrah's one of the two most-powerful and politically influential players in Nevada, a state that relied on casino taxes for more than half its state budget.

And yet, during the MGM Mirage-Mandalay Resort Group licensing hearings, members of the Control Board and Gaming Commission intimated that a key reason Kerkorian's supercompany was going forward rather smoothly was because most of its corporate footprint was in Nevada. The same could not be said for Harrah's, which had found success by applying a very different methodology. What was good for Harrah's in a dozen states wasn't necessarily good for Nevada's economy.

But by approving the MGM deal, state regulators were acknowledging that they weren't about to slow the industry giant's rapid consolidation.

They might put Loveman through his paces. His impolitic outspokenness about the need in the modern age for background investigations had angered some Gaming Control officials. But how does a state so dependent on gaming dollars say no to a major contributor of those dollars?

Combined, the two giants would account for approximately 30 percent of the state's general fund revenue.

The potential ramifications of having two all-powerful companies in the state's casino market concerned some Nevada politicians, who very privately said few elected officials would dare challenge the consummate clout created by building two monolithic organizations. (Not, they were compelled to add, that many politicians had been willing to take on Gaming Inc. at any time in previous years.)

Vendors in Las Vegas had often been at the mercy of their casino customers. Brokers of everything from tomato sauce to flowers would be even-more vulnerable to price setting by the two casino giants. Without them as customers, their business would be crippled. Without reasonable prices and timely bill paying, even midsized businesses that traded with the giants could suffer irreparable damage.

The supersized casino companies would be capable of wielding unprecedented clout. Even before the mergers, there were plenty of examples of casinos taking advantage of their financial importance on the balance sheets of feeder businesses by dictating political policy on such things as legislative tax plans and candidate endorsements.

It was no secret that many companies "provided" employees with preferred candidate lists and voter information in an attempt to strengthen their already mighty political positions. Like born-again Christians and environmental activists, the casino titans devoted time, personnel, and money toward consolidating their influence in local, state, and federal elections.

◆　　◆　　◆

And all of that was bound to increase once the Harrah's-Caesars Entertainment deal was eventually approved.

The Caesars Entertainment acquisition was more important for Harrah's than the Mandalay purchase was for MGM Mirage. Harrah's didn't need more casinos. It already ran more than any other company in the world. But it did need to start casting a formidable shadow on the Strip, which remains Ground Zero for all gambling marketing. The Harrah's resort was an impressive financial success, but it wasn't the sort of place most tourists dreamed of when they fantasized about their Vegas vacation. Thanks to an impeccably timed buyout, the MGM boys had the Bellagio, Mirage, and were on their way to adding the popular Mandalay Bay.

That left Caesars Palace, which had seen better days, but still carried one of the best brands in the business, on the Boulevard. And Loveman was well publicized as a man who knew his brands.

But what, many Strip observers wondered, would become of Caesars Palace? Not the building, but the brand name. Would the supremely confident Loveman appreciate and respect the identification a generation of gamblers still had for the place? Or would he do what others had done, look at the bottom line and assume the great Caesars name had become more legend than fact, that it was destined to fade like the Dunes, Sands, and Desert Inn.

The first place a new owner would be tempted to cut would be in the high-roller area. Previous operators had closed popular gourmet-style tourist restaurants such as the Bacchanal Room and had cut player limits in an effort to minimize the dramatic swings at the bottom line.

The *Review-Journal*'s Rod Smith was the first reporter to raise the issue in print and received a heated reply from Loveman, who denied he intended to change Caesars' tradition of catering to high rollers. That resulted in a lengthy clarification in the newspaper that, rather than vindicating the gaming executive, mired him in his own masked language. He had strongly hinted that, because the high-roller profit margins weren't "compelling," they would have to be improved. Harrah's 1999 acquisition of the Rio, the newspaper noted, resulted in a cutting back on its high-roller action.

It was also true that catering to high rollers was not only the fastest way for a casino to make a name for itself, but also the quickest way for corporate executives to sully their precious quarterly profit statements. It was an area where, perhaps coincidentally, the casinos that were most successful were those that employed executives with plenty of floor experience.

Loveman's rhetoric made some wonder whether he'd already given up on the Caesars image or didn't fully appreciate its place in the resort-industry pantheon.

The problem with Caesars wasn't of Loveman's making. He hadn't thinned the brand by failing at customer service, constantly shifting marketing personnel, cutting back on complementary services, and falling behind the Strip's era of rapid expansion. Previous operators could be credited with that dubious distinction.

How Loveman marketed the Caesars name, once the greatest in all gaming, would make or break his image as the Strip's newest genius.

## 35

# Flesh for Fantasy

The topless blonde lies across a blackjack table with a playing card in her mouth while her partner stares at her bikini bottom with the sort of attention most gamblers reserve for a brace of aces ready for splitting.

Leaving little to the imagination, the Hard Rock advertisement coos, there's always a temptation to cheat.

In another Hard Rock billboard display, panties are dropped around a pair of high-heeled ankles with the message, "Get Ready to Buck All Night," apparently intended for bronco-riding aficionados during National Finals Rodeo week.

Advertising for Peter Morton's Hard Rock Hotel and Casino had pressed the envelope since its opening. The Hard Rock was a haven for rock stars and Hollywood celebrities who exuded sex from its steamy poolside to its popular nightclubs.

Young people, some underage, converged on the resort in record numbers to chase good times and rub shoulders with the rich rockers and their flashy entourages. But the Hard Rock soon spawned imitators in the wicked and rapidly changing Las Vegas market. Other resorts added sexy nightclubs complete with everything from cage go-go dancers to bikini-clad bartenders.

In its attempt to maintain its reign as the hippest, sexiest resort in Las Vegas, the Hard Rock's advertising grew ever-more suggestive and undressed. In theory, a casino operator could lose his privileged license for embarrassing the state's most-powerful industry, but with the Las Vegas Convention and Visitors Authority promoting its racy "What Happens in Vegas Stays in Vegas" theme, how much trouble could the Hard Rock get in by leaving just a little less to the imagination?

Quite a bit, as it turned out.

In May 2004, the Gaming Control Board filed a three-count complaint against the Hard Rock. It charged that the casino's advertising reflected negatively on the industry.

Control Board Member Bobby Siller, a former FBI special agent in charge, was vocal in his criticism.

In response, Hard Rock President Kevin Kelley was adamant in his belief that the advertisements were not only effective, but didn't embarrass the industry or flout its regulations.

Although the commissioners doubted the ads actually would encourage cheating, Siller wasn't amused by Kelley's demeanor before the Control Board. It was his view that any encouragement of rule breaking was bound to lead to problems in the casino and send the wrong image to players.

Not only that, but it wasn't appropriate to sprawl topless on blackjack tables.

A $300,000 settlement of the issue was brokered. Then civil libertarians came to the Hard Rock's defense. Any gaming regulation used to prohibit certain kinds of advertising surely violated the First Amendment. The $300,000-settlement offer was withdrawn.

Meanwhile, Gaming Commission Chairman Peter Bernhard took the unusual step of scheduling a trial to address the policy issues involved. Namely, whether the Control Board ought to be involved in regulating casino advertising in the name of protecting either the industry or the community.

Hard Rock eventually modified the messages on its billboards. Still it continued to raise eyebrows with its portrayal of lipsticked lesbian party girls and ads that left little doubt that the resort's greatest commodity was its flesh and fantasy.

Although the hotel would claim it wasn't promoting illegal activity, undercover police officers observed young prostitutes flock to the resort's popular center-casino bar.

Hard Rock attorney Jeffrey Silver, himself a former member of the Gaming Commission, raised the issue of censorship, which even in heavy-handed Nevada set off alarms from constitutionalists. Silver also noted that the state had not created a guide for licensees who might raise similar issues in the future.

Would the future of sexy Las Vegas advertising truly be left to a state-sanctioned compliance committee?

American Civil Liberties Union of Nevada general counsel Allen Lichtenstein warned that to put anyone at risk for penalties that are unconstitutional is just flat-out wrong.

Gaming regulation in Nevada had often been criticized for skirting the Constitution on a variety of issues. Appeals courts had ruled years before that the industry could decide whom it allowed to hold a license and even work in the kitchen or behind a blackjack table.

But First Amendment speech was different—even in Las Vegas.

Siller found himself in the minority as he attempted to remind the industry that it was a different animal and that the rules were in place for a reason.

"There are some very interesting challenges in gaming," Siller said. "There's probably a good study to be done on the impact corporations are having on Nevada in gaming. I think it's like everything else. It's a pendulum, and I happen to believe it has swung too far in favor of the corporations.

"I happen to think they have too much influence now.

There's a difference in attitude. Their ethics is being redefined. It is ends-based ethics. The ends justify the means. Whatever they have to do to improve the bottom line is good. I care about what's good for the people of Nevada. They seem to care more about what's good for their bottom lines."

◆　　◆　　◆

Peter Morton's Hard Rock Hotel and Casino was an instant smash following its March 1995 opening. At a cost of just $92 million, and with only 340 rooms, it didn't rival the Strip's megaresorts. It did provide the equivalent of a working laboratory for attracting younger customers to Las Vegas casinos.

Those who were skeptical that a casino catering to twenty-somethings would do much business found themselves surprised. The casino floor was tiny by megaresort standards, but it was packed with youngsters trying their luck for the first time and with older players who fancied the hip atmosphere and hard-bodied appearance of the guests. In Las Vegas, as in the rest of America, few things sell better than sex and youth—and a hip logo.

At the Hard Rock, the famous logo plastered on T-shirts was an immense cash generator for the hotel. In its first year of operation, the company earned more from the sale of its logo shirts than from its few hundred hotel rooms. (The MGM Grand sells more than $1 million-worth of its logo T-shirts every year.)

After partnering with Harvey's Casino Resorts in 1997, Morton bought out that company's 40-percent share of Hard Rock for $45 million and embarked on a dramatic expansion plan. The business relationship had been described as stormy, but the fact was Morton believed he'd outgrown his partners and no longer needed them.

The Harvey deal was a bargain for Morton, whose smooth celebrity exterior masked a superaggressive businessman known for his rock-star ego.

However, unlike some of his counterparts in the casino

game, Morton maintained balance in his personal life by remaining close to his three children. Profile writers would note that his home had a distinct lack of the sort of over-the-top rock memorabilia that were the trademarks of his Hard Rock hotel and cafés.

Environmentalists might scoff at Morton's Hard Rock Save the Planet, which brought rock stars to perform on behalf of antipollution and conservation programs, but he clearly understood the importance of celebrity culture. His clubs and hotel practiced recycling and donated handsomely to charity. For his part, Morton was a National Resources Defense Council trustee.

At the Hard Rock hotel, in the middle of the city most known in the world for its waste of resources and conspicuous consumption, an electronic tote board counts down the time remaining for the world's rain forests.

Was this a pretentious and hypocritical statement in the middle of a casino resort?

Whatever the answer, Morton had tapped into a rich vein of liberal American consciousness. And he played it like a Stratocaster. Others might ask if there was room in the Hard Rock's hip world for players in wheelchairs. It's a question Ronald Ray Smith and Frank Stephens asked in a 1996 lawsuit against the hotel. They accused the Hard Rock of failing to make its shuttle buses handicapped accessible. Inexplicably, given its reputation as a green, clean operation, the hotel fought the lawsuit and lost two years later when United States District Judge Howard McKibben issued an injunction mandating the changes in the buses.

Morton would name-drop the Hollywood elite and be seen dining with the world's biggest rock and film stars, and yet he also appeared to have a soul away from the job he created after leaving his famous Chicago steakhouse family and embarking on a trip to London not long after Woodstock.

Morton continued to exude the laid-back air of a fellow to whom Lady Success might have kissed by accident. But it wasn't chance that put him among the top of the Vegas hipsters.

Behind dark glasses, he disguised well the fact he was raised in the family's famous restaurant business. He studied business administration at the University of Denver.

In London's Mayfair District, he found the breathing room a young man needed to explore the counterculture of the day and to decide the direction he wanted to take in the family calling. He kept it basic, opened the Great American Disaster hamburger haven, then grew it into the Hard Rock. And never looked back.

He opened the first Hard Rock Cafe in London in 1971 and wowed the masses with genuine American hamburgers. For extra income, he sold Hard Rock T-shirts. The burgers were tasty, but the T-shirts rapidly became coveted throughout Europe and the United States.

"We sold T-shirts out of a paper bag," Morton said of the business chain he eventually sold for nearly $1 billion.

He later opened Morton's steakhouse in Hollywood and continued to network with influential pals from the film and music industries. It wasn't until 1982, with help from Steven Spielberg and other Hollywood moguls, that Morton opened the first Hard Rock in the United States.

Although Morton eventually sold his interest in Hard Rock to the Rank Organization, he continued to be identified with it as he pursued Vegas perfection in an off-Strip location.

In the new century, Morton's expansion plans remain modest by Strip standards. With Harvey's out of the way, he called for an additional 350 guest rooms and four new restaurants. He also bought adjacent acreage to expand the resort's potential footprint to eighteen acres, large enough for a high-rise in the future.

Morton told a reporter, "As long as Las Vegas has great entrepreneurs like Steve Wynn and Kirk Kerkorian, I really believe in the long-term viability of the community."

# The Prince of the Palms

**M**eet the face of the new Las Vegas.

George Maloof's profile defines boyishly handsome. He has dark eyes that glint devilishly, and he has every reason to smile.

He has managed to successfully work casino marketing to capture the fickle attention of Las Vegas visitors. He's done so not with a multibillion-dollar megaresort or by flashing his wealth, but by bottling something akin to eternal youth and seizing the raw sexiness that has always been paramount in promoting Las Vegas.

The Hard Rock's Peter Morton retooled sexual imagery with great success, but he began with a brand name known throughout the world. Maloof started with a Mexican-themed slot palace in North Las Vegas and within ten years, parlayed it into the hottest boutique resort almost on the Strip. (The Palms stands on a slender island of property on Flamingo Road across the street from the Rio and Gold Coast casinos.)

349

Son of a wealthy New Mexico beer and liquor distributor whose brothers run the family's stake in the Sacramento Kings basketball team, George Maloof's name appears regularly in gossip columns. One day he's linked romantically to Britney Spears and the next he's observed dining with friends from the world of movies, sports, or pop celebrity.

On the surface, he appears to be living the life of a young Vegas playboy who just happens to have his own resort. Las Vegas history is riddled with the corpses of once-young playboys who believed operating a gambling den was simple and their youth and money would last forever.

But those who know Maloof say that his baby face is deceptive and that behind the easygoing manner lies a hard-working and fiercely competitive perfectionist. More than pleasing the paparazzi, Maloof seeks most to please his family and competitive brothers. It's that family tie, his friends and business associates say, that anchors George Maloof to the real world that exists below the penthouse suites and top-floor ultralounges.

Kerkorian's wealth and Wynn's track record as an innovator are greater, but with the slender, forty-two-story Palms, Maloof created the sizzle and sensation that's essential to capture the youth movement. The Palms is slutty, its gaming tables razzle-dazzle and silly (it pays 6 to 5 on blackjacks instead of the customary 10 to 5), but it brims with hard bodies and celebrity. And all this in a hotel with fewer than 500 rooms.

Maloof has managed to market successfully to two widely divergent customer groups: value-driven local slot players and twenty-something visitors with pockets full of currency and a weekend to kill in a 95,000-square-foot casino.

The result is most apparent in the Palms bottom line that reports a 20-percent profit margin. Imitation is flattery, and on the Strip, every megaresort has suddenly come up with ultralounges and nightclubs in an effort to lure away younger customers.

"It's a misnomer to say that the kids party, but don't gamble," one veteran casino expert said. "The key is, they spend. They might not play blackjack or shoot dice all night the way their fathers did, but they bring their money and they never sleep. Plus they're a lot easier on the eyes at poolside."

Maloof first saw Las Vegas as a boy during family vacations to the Aladdin and Riviera. He recalls being intrigued and captivated by the town's energy.

In the mid-1980s he returned to play cornerback for UNLV's football team and study at the hotel-management college. He graduated in 1987. The family fortune was in New Mexico, Colorado, Texas, and California. Young George was obsessed with Las Vegas.

The Maloofs had been in flashy, image-oriented businesses before. They'd owned the Houston Rockets from 1978 through 1983. (In 1998, they purchased 25 percent of the struggling Sacramento Kings franchise and eventually upped their stake to more than 50 percent. They also built the Arco Arena in Sacramento.) The Maloofs redefined the concept of the family business. Eldest son Joe and Gavin operate the Kings with mother Colleen adding her expertise. Phil and Adrienne also worked for Maloof Companies in executive capacities.

That made George the family's point man in Vegas.

But where Joe and Gavin gained reputations for their arrogance more than their high-wagering limits, George maintained a friendlier public demeanor capable of charming journalists and supermodels alike.

Wrote one enthusiastic newspaper profiler, "Maloof is the journalist's version of kryptonite, a life force so disarming that he weakens the willpower of approaching skeptics. Reporters routinely write glowing pieces about him, only to be ripped by their colleagues for being soft on the guy."

In his late thirties, with the hedonistic excesses of Las Vegas at his fingertips, Maloof still manages to draw comparisons to a Boy Scout—albeit one who'd earned merit badges in babe attraction.

In many respects, George Maloof is cut from the same tough cloth as the family patriarch he was named for. His grandfather, George J. Maloof, owned a Las Vegas, New Mexico, grocery store and was rumored to be a bootlegger. When he acquired the state's first Coors beer distributorship in 1937, he set his family on the highway to success.

Grandpa George didn't just haul beer. He bought stock and gradually broadened the family business portfolio. Although the Maloofs eventually would sell its liquor distributorship in the late 1990s, the profits it generated enabled them to buy banks, transportation companies, and motels, including the Anaheim Sheraton near Disneyland. They also owned the small but profitable Central Palace casino in Colorado.

With his family backing him, Maloof got his start in the casino business in 1994 with the creation of the Fiesta on downtrodden Rancho Road. Thanks to lively print and television advertising, the Mexican-themed casino became a favorite with locals for its food and reputation as the "royal flush capital of the world."

Maloof employed an effective marketing strategy: In a business in which operators were shortsightedly tight in the area of customer value, Maloof's slot machines were loose and generous and his restaurant and buffet prices were bargain laden.

Maloof's ownership of the Fiesta wasn't lacking in controversy. In October 1998, the company faced up to $1.7 million in fines when regulators suspected unlawful horse-race bets were being made in the casino's sports book. High-rolling horse bettor Andrew Berg placed more than $5 million in bets at the book and received rebates for his gargantuan wagers. The rebates were in clear violation of Nevada law.

The Fiesta survived the investigation and enjoyed considerable success, but no one gets into the gaming business to run a slot joint on the edge of North Las Vegas. In late 1997, the Maloof family made its second move. It bought 31.5 acres of property not far from the Strip near land formerly on the edge of a flood channel.

Maloof signed a three-year noncompete clause when he sold the Fiesta to the Fertitta family in 2000 for $185 million in cash. That excluded the Palms site from the deal. His intentions were clear: to raise his personal bar as a gaming developer and do battle at close range with formidable operations such as the Harrah's-owned Rio and the Gaughan-owned Gold Coast.

When the $265-million Palms project broke ground in October 2000, Maloof was just thirty-seven and already had built a reputation for marketing savvy and hard work. He was also smart enough to welcome minority partners in the form of the influential Fertitta and Greenspun family companies.

The Palms opened to throngs of celebrities, gamblers, and the just plain curious. From its first moment, it maintained a celebrity atmosphere far greater than its relatively small size. The Hard Rock, Bellagio, and Mandalay Bay had bigger names and plenty of stars, but the Palms was a smash hit, and its rooms and its casino were filled to capacity.

"People all over the country know the name," Maloof told a reporter in a candid moment. "They know the brand. And when I tell them I own a casino—the Palms—they smile."

At the Palms, television cameras are common, as are the celebrities they follow. Popular shows such as "The Real World" and "The Osbournes" shot episodes at the Palms, and any night Britney Spears or Paris Hilton party at the Ghost Bar of the Palms; the news was sure to wind up in the nation's gossip columns.

The Ghost Bar is known as Las Vegas's hottest celebrity hangout. Located on top of the forty-two-floor hotel, it is modeled on its Chicago namesake with a wide-eyed ghost who floats on the ceiling and changes color every half-hour.

Maloof had clearly targeted Peter Morton's Hard Rock crowd, but that didn't prevent Morton's brother, Michael Morton, and Scott DeGraff from operating the bar lounge, N9NE steakhouse, and a bar at the swimming pool. Las Vegas claims to have more than three hundred sunny days a year, and poolside at the Palms means Miami-type sunbathing on a two-acre Shangri-la. The area contains patches of white sand to give it a South Beach aura. Then there are the two-story cabanas that offer a view of the pool's bathing beauties and the Strip. A cabana on the weekends costs $195.

An unusual body chair allows one to float in the water. Then there are skinny-dip nights and the naughty naughty nights. The hotel tries to maintain a Mardi Gras flavor in the evening with stiltwalkers and jugglers.

The success of the Palms drew comparisons between Maloof and a Vegas rising star of a previous generation. Deutsche Bank analyst Andrew Zarnett observed, "He's very good in the operations side of the business. He puts a lot of effort into his product and his people, and it shows. His roots are in customer service, just like Steve Wynn's are."

One example of what's different at the Palms: The hotel created twenty-four special accommodations known as NBA suites. The ceilings in these are ten feet high instead of the usual eight feet and even the doors have been made higher. The beds are two feet longer than traditional beds. National Basketball Association players can sleep there without their feet dangling over the bed.

"He's passionate about what he does, about pleasing the customer. Clearly he's viewed as a young Steve Wynn in the industry, and even Steve agrees. That puts him in a great place," Zarnett said.

Not that his life is all work and no play.

As if the Palms didn't already attract more than its share of attractive women, in June 2004 Maloof announced a national search for its first official "Palms Girl," a model who would symbolize the resort and appear in commercials and on billboards. He had no shortage of applicants and in the end, true to his image, found not one worthy candidate, but twins.

With 20-percent profits and expansion plans for arguably the hottest property not on the Strip, George Maloof's greatest challenge will be keeping focused on the bottom line rather than on the unending parade of Las Vegas young beauties who flit about in his place.

# The Reverend

## 37

It was the kind of match-up you might have found in a first draft of a Biblical text: a wiry, gray-haired man of conviction speaks truth to power against a seductive and influential kingdom. But a strange thing happened to the Rev. Tom Grey on the way to felling the giant of Gaming Inc.: his best rock-throwing efforts failed to topple the behemoth or halt the rise of legalized casino gambling in America.

In a world where swords really were mightier than pens and money and power beat moral conviction the way aces beat deuces, there was almost no stopping the national gambling expansion. Sure, there was an occasional victory, but the industry had become far bigger than one man, or one hundred, could deter.

Grey was a Methodist minister and former Vietnam War army grunt who'd begun to criticize the gaming industry after casino corporations tried to build near his Illinois home. He headed the National Coalition Against Gambling Expansion, an organization that sent him around the nation by car. His opponents traveled in private jets.

Grey was energetic, articulate, and armed with no end of damning facts and suppositions. He made good newspaper copy and gained national headlines by crisscrossing the country in his battered Toyota, spreading the good word that legalized gambling was bad for America.

He was poorly funded and hopelessly outgunned. He was made to order for the gaming industry whose history in Nevada was littered with instances in which multimillionaires making 20 percent on their investments managed to cry and moan about an excessive tax burden.

In December 1997, the American Gaming Association, lobbying arm for the casinos, produced a study by Harvard University that downplayed the role of compulsive behavior and criminal activity in legalized gambling. The study reported that anywhere from two and seven gamblers out of every one hundred were problem gamblers.

True, this added up to many thousands of citizens with problems, but think of the other millions. For them, casino gambling was harmless adult entertainment.

In their eagerness to put the best face on their business, industry mouthpieces attempted to compare things like crime rates between Orlando, Florida, home of Disney World, and Las Vegas, home of more than sixty years of legalized gambling. They pointed out that parents might lose their children in a crowd at Disney World, but they didn't mention that parents could more easily lose their children's college fund in a bad night in a Las Vegas casino.

Grey sensed what most big casino officials were afraid to admit: That no seemingly official study can persuade even avid players that gambling is good for them. Those executives would never admit that their product came with a substantial sleaze factor or that their slots and table games preyed on human weakness. Or that a percentage of those who participated would fall victim to devastating compulsions.

And so Grey tried to apply pressure where he knew it stung the most. In the process, he made a national name for himself and was quoted regularly in major newspapers such as the *Washington Post*, as well as on television news magazines such as "60 Minutes."

His critics might mutter that he was little more than a one-man band, an Elmer Gantry in an endless search for heathens to save. Grey was cut from tougher cloth. The Vietnam veteran wasn't shy about admitting that he enjoyed a friendly game of poker now and then. Unlike others in the business of criticizing the casino crowd, Grey was no hypocrite.

He was precisely what so many in the casino industry were not. He was a straight-talking Methodist minister with no capped teeth, $100-haircuts, private jets, or Infinite Hubris cologne. He downplayed his Christian ideals and instead focused on gambling's social and economic impacts on a community.

He could spout statistics like the Rain Man one minute, crack jokes about himself and his battered Toyota the next.

"I think that probably the biggest misunderstanding has been that this was, quote, a religious-driven, motivated movement, and that worked to our advantage," Grey said. "I think we've gotten a lot of ground out of the fact the AGA and the press out of here saw it as being out of the right. . . . It was not a crusade against gambling. It was a defensive battle against gambling."

"When I first heard casino gambling was coming to my community, my thoughts were 'It's not good economics, it's not good public policy, and it's not good for the quality of life,'" he said. "I didn't think for a minute that people wouldn't gamble. And that's never changed."

For a short time in 1998, Grey found an unlikely ally in Las Vegas gaming maverick Bob Stupak. Stupak unsuccessfully tried to cash a stack of $5,000 gaming chips at the beleaguered Binion's Horseshoe Club. He gave one chip to Grey, whose attempt to exchange it for money was rebuffed. Horseshoe management suspected the chips had been stolen when the casino changed hands during a Binion family feud.

After the Gaming Control Board ruled in Stupak's favor, Grey's chip was cashed. In 1999, the money was donated to the Rev. James Reed of the Union Avenue United Methodist Church on the South Side of Chicago. Reed was dying of cancer, and his parish needed the money, Grey said.

Grey was an occasional Las Vegas visitor and had been befriended by firebrand former City Councilman Steve Miller. Miller was a critic of gaming expansion outside Nevada. Grey was also vocal when Nevada-based casino corporations spent millions to defeat Native American gaming expansion in California. After losing on Election Day, they spent millions more to partner with the Indians in their casino gold mines.

Grey was spot-on in his cataloguing of Gaming Inc. hypocrisy, yet he failed to admit that the casino men were getting their way in most jurisdictions. As he was predicting the national gambling explosion would be the downfall of the Las Vegas gambling lords, he appeared to underestimate their ability to adapt to changing political tides and public perceptions.

"The truth's on our side," Grey liked to tell his audiences and members of the press.

But time and money were on the industry's side.

◆  ◆  ◆

"If casinos are the best we can do for jobs and a future, I don't want any part of that," Grey said. "My zeal is about a product that has a place, but they've taken it out of the box that it was in and marketed it across the nation."

The National Gambling Impact Study Commission released its report in June 1999. Grey, a commission member, sounded like the lone voice of criticism against an industry that had managed to influence and manipulate the most-extensive congressional gambling panel study since Estes Kefauver.

The commission's report listed in detail the many issues facing legalized gambling expansion. It called for the elimination of campaign contributions by the industry and discontinuing the practice of allowing college sports betting. Still it had fallen short of Grey's hopes. Although he claimed to "love" the report, he was once again shouted down by the larger voices in the gaming industry.

Lobbyist Frank Fahrenkopf was ecstatic. "The verdict is in, and the accused has been exonerated," he said in an AGA press release. "When this commission was launched, critics predicted our industry would be found guilty of all types of evils. But their charges have been proven wrong. I hate to say I told you so, but the commission report is replete with positive references to commercial casino gaming."

After two years and $5 million in taxpayer money, the industry was untouched and could now look forward to many more years without scrutiny by Congress.

"This is a love-in," Grey said. "Everyone loves this report. They love it, and we love it. That means, as in the game of poker, everyone says they've got a winning hand. I want to tell you. Our hand is the winner."

The winner? Despite the lack of a federal tax recommendation? Despite an admission that America wants to gamble? Despite the acknowledgment that gambling isn't just a vice, but "has emerged as an economic mainstay in many communities and plays an increasingly prominent role in state and even regional economies"?

"How people in the industry can sign a report and embrace a report that trashes their own product is beyond me," Grey said.

He planned to use the report to remind all who will listen of gambling's dangers. He faced a Gallup Poll that said two-thirds of American adults approve of legalized gaming.

The reverend might have had right on his side, but his warning was drowned out by the shouts of a nation of players and the white noise of the industry's relentless and persuasive lobbyists, as well as its not-so-secret weapon: the promise of easy riches and the return of prosperity in regions rattled by recession.

He reminded some of a Biblical David. In truth, his best rocks were no match for the gaming Goliath.

# 38

# Riding for the Brand

Las Vegas has marketed itself through mass media and Hollywood movies for generations. The Las Vegas News Bureau's cheesecake photo images of bikini-clad showgirls at poolside have found their way into newspapers for more than fifty years. Blockbuster films such as *Viva Las Vegas* and the original *Ocean's 11* promoted not just Elvis and Sinatra, but the hip gambling party going nonstop on the Strip when casinos weren't allowed to advertise.

The image game has become more sophisticated since Danny Ocean cased Las Vegas Boulevard, but the message is the same: The Strip is where anything goes, a place where the seven deadly sins are just another way to spend a long weekend.

Although each resort has its own advertising staff, and major casino operators often hire Los Angeles and New York agencies, homegrown R&R Partners is responsible for crafting the collective Las Vegas message. Its $60-million contract with the Las Vegas Convention and Visitors Authority has been controversial—the authority was originally created so casino operators could pay for parks and fairs through a hotel-room tax levy—but there's no disputing R&R's impact. Its LVCVA advertising budget is larger than that of many states. Although, for legal reasons, the advertising contract seemingly is put out for bids, the process is little more than clever theater. The end result is that the local firm always prevails over some of the largest advertising companies in the world.

Through the years, R&R has performed competently, although results have sometimes been less than dazzling. That changed in 2003 when Las Vegas was emerging from the damage to tourism associated with the September 11 terrorist attacks.

A series of television ads featuring an ethnic mélange of Vegas visitors began to air. All had visited the Strip and had done something impulsive, something a little crazy, something the folks back home might not approve. It was beautifully captured in the slogan: "What happens here, stays here."

"Almost everyone knows what Las Vegas looks like," R&R creative director Randy Snow observed, "but fewer know how it really feels."

Not even the creative heads at R&R realized how effective those five words would be. On a May 2004 broadcast of "The Tonight Show," a guest appearance by first lady Laura Bush cemented the slogan's place in the pantheon of advertising pitches.

Laura Bush had traveled to Burbank, California, from Las Vegas where she had made a campaign stop. After teasing her about rumors that she'd been "partying until dawn," host Jay Leno asked, "Did you gamble while you were there? Did you pull a slot machine handle? Did you go to a Chippendales show?"

Grinning slyly, the first lady replied, "Jay, what happens in Vegas stays in Vegas."

When a city's mantra finds its way into the public pronouncements of the first lady of the United States, even the industry's staunchest critics must recognize that R&R has hit a home run in ad effectiveness.

In the months that followed, scores of movie stars, politicians, and other public figures would mouth the line. Host Billy Crystal used it on Motion Picture Academy Awards night. On college campuses, commercial flights, and corner bars, the slogan became the latest catch phrase in a nation that embraces advertising clichés.

It was even uttered sarcastically by the former education secretary and self-appointed national morality czar, William Bennett. Bennett had been scandalized by his inability to control his multimillion-dollar slot-machine addiction. This had exposed him as a hypocrite. Bennett whined to Tim Russert of "Meet the Press," "Apparently, 'what happens here stays here' applies to everyone but me."

The Maloofs tried to kidnap the catchy line by promoting the theme "What happens at the Palms stays at the Palms."

The line, incidentally, was penned by R&R Partners copywriters Jeff Candido and Jason Hoff as part of a series of offbeat commercials meant to wink at the way Las Vegas feels to visitors—tourists who come by the millions to party and gamble and not feel guilty about pleasures in which they partake.

The catchy campaign was not without its critics. Harrah's executive Jan Jones, *Las Vegas Sun* columnist Jeff German, and an array of conservative Southern Nevada residents were angry. Sure, perhaps half of the young married women in Las Vegas turned occasional tricks. Sure, every kind of dope was available. But these things weren't to be suggested, and now a slogan placed Las Vegas on the lips of millions and put R&R Partners chief executive Billy Vassiliadis in a place he'd rarely been. In nearly a quarter-century of manipulating the political and advertising landscape for the great Las Vegas gambling machine, the spotlight had finally turned on him. He reveled in it.

*Advertising Age* called the Las Vegas campaign a cultural phenomenon, and *USA Today* said it resulted in the most-compelling ad spots of 2003.

When "Saturday Night Live" spoofs your commercials and Jay Leno uses the line night after night, you have arrived.

Vassiliadis had come from Chicago to Las Vegas as a university student. He broke into the ad business with the well-connected Martin Black Advertising Agency. After being credited with electing John Moran sheriff, Vassiliadis's partnership with Sig Rogich at R&R increased his political contacts.

Rogich is a Republican Party operative and opinion maker who has worked as a senior adviser to presidents Ronald Reagan and George H. W. Bush. Vassiliadis eventually bought out Rogich and emerged as the state's top imagemaker and most-wanted political consultant. Like those who have come before him, he speaks candidly while downplaying maladies wrought by the casino culture on the Southern Nevada community.

If Las Vegas ranks among the worst metropolitan areas in such categories as public education, juvenile delinquency, teen pregnancy, suicide, smoking, and obesity, the vacationing world will never learn about it from the polished propagandists at R&R Partners.

◆　　◆　　◆

"Our business has evolved dramatically over the years," Frank Fahrenkopf observed. Fahrenkopf, former chairman of the Republican National Committee, is the president of the American Gaming Association. This organization polishes the industry's image and delivers its political message to politicians.

To illustrate his point, Fahrenkopf reels off a lengthy list of accomplishments that makes the gaming crowd sound like the most-enlightened souls on the planet. From eliminating the mob from the casinos and grooming happy employees to recognizing compulsive gamblers and battling naysayers seeking to outlaw college sports betting, the AGA is omnipresent. It can deliver a withering stack of reports, studies, and documents to defend its claims that the gambling culture isn't bad for a community.

Part of its dog-and-pony show is to tell all who will listen that the gambling business isn't really about gambling, it's about entertainment. To defend its position, the AGA notes that nongaming revenue in Las Vegas now accounts for 57 percent of total revenue, up from 43 percent in 1994.

When it was created, AGA membership was limited to corporations. In 2004, it opened its rolls to individuals.

Harvard Medical School addictions expert Dr. Howard Shaffer has done much research on compulsive gambling. Shaffer cuts down critics who approach the subject of addiction on moral grounds by using formidable statistical and medical arguments. For every anecdotal tale of addiction, bankruptcy, and human misery generated by gaming's underfunded critics, there would be a thick collection of documents tearing such complaints to shreds produced by this Harvard professor.

In 2004, Shaffer delivered a keynote address to the National Center for Responsible Gaming (NCRG) conference at the MGM Grand. It was titled "Addiction as Syndrome: A New Model for Understanding Excessive Behaviors."

Shaffer concluded that compulsive gamblers and alcoholics have much in common. Although the addictions are different, they stimulate the same place in the brain.

"If pathological gambling is an expression of an addiction syndrome, should health insurers extend coverage to the treatment of pathological gambling?" one of Shaffer's advocates asked in an industry publication. "Should licensing agencies require health care providers be educated on gambling disorders as well as alcohol and drug disorders?"

The effect on compulsive gamblers of the proliferation of casinos and the explosion of gaming resort-related advertising wasn't high on anyone's discussion agenda.

For Fahrenkopf, the bottom line is clear: "Our marketing, construction, and investment strategies must adjust if we are to keep pace with the demands of our increasingly sophisticated customer base."

But one thing hadn't changed since the days of Benny Siegel and Moe Dalitz. The gambling industry is only as strong as its ability to influence political policy and public perception.

# 39

# Tomorrow is Forever

Gaming's main man in Washington is Senate Minority Leader Harry Reid. Reid, a devout Mormon who neither drinks nor smokes, would at first blush seem to be an unlikely partner with the industry.

The son of a Searchlight, Nevada, miner has been a reluctant supporter of the casino crowd. Politically, he grew up at a time when legitimate operators and mob fronts were almost impossible to distinguish, and Reid tangled with the legitimate and illegitimate alike.

As chairman of the Nevada Gaming Commission, he led the fight to deny a license to Frank "Lefty" Rosenthal. Kansas City and Chicago mobsters gave him the nickname "Clean Face." The rumor was spread that Reid was in the mob's pocket. An investigation concluded otherwise, and in the end, Reid rose from the commission to the U. S. Senate, where he quickly became a savvy and smooth player.

Although he was a fierce defender of the industry, working to hammer out compromises in anticipation of the National Gambling Impact Study Commission, Reid wasn't above sparring with casino magnates when he believed their egos had gotten the best of them. He once challenged Steve Wynn to run against him.

Reid also was opposed to Indian reservation gaming—although he helped to draft the enabling legislation—and was adamantly opposed to Internet gambling. That position put him at odds with gaming corporations.

"What you have got to understand about gamblers is that gamblers go where the money is," Reid told *Roll Call*'s Mark Preston. "Nevada gamers were opposed to Indian gaming until they realized they could make money in it. Nevada gamers were opposed to the Internet until they decided they could make money in it."

It's a stance that would sound even more unlikely coming from Reid's counterpart in the Senate, Republican John Ensign. The son of Mandalay Resort Group boss Michael Ensign, the senator was a veterinarian who also had run casinos for his father before winning a seat in the House of Representatives in 1994. This was during the height of House Speaker Newt Gingrich's power and the Republican Party's "Contract With America" program. Observers were often amused by Ensign whose conservative politics and Christian beliefs never put him in opposition to the gaming industry's heavily marketed hedonism.

Without a hint of irony, Ensign told a reporter, "We don't try to do anything for them. We just try to keep them from being attacked."

In early 2005, Republican Jim Gibbons and Democrat Shelley Berkley emerged as cochairs of the Congressional Gaming Caucus. Berkley was the daughter of a casino restaurant waiter and had served cocktails at the Sands to help put herself through college. She had shown uncommon courage when she was critical of Venetian casino magnate Sheldon Adelson, her former boss.

"Our goal is to ensure that the gaming industry and all those it employs are represented as we make public policy here in the nation's capital," Berkley vowed.

Like most savvy Nevada politicians—and all the successful ones—she was fiercely protective of the state's largest employer despite the fact many operators were big contributors to the Republican Party and had made little secret of their disappointment at seeing the liberal Democrat elected to the House.

Although Nevada casinos pay a lower gaming-tax rate than other states, it didn't prevent operators from pushing for a shared burden with nongaming businesses. To that end, Gov. Kenny Guinn, a supporter of the gaming industry, proposed a gross-receipts tax on business.

When the plan foundered due to a lack of legislative leadership and the palpable arrogance of the industry's veteran lobbyists during the 2003 legislature, Terry Lanni and others vowed to make substantive changes.

The industry was accustomed to enjoying the kind of assistance provided by then-District Attorney Stewart Bell. His unprecedented debt-collection efforts on the part of major casino corporations resulted in locating and jailing deadbeat gamblers across the United States. Although some skeptics wished Bell had worked as hard at grabbing deadbeat fathers as busted-out high-rollers, the collection efforts paid off for the industry. And Bell rose from district attorney to district court judge and to the Nevada Supreme Court.

Even legislation portrayed as a victory for residents such as Senate Bill 208, a law passed in 1997 that sought to limit neighborhood casino sprawl out of a concern for the quality of life of residents, came with a catch. Smart operators such as the Fertittas, Michael Gaughan, and Bill Boyd had acquired real estate prior to SB208's passage and in some cases already had begun the rezoning process. In the end, the law designed to protect neighborhoods from invading casinos served to protect neighborhood casino operators from increased competition.

369

In Las Vegas, the deck is so stacked against residents that they must take their small victories where they find them.

While the number of times Nevada's congressional delegation and governor have gone against the gaming industry can be counted on one hand with fingers left over, in 1998, former mob mouthpiece Oscar Goodman was elected Las Vegas mayor. His landslide victory came in part because he was willing to criticize what he called the corporations' stinginess and near-abandonment of the Fremont Street gambling corridor.

Goodman was brutalized by the industry's pet media pundits and scoffed at as a "loose cannon" by its paid spin doctors. When he expressed dismay over massive layoffs of wage earners following the 9/11 attacks, he was ridiculed for not understanding how business worked. When he called for downtown casino owners to do more for themselves by fixing up their tawdry properties, he was again marginalized.

It was only after he stepped forward to endorse the general agenda of Gaming Inc. that Goodman started seeing some of his lofty plans for a downtown renaissance realized. After being reelected in a landslide, he appeared to have nothing to fear from the community's casino bosses—as long as he remembered his place in the political pecking order.

Outside of Nevada, gambling revenues have become what the *New York Times* described as "a critical stream of income." It quoted Republican Wayne A. Smith, majority leader in the Delaware General Assembly. "Gambling revenues are like free money." In Rhode Island, gambling revenues surpassed corporate taxes. In South Dakota, because of gaming revenue, the state reduced property taxes by 20 percent. And so it goes in state after state.

A South Dakota state senator, David L. Knudson, observed that individuals weren't the only ones with gambling addictions. "The biggest gambling addict turns out to be the state government that becomes dependent on it."

◆　　◆　　◆

In Las Vegas, Culinary Local 226 had been a warm and friendly partner of the gaming industry for many years. It supplied thousands of service workers to fill the never-ending calls for waiters, busboys, maids, and porters.

Although the Venetian successfully fended off formidable attempts at organization and vilification by the union, the MGM Grand gradually thawed its frosty feelings toward the Culinary during the booming 1990s.

The pressure that accompanied casino consolidation threatened to change that equation. The Culinary Union secured a living wage for thousands of service workers in Southern Nevada, but under the leadership of John Wilhelm, president of the Hotel Employees and Restaurant Employees International Union, the Culinary Union's parent union, it also developed a hand-in-glove closeness with the casino industry that shattered the adversarial labor-management model. And while the union was quick to bully tiny, struggling casino operators such as Mark Brandenburg of downtown's diminutive Golden Gate casino, it carved out handsome concessions to industry giants MGM Mirage and Mandalay Resorts.

Devoted Culinary organizers and activists Glen Arnodo and D. Taylor were quick to criticize the behavior of nonunion operations such as Station Casinos and the Venetian, but their rhetoric added up to words spoken against the wind. Its effort to organize 15,000 service workers in a dozen neighborhood casinos as well as the Venetian, Palms, and Aladdin had mixed results.

In a business with double-digit annual net profits, the easiest way for management to keep its nonunion workers loyal was to pay them more than union workers received. Adelson liked to brag that his medical and retirement plans were also superior employee deals that, if he did say so himself, were better administered than those offered by the Culinary.

While the Culinary, with its 45,000 members, remained the most-powerful political force in Nevada labor, it also appeared that most Strip properties maintained their relationship more out of a sense of headache prevention than any devotion to the needs of their legions of service workers.

The Culinary had shown it was willing to strike Strip casinos even if the one it selected was the secondary Frontier property. But casino industry consolidation raised an essential question for the union: Could it afford to take to the sidewalks against one of the giants?

A union that had been unsuccessful in organizing the Station Casinos locals operations would have little chance to outlast an opponent the size of the MGM Mirage.

The image of Las Vegas as a two-headed casino monster with Harrah's on one side and MGM Mirage on the other has its appeal, but it didn't take into account the nature of the players involved. While projecting lusty high-net profits was easy, the modern age made the thirst for ever-increasing profits essential to the publicly traded company's health. Fluctuations in the Asian currency market alone could be enough to stagger the giants.

The casino business was consolidating, but the final shape of its growth was anything but predictable.

Historian Michael Green observed, "Kerkorian, MGM Mirage and Mandalay are part of the story of modern Las Vegas and modern America. That's the fun part of this history: It's being written as you read it."

Casino companies ran the risk of forgetting that they still had to attract a customer's business. With a few giants controlling the street, there was a genuine risk of arrogance and a sense of entitlement replacing customer service.

"You want to survive in Vegas? In Nevada you've got to be careful what boats you rock when all the power's in the hands of so few people," casino observer Anthony Curtis told a reporter.

Geoff Schumacher concluded in *Sun, Sin & Suburbia: An Essential History of Modern Las Vegas*: "While Wall Street analysts saw the potential to increase shareholder value, casino workers worried about layoffs, vendors fretted about contracts and political pundits pondered what effects the mergers would have on state and local government policy. In the bigger picture, however, the mergers were a strong indication that as legal gambling spreads across the land, Las Vegas-based companies will continue to dominate the industry and dictate its agenda, ensuring that Las Vegas is never eclipsed as the main attraction."

With the gaming industry more powerful than ever in Nevada, it takes even less time for politicians to tumble and small businesses to knuckle under to price pressures delivered by the mighty casino corporations.

Yet, within the monolith, competition remains keen.

There were titans such as Wynn and Adelson, the Fertitta and Maloof families, and even Bill Boyd, Phil Ruffin, and the Vegas newcomers like Carl Icahn who were forces to be reckoned with in their own right. (Only in Las Vegas would businessmen the size of Icahn and Donald Trump be considered minor players.) They might not rival the scale of MGM Mirage and Harrah's Entertainment, but one slip, and they'd take a big bite out of the giants.

Those who believed gaming's trend toward consolidation eventually would result in a couple noncompeting super-companies underestimated the growth of the market and the nature of the players.

Although historian Eugene Moehring contends, "The city's pioneers could never have envisioned that their sleepy little whistlestop in the remote Mohave Desert would someday host this shrine to the glorification of leisure." Authors Sally Denton and Roger Morris would counter that the legitimization of a seductive vice was precisely what godfathers Benny Siegel and Moe Dalitz had in mind.

For author Marc Cooper, Las Vegas was "The last honest place in America." For *Time*'s Richard Corliss, the city is "an epic movie with casino chips for special effects; a tragedy of addiction and a burlesque with the smoothest showgirls around."

But even Las Vegas's occasional critics come out sounding like secret admirers as they concede that the place remains one thing above all else.

Irresistible.

# Epilogue

Time passes and things change. In Las Vegas, they change rapidly. Nevada casinos, while still the state's biggest employer, account for 21 percent of the total job market, down from 26 percent, according to the Nevada Resort Association, which bragged that the industry still accounts for 50 percent of the state's general fund. On the political clout scale, Gaming Inc. remains the ultimate 800-pound gorilla.

In March 2005, the Nevada Gaming Commission hearing for the Wynn Las Vegas lacked only trumpets and timpani for a royal announcement.

Afterward, Steve Wynn told reporter Howard Stutz, "These men and women were giving regulatory approval to the most expensive, the most complex, the most ambitious structure ever built in the world, including the pyramids of Egypt. We're not talking about Las Vegas; we're talking about everywhere.

"...And on top of that, it's done with a balance sheet that's like the Bank of England."

Steve Wynn had gone from being bought out by Kirk Kerkorian to "the Bank of England" in less than five years.

Then Wynn Las Vegas opened to overwhelming crowds and underwhelming reviews. For example, the *Los Angeles Times*, Christopher Hawthorne wrote, "It turns out the Wynn does have a theme—just a very odd one: The theme is mid-rise office tower in Houston, circa 1983." And even a polished puff piece in *Vanity Fair* showed Wynn as a man with a volcanic temper who was obsessed with his "creative vision."

Before the paint was dry at Wynn Las Vegas, Wynn announced a $1.4 billion, 2,000-suite second tower to be named Encore. At a stockholder meeting, even as the price of his company's stock plunged, Wynn hinted that someday in the unforeseeable future, the stock might even pay a dividend.

Meanwhile, the first disaster struck. The hotel's big show, *Le Reve*, created by Franco Dragone, was such a clinker that customers were leaving the showroom minutes after the curtain went up. Two shows a night became one show a night until, as Wynn explained, "we can attract enough people."

Middle managers were terminated. The director of the hotel's major nightclub was replaced. A design flaw at the property's entrance blocked traffic on Las Vegas Boulevard.

As usual, Wynn promised the public opulence beyond imagination—or at least beyond the accommodations offered by the competition.

Meanwhile, Sheldon Adelson vaulted ahead of Kerkorian on the list of the nation's wealthiest tycoons. His $1.6-billion Palazzo would be fifty stories high and offer 3,025 additional rooms. Adelson roared ahead even as Macau's Stanley Ho cut into his success on the Asian island, where holding onto fortunes has often proven difficult for outsiders.

George Maloof and his family at the Palms showed they had no intention of giving up the unofficial title of hippest operators in Las Vegas. They broke ground on a condominium high-rise.

Peter Morton kept pace by saying he would build a $1-billion, 1.5-million-square-foot hotel and condominium tower expansion at his Hard Rock, and he would finance it from his profits.

Rather than taking his windfall and retiring, former Mandalay Resort Group executive Glenn Schaeffer resurfaced as a player in the creation of the Fontainebleau resort project on the Strip. The Iowa Writers Workshop was in his background, but Vegas was in his blood.

Kerkorian, the ultimate predator, busied himself buying up substantial shares of General Motors. In a single day, he made more than $60 million on his GM stock. Thanks to his main man, Terry Lanni, Kerkorian could, with confidence, take his eye off this Strip empire. Harrah's Entertainment has become the largest casino corporation on the planet. Gary Loveman maintained Harrah's prominence amid the endless feeding frenzy and a competition intensity unknown at Harvard.

# Acknowledgments

I have often watched the gaming industry over the years with a sense of wonder others might reserve for the carnivores in the zoo, but have grown to respect their underrated business savvy and understanding of the motivations that drive their customers. Casino operators need to be one part shark, one part psychologist in order to be successful. In that way, they are far more like the classic titans of American business than some of the nation's more reserved capitalists would care to admit.

In an era that finds legalized gambling increasingly acceptable in nearly every corner of the country, casino men have become all but indistinguishable from their counterparts in other forms of American entertainment.

And that's what they had in mind all along.

No one writes a book of this scope without the collective effort and memories of scores of journalists, gaming regulators,

*Acknowledgments*

casino officials, and members of law enforcement, some of whom preferred to assist me anonymously. Their help is no less appreciated.

At the *Las Vegas Review-Journal*, where I have been employed as a daily columnist for 20 years, Publisher Sherman Frederick and Editor Thomas Mitchell continue to encourage my growth as a writer. The *Review-Journal*'s staff is one of the most underrated groups of professionals in the business. They cover what is pound-for-pound the most dynamic news town in America with uncommon tenacity. I'm proud to work alongside them and will always be grateful for their kindness during my daughter Amelia's medical travails.

News coverage of the gaming industry has evolved mightily in recent years. Where once the casino reporter was expected to cover the Gaming Control Board meetings and not rock the boat, today much has changed thanks to a maturing management and the efforts of top-notch reporters.

The work of current and former *R-J* staffers Dave Berns, Jeff Burbank, Pamela Busse, Norm Clarke, Ned Day, K.J. Evans, A.D. Hopkins, Chris Jones, Sergio Lalli, Jane Ann Morrison, Padmini Pai, Dave Palermo, Glenn Puit, Jeff Simpson, Hubble Smith, Rod Smith, Howard Stutz, and Al Tobin provided insight for this project. A special thanks to Palermo and Mitchell for taking time to read rough draft chapters.

Thanks also to the efforts and expertise of Ed "The Sage" Becker, Bobby Bennett, Shelley Berkley, Myram Borders, Mahlon Brown, Richard Carr, Gwen Castaldi, Deke Castleman, Keith Copher, Anthony Curtis, Sally Denton, Thalia Dondero, William Eadington, Anthony Fiato, Jackie Gaughan, Michael Gaughan, Mary Ellen Glass, Oscar Goodman, Michael Green, Roger Gros, Andrew Gumbel, Phil Hagen, George Knapp, Robert Maheu, Marydean Martin, Herb McDonald, Roger Morris, Robert Panaro Sr., Rob Powers, Rossi Ralencotter, Frank Rosenthal, Hal Rothman, Amy Schmidt, Geoff Schumacher, Jack Sheehan, Bobby Siller, Mike Sloan, Loren Stevens, William Thompson, Herb

*Acknowledgments*

Tobman, George Togliatti, Billy Vassiliadis, Barney Vinson, and Claudine Williams. Becker also took time to review the manuscript.

Although they are no longer on the Boulevard, this book benefited from my conversations with Bill Bennett, Fred Benninger, Ted Binion, Herb Blitzstein, Joey Boston, Harry Claiborne, Ralph Engelstad, Mel Exber, Willie Fopiano, Don Garvin, Marty Kane, Esther Kelley, Joe Kelley, Frank Maggio, and Herb McDonald.

I'd also like to thank Lyle and Carole Stuart of Barricade Books for their friendship and support during difficult times. Lyle and Sandy Stuart whipped a 600-page manuscript into shape, and Jeff Nordstedt and the staff at Barricade did a great job in ushering this project from first draft to finished product.

As ever, thanks to my wife (and editor), Tricia, and daughter, Amelia, for their patience and support.

# Bibliography

Adams, James Ring. *The Big Fix*. New York: John Wiley & Sons, 1990.

Ader, Jason N., and Marc J. Falcone. *Bear Stearns North Atlantic Gaming Almanac, 2001-2002*. Las Vegas: Huntington Press, 2001.

Allen, Steve. *Ripoff: A Look at Corruption in America*. Secaucus, New Jersey: Lyle Stuart, 1979.

Alvarez, A. *The Biggest Game in Town*. Boston: Houghton Mifflin Company, 1983.

Bailey, Fenton. *Fall From Grace – The Untold Story of Michael Milken*. New York: Carol Publishing Group, 1991.

Barlett, Donald L., and James B. Steele. *Empire: The Life, Legend, and Madness of Howard Hughes*. New York: W.W. Norton, 1979.

Barrett, Wayne. *Trump – The Deals and the Downfall*. New York: Harper Collins Publishers, 1991.

Berman, Susan. *Easy Street*. New York: Dial Press, 1981.

Bonanno, Joseph. (With Sergio Lalli.) *A Man of Honor*. New York: Simon & Schuster, 1983.

Brill, Steven. *The Teamsters*. New York: Simon & Schuster, 1978.

Bruck, Connie. *The Predators' Ball – The Inside Story of Drexel Burnham and the Rise of the Junk Bond Raiders*. New York: Penguin Books USA Inc., 1994.

Burbank, Jeff. *A License to Steal: Nevada's Gaming Control System in the Megaresort Era*. Reno, Nevada: University of Nevada Press, 2000.

383

# *Bibliography*

Cartwright, Gary. *Dirty Dealing*. New York, Atheneum, 1984.

Cohen, Mickey, and John Peer Nugent. *In My Own Words*. New York: Prentice-Hall, 1975.

Conrad, Harold. *Dear Muffo: Thirty-Five Years in the Fast Lane*. New York: Stein and Day, 1982.

Cowan, Rick, and Douglas Century. *Takedown: The Fall of the Last Mafia Empire*. New York: G.P. Putnam's Sons, 2002.

Demaris, Ovid. *The Boardwalk Jungle*. New York: Bantam Books, Inc., 1986.

_____. *The Last Mafioso: The Treacherous World of Jimmy Fratianno*. New York: Bantam, 1981.

Dombrink, John, and William N. Thompson. *The Last Resort*. Reno, Nevada: University of Nevada Press, 1991.

Drosnin, Michael. *Citizen Hughes – the Power, the Money, the Madness*. New York: Bantam Books, 1986.

Early, Pete. *SuperCasino: Inside the "New" Las Vegas*. New York: Bantam Books, 2000.

Edmonds, Andy. *Bugsy's Baby: The Secret Life of Mob Queen Virginia Hill*. Secaucus, New Jersey: Carol Publishing, 1993.

Feder, Sid and Joachim Joesten. *The Luciano Story*. New York: David McKay, 1954.

Findlay, John M. *People of Chance: Gambling in American Society From Jamestown to Las Vegas*. New York: Oxford University Press, 1986.

Fopiano, Willie, and John Harney. *The Godson: A True-Life Account of 20 Years Inside the Mob*. New York: St. Martin's Press, 1993.

Frey, James H., and William R. Eadington. *Gambling: Views from the Social Sciences*. The Annals of the American Academy of Political and Social Science. Beverly Hills, Calif.: Sage Publications, 1984.

Gage, Nicholas. *The Mafia is Not an Equal Opportunity Employer*. New York: McGraw-Hill, 1971.

Garrison, Omar V. *Howard Hughes in Las Vegas*. New York: Lyle Stuart, 1970.

Gentry, Curt. *J. Edgar Hoover: The Man and His Secrets*. New York: W.W. Norton, 1991.

Gerber, Albert B. *Bashful Billionaire – A Biography of Howard Hughes*. New York: Lyle Stuart, Inc., 1968. Malden, Mass.: Blackwell Publishers, 1999.

## Bibliography

Glass, Mary Ellen. *Nevada's Turbulent 50s: Decade of Political and Economic Change*. Reno, Nevada: University of Nevada Press, 1981.

Goodman, Robert. *The Luck Business: The Devastating Consequences and Broken Promises of America's Gambling Explosion*. New York: The Free Press, 1995.

Gottdiener, M., and Claudia C. Collins, David R. Dickens. *Las Vegas: The Social Production of an All-American City*. Blackwell Publishing, 1999.

Greenspun, Hank, and Alex Pelle. *Where I Stand: The Record of a Reckless Man*. New York: David McKay, 1966.

Hanna, David. *Frank Costello: The Gangster with a Thousand Faces*. New York: Belmont Tower Books, 1974.

Hopkins, A.D., and K.J. Evans, editors. *The First 100: Portraits of the Men and Women Who Shaped Las Vegas*. Las Vegas, Nevada: Huntington Press, 1999.

Hulse, James W. *The Nevada Adventure*. Reno, Nevada: University of Nevada Press, 1966.

Jennings, Dean. *We Only Kill Each Other: The Life and Bad Times of Bugsy Siegel*. London: John Long, 1968.

Johnston, David Cay. *Temples of Chance – How America Inc., Bought Out Murder Inc. for Control of the Casino Business*. New York: Doubleday, 1992.

Keats, John. *Howard Hughes*. New York: Bantam Books, 1966.

Kessler, Ronald. *The Richest Man in the World*. New York: Warner Books, 1986.

Kling, Dwayne, and R.T. King, editor. *Every Light Was On: Bill Harrah and His Clubs Remembered*. Reno, Nevada: University of Nevada Oral History Program, 1999.

Kornbluth, Jesse. *Highly Confident – The Crime and Punishment of Michael Milken*. New York: William and Morrow, 1992.

Kwitney, Jonathan. *Vicious Circles: The Mafia in the Marketplace*. New York: W.W. Norton, 1979.

Lacey, Robert. *Little Man: Meyer Lansky and the Gangster Life*. Boston: Little, Brown, 1991.

Lehr, Dick, and Gerard O'Neill. *Black Mass: The Irish Mob, the FBI, and a Devil's Deal*. New York: Public Affairs, 2000.

Levy, Shawn. *Rat Pack Confidential: Frank, Dean, Sammy, Peter, Joey, and the Last Great Showbiz Party*. Doubleday, 1998.

385

Linn, Edward. *Big Julie of Vegas.* Greenwich, Connecticut: Fawcett
Publications, 1974.

Lintner, Bertil. *Blood Brothers: The Criminal Underworld of Asia.* New York:
Palgrave/Macmillan, 2002.

Littlejohn, David, editor. *The Real Las Vegas.* New York, Oxford University
Press, 2000.

Maheu, Robert, and Richard Hack. *Next to Hughes: Behind the Power and
Tragic Downfall of Howard Hughes by His Closest Advisor.* New York:
HarperCollins, 1992.

Maas, Peter. *The Valachi Papers.* New York: Putnam's, 1968.

McClellan, John L. *Crime Without Punishment.* New York: Duell, Sloan,
and Pearce, 1962.

Messick, Hank. *Lansky.* New York: Putnam's, 1971.

_____. *The Silent Syndicate.* New York: Macmillan, 1967.

_____. *The Syndicate Abroad.* New York: Macmillan, 1969.

Miller, Kit. *Inside the Glitter: Lives of Casino Workers.* Carson City, Nevada:
Great Basin Publishing, 2000.

Moehring, Eugene P. *Resort City in the Sunbelt: Las Vegas, 1930-1970.*
Reno, Nevada: University of Nevada Press, 1989.

Moldea, Dan. *The Hoffa Wars: Teamsters, Rebels, Politicians, and the Mob.*
New York: Paddington Press, 1978.

_____. *Dark Victory: Ronald Reagan, MCA, and the Mob.* New York:
Penguin, 1987.

_____. *Interference: How Organized Crime Influences Professional Football.*
New York: William and Morrow, 1989.

Neff, James. *Mobbed Up: Jackie Presser's High-Wire Life in the Teamsters, the
Mafia, and the FBI.* New York: Dell, 1989.

O'Brien, Timothy L. *The Insider Story of Glamour, Glitz, and Danger of
America's Gambling Industry.* New York: Random House, 1998.

O'Donnell, John R. *Trumped! – The Inside Story of the Real Donald Trump.*
New York: Simon & Schuster, 1991.

Paher, Stanley W. *Las Vegas: As It Began, As It Grew.* Las Vegas: Nevada
Publications, 1974.

Peterson, Virgil W. *The Mob: Two Hundred Years of Organized Crime in
New York.* Ottawa, Illinois: Green Hill Publishers, 1983.

Pileggi, Nicholas. *Casino.* New York: Simon & Schuster, 1995.

# Bibliography

_____. *Wise Guy: Life in a Mafia Family.* New York: Pocket Books, 1985.

Puzo, Mario. *Inside Las Vegas.* New York: Charter Books, 1976.

Rappleye, Charles, and Ed Becker. *All American Mafioso – The Johnny Rosselli Story.* New York: Doubleday, 1991.

Reid, Ed. *The Grim Reapers: The Anatomy of Organized Crime in America.* Chicago: Henry Regnery, 1969.

Reid, Ed, and Ovid Demaris. *The Green Felt Jungle.* New York: Trident Press, 1963.

Renay, Liz. *My Face for the World to See.* Fort Lee, New Jersey: Barricade Books, 2002.

Roemer, William F. Jr. *Man Against the Mob.* New York: Donald I. Fine, 1989.

_____. *The Enforcer: Spilotro, Chicago's Man Over Las Vegas.* New York: Donald I. Fine, 1995.

Rothman, Hal K. *Devil's Bargains: Tourism in the Twentieth-Century West.* Lawrence, Kansas: University of Kansas Press, 1998.

Rothman, Hal K., and Mike Davis, editors. *The Grit Beneath the Glitter.* Berkeley: University of California Press, 2002.

Russo, Gus. *The Outfit: The Role of Chicago's Underworld in the Shaping of Modern America.* New York: Bloomsbury, 2001.

Salerno, Ralph, and J.S. Tompkins. *The Crime Confederation.* New York: Popular Library, 1969.

Schumacher, Geoff. *Sun, Sin & Suburbia: An Essential History of Modern Las Vegas.* Las Vegas, Nevada: Stevens Press, LLC., 2004.

Schwartz, David G. *Suburban Xanadu: The Casino Resort on the Las Vegas Strip and Beyond.* New York: Routledge, 2003.

Sheehan, Jack, editor. *The Players: The Men Who Built Las Vegas.* Reno, Nevada: University of Nevada Press, 1998.

Shook, Robert L. *Jackpot! Harrah's Winning Secrets for Customer Loyalty.* New York: John Wiley & Sons, Inc., 2003.

Sifakis, Carl. *The Mafia Encyclopedia.* New York: Facts on File Publications Inc., 1987.

Solkey, Lee. *Dummy Up and Deal.* GBC Press, 1980.

Skolnick, Jerome H. *House of Cards.* Boston: Little, Brown, 1978.

Smith, Harold S., Sr. *I Want To Quit Winners.* Englewood Cliffs, New Jersey: Prentice-Hall, 1961.

Smith, John L. *The Animal in Hollywood: Anthony Fiato's Life in the Mafia.* New York: Barricade Books, 1998.

_____. *Las Vegas – The Story Behind the Scenery.* Las Vegas, Nevada: KC Publications, 1995.

_____. *Of Rats and Men: Oscar Goodman's Life from Mob Mouthpiece to Mayor of Las Vegas.* Las Vegas, Nevada: Huntington Press, 2003.

_____ *On the Boulevard: The Best of John L. Smith.* Las Vegas, Nevada: Huntington Press, 2000.

_____. *No Limit: The Rise and Fall of Bob Stupak and Las Vegas' Stratosphere Tower.* Las Vegas, Nevada: Huntington Press, 1997.

_____. *Quicksilver: The Ted Binion Murder Case.* Las Vegas, Nevada: Huntington Press, 2001.

_____. *Running Scared: The Life and Treacherous Times of Las Vegas Casino King Steve Wynn.* New York: Barricade Books, 1995.

Smith, John L. and Patricia G. Smith. *Moving to Las Vegas.* New York: Barricade Books, 1998.

Spanier, David. *All Right, Okay, You Win – Inside Las Vegas.* London: Secker & Warburg, Ltd., 1992.

Stein, Benjamin J. *A License to Steal. The Untold Story of Michael Milken and the Conspiracy to Bilk the Nation.* New York: Simon & Schuster, 1992.

Stevens, Mark. *King Icahn: The Biography of a Renegade Capitalist.* New York: Penguin/Dutton, 1993.

Stuart, Lyle. *Casino Gambling for the Winner.* Secaucus, New Jersey: Lyle Stuart, Inc., 1980.

_____. *Lyle Stuart on Baccarat.* Secaucus, New Jersey: Lyle Stuart, Inc., 1984.

_____. *Winning at Casino Gambling.* New York: Barricade Books, 1995.

Stuart, Mark. A. *Gangster #2: Longy Zwillman, the Man Who Invented Organized Crime.* Secaucus, New Jersey: Lyle Stuart, 1985.

Summers, Anthony. *Official and Confidential: The Secret Life of J. Edgar Hoover.* New York: G.P. Putnam's Sons, 1993.

Thomson, David. *In Nevada: The Land, the People, God, and Chance.* New York: Alfred A. Knopf, 1999.

Torgerson, Dial. *Kerkorian: An American Success Story.* New York: The Dial Press, 1974.

Trump, Donald J., and Tony Schwartz. *Trump: The Art of the Deal.* New York: Warner Books, 1987.

# *Bibliography*

Tuccile, Jerome. *Trump: The Saga of America's Most Powerful Real Estate Baron.* New York: Donald I. Fine, 1985.

Turkus, Burton B., and Sid Feder. *Murder Inc.* New York: Farrar, Straus, and Young, 1951.

Turner, Wallace. *Gamblers' Money—The New Force in American Life.* New York: The New American Library, 1965.

Venturi, Robert, and Denise Scott Brown. *Learning From Las Vegas.* Cambridge, MA: The MIT Press, 1993.

Vinson, Barney. *Las Vegas Behind the Tables, Part I.* Grand Rapids, Michigan: Gollehon Books, 1985.

_____. *Las Vegas Behind the Tables, Part II.* Grand Rapids, Michigan: Gollehon Books, 1988.

Vogel, Jennifer, editor. *Crapped Out: How Gambling Ruins the Economy and Destroys Lives.* Monroe, Maine: Common Courage Press, 1997.

Wilkerson, W.R. III. *The Man Who Invented Las Vegas.* Beverly Hills, California: Ciro's Books, 2000.

Wright, Frank. *World War II and the Emergence of Modern Las Vegas.* Las Vegas, Nevada: Nevada State Museum and Historical Society, 1991.

Zuckerman, Michael J. *Vengeance is Mine.* New York: Macmillan, 1987.

## Freedom of Information (Partial and complete files)

Benny Binion
Marshall Caifano
Moe Dalitz
Sam Giancana
Meyer Lansky
John Rosselli
Benjamin Siegel
Anthony Spilotro

## Magazines and Newspapers

*Arizona Republic*
*Barron's*
*BusinessWeek*
*Casino Journal*
*Casino Player*
*Chicago Tribune*

# Bibliography

*Chicago Sun-Times*
*Cigar Aficionado*
*The Economist*
*Far Eastern Economic Review*
*Financial World*
*Forbes*
*Fortune*
*GQ*
*Gambling Times*
*Gaming and Wagering Business*
*Henderson Home News*
*Hotel and Motel Management*
*Independent*
*Indian Country*
*International Gaming & Wagering Business*
*LV*
*Las Vegas Review-Journal*
*Las Vegas Sun*
*Las Vegas Today*
*Los Angeles Times*
*M. Inc.*
*Meetings and Conventions Magazine*
*Nevada*
*Nevada Casino Journal*
*The Nevadan Today*
*New Republic*
*Newsweek*
*New York Magazine*
*New York Post*
*New York Times*
*Overdrive*
*Penthouse*
*Spirit Magazine*
*Time*
*U.S. News and World Report*
*Valley Times*
*Vanity Fair*
*Wall Street Journal*
*Washington Post*

# Index

**395**

**397**

**400**